Table
4
at
The
River
Cafe

GALLERY BOOKS
New York   Amsterdam/Antwerp   London
Toronto   Sydney/Melbourne   New Delhi

Ruthie Rogers

# Table 4 at The River Cafe

Conversations about Food and Life

Photography
Matthew Donaldson

## Food Is Family 9

| | | | | | |
|---|---|---|---|---|---|
| Paul McCartney | 11 | Salman Rushdie | 37 | Elton John David Furnish | 55 |
| Mary McCartney | 15 | Rachel Eliza Griffiths | 43 | Michael Elias | 61 |
| Stella McCartney | 21 | Keri Russell | | Roo Rogers | 67 |
| Victoria Beckham | 27 | Matthew Rhys | 47 | Emily Mortimer | 73 |
| David Beckham | 31 | | | | |

## Food Is Tradition 79

| | | | | | |
|---|---|---|---|---|---|
| Greta Gerwig Noah Baumbach | 81 | Wyclef Jean | 107 | Trudie Styler | 137 |
| Linda Evangelista | 89 | Tina Fey | 115 | Tom Hollander | 145 |
| Edward Enninful | 95 | Alfonso Cuarón | 121 | Francis Ford Coppola | 151 |
| Mel Brooks | 99 | Bob Pittman | 125 | | |
| | | J.J. Abrams | 131 | | |

## Food Is Discovery 157

| | | | | | |
|---|---|---|---|---|---|
| Michael Caine | 159 | Carey Mulligan | 179 | Bob Iger | 201 |
| Jake Gyllenhaal | 163 | Jeff Goldblum | 185 | Stephen Fry | 207 |
| Sarah Jessica Parker | 169 | Fisher Stevens | 191 | Austin Butler | 213 |
| Wes Anderson | 175 | Olivia Colman | 197 | | |

## Food Is Art 221

| | | | | | |
|---|---|---|---|---|---|
| Norman Foster | 223 | Frank Gehry | 231 | Frida Escobedo | 245 |
| Tracey Emin | 227 | Jony Ive | 237 | Ed Ruscha | 249 |

## Food Is Politics 255

| | | | | | |
|---|---|---|---|---|---|
| Nancy Pelosi | 257 | Simon Sebag Montefiore | 275 | Mark Carney | 291 |
| Al Gore | 263 | Darren Walker | 283 | Adam Schiff | 295 |
| Mala Gaonkar | 269 | | | Michael Bloomberg | 301 |

## Food Is Food 307

| | | | | | |
|---|---|---|---|---|---|
| Martha Stewart | 309 | Wolfgang Puck | 333 | Sian Wyn Owen Joseph Trivelli | 363 |
| Danny Meyer | 315 | Eric Ripert | 341 | | |
| Nigella Lawson | 321 | Alice Waters | 347 | | |
| Yotam Ottolenghi | 325 | Jamie Oliver | 355 | | |

# INTRODUCTION

"When I see you," Mel Brooks once told me, "I get hungry."

I can see why. When you meet an artist, you want to go to a gallery. When you meet an actor, you want to go to the theater. So I understand how meeting me might make Mel want to eat. As much as preparing and cooking is part of being a chef, so is listening. Over the years, I have spoken with many people who have great stories to tell about food.

Michael Caine remembers chasing and catching rabbits for his mother to cook when he was evacuated from London to the countryside during World War II. As for Mel, he could vividly describe to me, in his nineties, the first decent spaghetti he had ever eaten, more than eighty years earlier, and who cooked it for him.

At The River Cafe, the restaurant I cofounded with Rose Gray in 1987, we ask our waiters to really consider the people who come for lunch or dinner. What stories might they have to tell? Are they celebrating the birth of a new baby? Was there a lot of traffic on the way to the restaurant? Did they save up to bring in someone they love for a special meal? Food stories and memories are what my podcast, *Ruthie's Table 4*, is all about.

The same goes for this book. The origins of both lie in an evening my husband, Richard, and I hosted in 2003. A receptionist at the restaurant, a recent Oxford graduate, Nina Raine, was just getting her start in the theater, where a bright future as a director and playwright awaited. Nina asked if she could stage a performance of a Harold Pinter play in the living room of our London home.

Nina's event went so well that it inspired a series in our house, where we invited actors and musicians to perform, and friends and family to attend. Judi Dench sang and told stories of her life onstage and in film. Ralph Fiennes performed a Samuel Beckett monologue. Ian McKellen delighted us with an evening of poetry, recitals of Shakespeare's sonnets, and amusing memories of his early career in rep. For the last part of his performance, he stood on the staircase overlooking our living room and read aloud a recipe for ribollita, a Tuscan soup. Richard and I had no idea he was going to do this. But his performance brought down the house. It confirmed my belief that a recipe, properly written, is part science and part poetry. And, in this case, part theater.

It had always been a dream of mine to have a River Cafe radio station, where the people who visited the restaurant could share stories about and over food. When the pandemic and the subsequent lockdown hit, the memories of these evenings at our home reasserted themselves. People were isolated from each other. What could we at The River Cafe do to bring the world of food and community to them?

Zad Rogers, my stepson, and the team at his production company, Atomized, started working on the concept. The initial thought was simple: we'd ask friends of the restaurant to read one recipe a day, 365 days a year, and put these recordings online. The first three people we approached were Michael Caine, Jake Gyllenhaal, and Wes Anderson. Amazing as it was to hear these distinctive voices reading our recipes aloud, it was clear we needed more from the conversation. As soon as lockdown restrictions were eased, Michael and I met at his home to talk.

His stories were everything I'd hoped for: memories of what he ate growing up in World War II; the thrill of moving to a postwar prefab house that came complete with such luxuries as an electric stove and refrigerator; and his claim that he makes "the best roast potatoes that anybody who has come over has ever eaten." All told in his trademark voice. So began the *Ruthie's Table 4* podcast.

Why did we call it that? Everyone who knows me calls me Ruthie. As for the *Table 4* part, Matthew Freud suggested it. In a nicely Freudian way (Matthew is a great-grandson of Sigmund), it has a double meaning: as the name of an actual table in the restaurant and as a pun. Every time we have a guest on the podcast, we have a table for them: a table for Wes Anderson, a table for Carey Mulligan, a table for Edward Enninful. The actual Table 4 also happens to be Michael Caine's favorite. This book welcomes you to that table.

On the podcast, I often recite a litany: Food is love. Food is memory, family, politics, art, discovery. And food is comfort. The conversations collected here, adapted from *Ruthie's Table 4*, tell the stories that food has played in our guests' lives. They are also full of surprises. Who knew that Nancy Pelosi, the former speaker of the U.S. House of Representatives, grew up in a household where every single meal was served atop a tablecloth, while Martha Stewart, the doyenne of good taste, crowded with her siblings and parents around a homely pink Formica table? Would you ever have guessed that Stewart, Mel Brooks, and the architect Frank Gehry all had in common that their mothers kept a live carp in the bathtub, ensuring that the fish stayed swimmingly fresh until it met its final fate in the kitchen?

None of my guests, I've learned, has been jaded or entitled about food. To this day, Tracey Emin's greatest culinary pleasure is eating multiple apples at once—slicing them into irregular shapes and piling the pieces high on a plate. Asking Paul McCartney to talk about the Beatles might have made him yawn, but since we were talking about food, he told me stories he had never told before.

People often ask me what my last meal would be. It's not a question I like. There is so much life in food. Looking for a way to end each episode of the podcast, I wanted to find a more uplifting final question. Kirsty Young, who for many years presented the treasured BBC radio program *Desert Island Discs*, had a suggestion. "Keep it simple," she said. "Ask every guest the same one question. Something they really care about." We decided it would be to ask everyone what their comfort food is.

Of all the roles that food plays in our lives, its most immediate and intimate is as a source of solace. Comfort food is what sees us through the bad times. And it's often enjoyed alone. Pasta—in one form or another—is by far the most commonly chosen comfort food on *Ruthie's Table 4*. The question also receives some highly esoteric answers. One guest said her comfort food was a chicken casserole made with a crust of Weetabix and cheddar cheese. Another chose a peanut butter and jelly sandwich.

My life in food begins in Monticello, a small village in the Catskill Mountains in upstate New York. When I was twelve, we moved to Woodstock, fifty miles away. This was years before the famous music festival, but the area was already known as a community of creative people. And our house was a place where artists, writers, musicians, and other friends gathered. Both of my parents were the children of immigrants—my father's family from Hungary, my mother's from Russia—and I was the youngest of three children. Since my parents worked long hours (my father was a radiologist, and my mother a teacher), we ate simply: meatloaf, roast chicken, sweet corn from local farm stands in the summer. Classic American fare, unambitious but considerately prepared.

When I was a teenager, newly in thrall to Julia Child, I tried to make her version of beef bourguignon. It cracked open not just my palate, but also my mind—introducing the idea and desire to cook for other people. Julia inspired me because of her enthusiasm, her faith in her readers, and her precision. If you followed her recipes to the letter, as I did, you never had a failure. This made me confident in the kitchen: ready to branch out, take risks, and create recipes and techniques of my own.

As a student on a semester abroad in London, I met Richard Rogers, an architect. His family had moved to England from Florence when he was five, forced into exile by Mussolini. Richard's father, Nino, was a doctor, and his mother, Dada, was an elegant woman from Trieste. Dada was a great, great cook. Up until then, my experience of Italian food had been the American version, basically a heavy, rich variation on Southern Italian cooking: veal parmigiana, spaghetti and meatballs. To eat my mother-in-law's cooking—and, later on, to visit Florence with Richard, tasting a classic pappa al pomodoro or fish prepared simply, grilled with just lemon and local herbs—was a revelation.

Not long after I met Richard, I became friends with Rose Gray, an imposing beauty who was a brilliant and passionate cook, interested primarily in Italian food. It would be a long time, though, before we joined forces to launch a restaurant. When Richard won the competition to design the Centre Pompidou with his Italian partner Renzo Piano, we moved to Paris. Our son Roo was born there in 1975. I became immersed in French cuisine, both new and classic. At the same time, Rose was living in Tuscany, with her husband, David, and their four children. Though we were in different countries, the focus of our days was on going to the seasonal food markets, choosing what we were going to cook for our families.

In 1977, after the Pompidou opened, Richard and I moved back to London. Richard wanted to find a light, open environment in which he and his team could thrive creatively. They found a disused oil warehouse in Thames Wharf on the river in Hammersmith. Soon they were joined by other architects, graphic designers, and artists. Now all they needed was somewhere to eat. He and Renzo, Richard liked to say, had done most of their design of the Pompidou Centre on the tabletop of a Paris café. A few proposals came in from restaurateurs, but none of them were particularly impressive. Reading them, I remember saying to Richard, "The only thing worse than not having a place to eat would be to have a mediocre one. Why don't we do it ourselves?"

Rose had just moved back to London from New York, where she had helped a friend, Nell Campbell, open her eponymous nightclub owned by Keith McNally and Lynn Wagenknecht. I had heard Rose's ambition was to open a restaurant. We met to talk things over in a wine bar in Chelsea that is now a McDonald's. So you could make the claim that The River Cafe was conceived in a McDonald's.

To say that we weren't particularly qualified is an understatement. Rose's kitchen résumé was slim, with only the stint at Nell's to her credit. As for me, I had no professional experience as a chef whatsoever. Undaunted, we opened our first iteration of The River Cafe in 1987, strictly as a lunch-only place, its customer base limited by local planners to workers in the Thames Wharf complex. Richard designed the space and Rose's husband designed its logo. Bo, our youngest child, turned three.

I'm often reminded that the menu wasn't so rigorously Italian in those early days, serving hamburgers and sandwiches. But as our confidence in cooking like real Italians grew, so did The River Cafe. Little by little, we expanded the menu and hours. By the summer, we were able to welcome people coming in from outside of Thames Wharf. Word spread that these two women might be onto something. We went from being an office canteen open only for lunch to a restaurant serving until eleven at night.

Chefs, experienced ones, came to work for us, and developing the the wine list took us to all regions of Italy, meeting the new generation of wine producers, many of whom remain close friends thirty-seven years later. Our first cookbook, simply entitled *The River Cafe Cookbook*, was published in 1995. Today we call it *The Blue Book* because it has been followed by a further thirteen volumes, with covers in bright colors.

In 2008, after The River Cafe was damaged by a fire, Richard redesigned the space to have a completely open kitchen, visually anchored by a shocking pink wood-burning oven. The open plan creates a sense of intimacy and warmth among everyone in the room: the people working there, and the people eating there.

Everything about The River Cafe inspires me: the room, the food, our brilliant team, the people who join us every day for lunch and dinner.

In answering the final question put to all my *Table 4* guests, my choice will always be chocolate. Taking a taxi home at the end of the night, I'll ask the driver to stop so I can buy a bar of chocolate. I rarely finish it, breaking off a few pieces and offering the rest to the driver.

Recently, when I did this, the driver was unsurprised. "You gave me a piece of chocolate the last time I took you home," he said.

I didn't realize I'd been in his cab before. But I guess that's the story of my life in food.

At home, at work, even in transit, I always like to share something delicious.

—Ruthie Rogers

# Food Is Family

Families are integral to both The River Cafe and *Ruthie's Table 4*. In *Anna Karenina*, Tolstoy suggests, "Every happy family is alike," but what I have learned from these interviews is that family memories are often unalike: David and Victoria Beckham; or Paul, Stella, and Mary McCartney—each has their own impressions from their childhoods, distinct and special.

It is moving for me to listen to my brother, Michael Elias, describe our mother's cooking. And to hear my son Roo talk about his early memories of going to the markets with his father in Paris, offering a perspective different from my own memories of that time.

For the past four years, I have worked on this podcast with Zad Rogers as producer—traveling to Los Angeles, New York, Venice; meeting new people, listening to their stories, writing, recording, editing their interviews.

And most of all, experiencing the joy of making something lasting and meaningful with someone you love.

Family is food, food is family.

# PAUL McCARTNEY

One of my most prized possessions is a photograph Paul McCartney sent me during the pandemic. It shows him and one of his grandsons, Mark, proudly standing with a plate of tomato pasta they have prepared together from our River Cafe recipe.

Paul and Linda McCartney made being a vegetarian "rock and roll" and influenced a huge amount of people who thought the opposite. Today he also relishes making his own beer, which he named after a particularly phallic-looking mushroom. He read our recipe for Roast Aubergine Parmesan.

Cooking in Liverpool, in my working-class family, there was not much variety.

The vegetables would be potatoes, carrots, onions, and broad beans, which we called butter beans. I like them to this day, in a nice butter-bean soup. But our diet was pretty bland, very limited.

My mum was a nurse. I think she enjoyed cooking, but in those days, there was really no question about it, it was the woman's role to cook. She was a proper cook, a good one. The only time I didn't eat what she had prepared was when she presented a bloody big cow's tongue on a plate. I was not persuaded to eat that.

The sadness of my life was the death of my mother when I was fourteen. My dad and me and my younger brother, Mike, were left to look after ourselves. Sometimes I'd get home from school before Dad was home from work at the port, where he was a cotton salesman. I'd have to knock up a little bit of a meal. I became very good at mashed potatoes. These days my recipe would need to be a little bit health-erized. I mashed the potatoes with a fork—we didn't have many cooking implements—until I got all the lumps out. Then I would pile in a lot of butter, a little bit of milk, and whip that sucker up. Sometimes, if I was trying to be exotic, I'd put in some finely chopped onions, raw, which was kind of nice. Dad would buy either some sausages or some chops to go with it.

It was only when I went to London, when the Beatles came down to make records, that I started going to fine restaurants and tried to navigate my way through their menus. Food was pretty much fuel until then. For instance, I hated wine. We never had it at home. The nearest we came to alcoholic beverages was when we had a glass of cider with Sunday lunch, but that was it. Whenever I tasted wine, I hated it.

One time, John and I hitchhiked to Paris. He'd been given a fabulous birthday present by his rich relatives in Scotland: £100. We hitchhiked to Paris and thought, "Oh, we're in France, we've got to have a wine experience!" So we went into a corner café, sidled up to the bar, and said, *"Deux verres vin ordinaire, s'il vous plaît."* They gave us two glasses of red wine. We took a sip, and John and I were like, "This is terrible, it's like vinegar! What is the fuss about? All these people going on about wine—they're crazy and we're sane."

The first time I remember liking wine was with our producer, George Martin. My girlfriend at the time was Jane Asher. We went out with George and his wife, Judy, to a little restaurant in Charlotte Street called L'Étoile. I was treating, so the sommelier came up to me and leaned in, very intimately, whispering, "Would you like a wine, sir?" I said, "I'd like you to recommend something. I don't know much about wine." He brought back a bottle of Louis Latour Château Corton Grancey 1959 and I took a taste of it. Oh, it was like velvet. I thought, *"Now* I get it. Now I see why people go crazy about wine."

We are a vegetarian family, all of us. My children and grandchildren do not eat meat or fish at all. The way it started was, Linda and I were at our farm in Scotland. The farm was in a place called Campbelltown, down in the Argyll

Peninsula south of Glasgow. The Beatles' breakup got a bit heavy and I just couldn't deal with it, so we escaped there.

One day, we were looking out the kitchen window and it was lambing season, early in spring. The lambs were gamboling around, so full of life. There was a pack of about twenty of them. They'd start at one end of the field and then—as if one them had said, "Let's go!"—they'd all run to the other side of the field. And then back again. Linda and I were watching them and saying, "Isn't this cute and great?" Then we suddenly realized we were eating . . . leg of lamb. That was when the penny dropped.

We had a conversation: "Should we try and not eat meat? Should we try and go veggie?" In those days, it was difficult. But we decided to make it a fun challenge: "Okay, what do we do?" It was about filling the hole in the middle of the plate. We kept everything else on the plate and just worked on things to take the place where the meat had been. At Christmas, I had always loved the role I had been given in the family to carve the turkey. And Linda did indeed cook a great turkey. But suddenly, here we were without anything for me to carve. Linda had the brilliant idea of making macaroni and cheese. She let it cool and go solid, and then we put it in the fridge overnight. The next day, I had this big block that I could carve into turkey-sized portions.

It became an interesting challenge to work out how to be a vegetarian in the 1970s, because not many people were bothering. I remember going with Linda's father one night to Claridge's Hotel and thinking, "Great, they're going to know how to do it!" We told them, "We're vegetarian, can you make some suggestions?" The waiter gave us a very sniffy look and came back with a plate of vegetables, steamed. That was the limit of his imagination.

For a time, the only significant vegetarian restaurant in London was a place named Cranks. I thought it was very cool that they called it that. It used to come with the territory—that if people were veggie, they were cranks. But that soon left the arena. Things started to change very quickly. In Liverpool, there's a stew called scouse. It's basically an Irish stew with everything thrown in. When Linda and I became vegetarians, we went up to visit my auntie, who very kindly made scouse without the meat, which Liverpudlians call blind scouse.

We have another farm in East Sussex. When I first bought it, there were some fields they didn't plant in. My farm guys said, "There are no worms in these fields, because basically all we did was put pesticides and fertilizer in." So I thought, "We're going to go organic." I talked to the Soil Association and they gave us some tips. Now we grow all sorts of crops. I like doing things like spelt wheat just because it's a little bit different. We also grow rye and peas. And we make our own ale. Through the years, I would hear of neighbors who were looking to sell some of their land adjacent to ours. One of them had a hops garden. Long story short, I bought it. And then I thought, "Well, I've got to start doing hops. I've got to bring them back, because the region we're in, in Sussex, was a very big hop-growing area." So I went to a local brewer in the village near us and asked if he would make beer for me. I said, "I'll grow the hops and you put it all together. And it must be organic." And so he did. We were looking for a name for the beer. You know how it is with artisanal beers, they have to have crazy names. So I was riding with Linda one day through our woods. She was behind me, and I stopped and said to her, "You're not going to believe what you're about to see." It was a fungus that was white and very phallic—it looked like an erect penis. Beside it, even better, was another one that looked like a limp penis. When I tell people this story, I say, "Don't blame me, this is nature—it's not me being dirty." We found out that this mushroom is called a stinkhorn. So that's why we named our beer Old Stinkhorn. We don't produce enough to go commercial, just enough for family and friends.

*Paul, what is your comfort food?*
A quesadilla. It's like a pizza turned inside out. I love it.

# MARY McCARTNEY

Mary McCartney and I have had breakfast, lunch, and dinner together. Most recently, it was breakfast. Arriving for a visit bearing her own porridge, she said, "Ruthie, you're going to love this: it has vanilla, almonds, pecans, and plums poached in maple syrup." How could I possibly disagree?

Mary is a cookbook author, photographer, and documentary filmmaker—as always, she had her camera in tow.

She consults for the visionary vegetarian food company her mother, Linda, launched in the early 1990s. In 2009, Mary, with her father and her sister Stella, launched Meat Free Monday, which combats the environmental impact of animal farming and fishing.

Mary joined me on a particularly lovely summer's day, when the zucchini in our garden were in full bloom, inspiring her choice of recipe to read: Risotto with Zucchini Flowers.

Growing up, Mum did the cooking. Dad would help. If you give him a job like, "Can you chop this?" he'll do it meticulously. Mum described herself as a peasant cook: go to the cupboard, find what's in there, and make something delicious with it.

Mum and Dad kept us all together as a family. When they went on tour, we would go with them, which is why we siblings are all so close. We were never left at home with other people. We would explore. For my sister Heather's birthday, we went to a Japanese restaurant and ordered the seaweed salad. We thought it was going to be like a crispy Chinese thing, but it was literally wet, slimy seaweed—we were like, "Eiuwww." But it was great for us. It wasn't the most delicious meal, but it opened our minds.

We spent summer holidays in Scotland, on this beautiful but remote farm, or in Arizona, because Mum went to the U of A and became a photographer there. When we went to these places, it was just us, so we did the cooking together and then sat down together to eat. We didn't have housekeepers, chefs, chauffeurs, or any of that kind of stuff, which I really value now, because I know how to cook. I spent my childhood with my family around a table, talking endlessly about food and flavors.

I remember that we had a family discussion when I was quite young, five or six. Mum and Dad said, "Let's sit down. We want to talk to you." They said, "Look, we've decided we don't want to eat meat anymore. You can choose what you want to eat when you're out, but at home, this isn't going to happen."

It wasn't a problem because my mum was a great cook. The big thing was, we would always talk about it. My dad was very clever. He'd say, "Look, if we are not going to eat a turkey, then what are we going to eat? Because we want something you can slice and put at the center of the plate." Mum was like, "Well, I could do this macaroni thing and we could slice it."

It all sounds a bit crazy, but that was the beginning of how it carries on to this day. I'll do it with my husband and my family. I don't ever want to feel like I'm missing out as a vegetarian. I don't want to go to a restaurant and have someone look at my entrée and say, "Oh, I'm sorry you have to eat that." I want it to be more like, if we get it right, somebody will say, "Oh, I wish I had ordered that rather than this steak."

My husband always jokes that I'm a vegetarian who doesn't really love vegetables, because I will never be found eating a plain piece of steamed broccoli. I like a dressing. I like a soup. It's all about little flavors.

Also, I'm not judgy about vegetarianism. I have tasted meat and I understand the appeal. When I left home to work in London as a photographer, I tried a tuna salad sandwich at my lunch hour. I loved the taste of it. But then all I could think about was, "I know how to cook differently. I don't need to eat this." Because I've grown up a certain way, I've never considered meat or fish a food.

I didn't realize that this was unusual until we started promoting Meat Free Monday. It's all word of mouth. We often think that we can't do anything for the planet and we get overwhelmed. What I love about the idea for Meat Free Monday is that you can have one day where you don't eat meat or fish and you're not giving in to that industry. It's a really easy way of reducing your carbon footprint and being kinder to animals, if you want to.

What I found is that when people start doing Meat Free Monday, it grows into a part of their lifestyle and makes them consider what they're eating a bit more. At work, if I was on a photo shoot, people started coming up to me to say, "I love Meat Free Monday and we're trying to do it with our family, but I don't know what to cook."

That really surprised me because I'd grown up talking about food and asking questions like, "What are we going to do with that gap on the plate if we're not having meat or fish?" So then I thought, "Okay, I can share these recipes." That's what Mum did. That's why she did her cookbooks, because whenever people came to our house for dinner, they'd say, "I would definitely eat this way."

Mum grew up in America, New York City and Scarsdale. They had a cook in the house and she gravitated toward the kitchen. It was very much meatloaf and 1950s-style American cooking. In a way, that kind of went into her approach to vegetarian cooking. She would say, "Meat is often a matter of how you flavor it." So her recipe ideas stemmed from that.

I always considered myself half Liverpudlian and half American. In Liverpool, it was all, "Going to the chip shop," chip butties, very simple food. In New York, it was deli sandwiches and pizza. The minute we would get to New York to visit our Eastman grandparents, it would be straight out to get pizza.

My mum's mum died in a plane crash in the early '60s. Then my grandfather remarried, to a French American woman named Monique. We thought of her as quite strict. She believed in the idea of "Children should be seen and not heard." But when I became a teenager, Monique and I bonded in the kitchen. Whereas Mum taught me about instinctive, peasant cooking, Monique taught me how to make pastry and soufflés. She taught me how to make a pâtisserie apple tart—things in my cooking that I still use. Like, in my new cookbook, I bring an apple tart to Dame Judi Dench. It's four ingredients, because I'm not making the pastry. It's just ready-rolled pastry, thinly sliced apples, olive oil, and a glaze of apricot jam.

I'm always trying to myth-bust the idea that plant-based or vegetarian cooking involves more ingredients and takes longer. With all of the recipes I develop, I try to use the fewest ingredients and make it in the quickest, easiest, and most pleasurable way. I love a shortcut and I love make-ahead, especially if I'm having a dinner party. You can prep it all the night before and then have it ready to cook.

I often start with the name of a recipe and think, "Now how would I make that?" A lot of the answers are surprisingly simple. I did a Caesar salad dressing with torn sourdough croutons. When I put the croutons in, I was like, "Oh my God, I can't believe I've made such delicious dressing. This took me thirty seconds!" My mouth was watering.

The more I do it, the more surprised I am with how simple and delicious vegetarian cooking can be. I'm not fully vegan, but I'm exploring more plant-based vegan ideas, too. For my new recipe book, I made a beurre-less beurre blanc sauce. I thought, "I wonder if I could use olive oil instead of butter?" I used plant-based cream instead of cream, a little bit of cornstarch to make it glossy, and some mustard and white wine. It was incredible.

You really put your heart on the line when you're cooking for someone, because you want to please them. You can see when somebody takes that first bite: if they light up, it's like an electric shock of joy. That's why *The Great*

*British Bake Off* is one of my all-time favorite shows. Because there's that drama. The cake can look beautiful, but if you overbake it by two minutes, it can be dry and a chore to eat. The pleasure of feeding people, I think, is my main motivation. Anyway, you can tell that I'm obsessed with food.

*Mary, what is your comfort food?*
There is one hands-down comfort food for me: my mum's cream of tomato soup. She actually taught me how to make it. It was inspired by a lobster bisque. It's got tomatoes and onions and celery. She would cook it all down and put it through one of those Mouli food mills, and then put cream and herbs in it. I've kind of adapted and grown that recipe over the years. If I'm a little flat or down, that soup is my sunshine. It brings me joy.

# STELLA McCARTNEY

Stella McCartney's been coming to The River Cafe for thirty years, and 99 percent of the time, it has been with her husband, Alasdhair, and their children. When not them, then with her sister Mary, or brother, James, or Paul, her father. They're a strong family and the happiest times are when they're all here together.

Stella's mother, Linda, was, like her daughter, a woman with conviction, imagination, and passion. I wish I'd known her.

Stella founded Stella McCartney in 2001, a cruelty-free company using no animal products in its clothing. She's a fashion designer with ethics, a spokesperson for sustainability, a supporter of young designers, an entrepreneur who takes on risks for a cause.

She's also mischievous, a natural performer. Choosing the Chickpea and Fennel Farinata—a Ligurian street food—she announced she would recite the recipe in her sexiest voice. And she did.

My very early years were in Scotland. We had a tiny little vegetable patch. Mary and I would get into trouble because there were sugar snaps and carrots in the patch, and we would nick them and eat them before the plants could yield any kind of significant crop. Also, we had horses, so were always like, "Right, we'll eat the carrots and give the carrot tops to the horses."

When we got a bit older, my parents got the farm in East Sussex and then we had a proper vegetable patch. It's funny, I grew up on an organic farm and now I have one of my own, and it's always the vegetable patch that is the most exciting place to be. It's an incredible blessing to grow up that way, understanding when a lettuce is coming into season or when the cabbages and the beetroots are ready.

You have this adventure between picking the vegetable, feeling the soil, getting your fingernails dirty, feeding the carrot tops to the horses, and getting horse slobber all over your hands. So many different smells as well. I've worked on creating perfumes, and, it's interesting how the scents of foods have inspired a lot of the things that I've created. I did a perfume with truffle in it. When you're a vegetarian, there are so few moments of extravagance, whereas with meat, it's so associated with wealth and cost. For a vegetarian, it's only in truffle season that you think, "Right, okay—*this* is the moment." That scent! Everything associated with it seems sexy and mysterious and incredible.

We always ate together as a family, in the kitchen or the living room, on the sofa with a plate in your lap. It was the moment where we all reunited after whatever we'd been doing during the day. We also did a lot of road trips when I was young. We'd go up to Scotland in the car and have car-based sandwiches.

We were a big sandwich family. That's more my American side, because in those days, a British sandwich was butter on a piece of white bread and a slice of cheese. Our sandwiches were very layered, with lettuce and pickles and mayo. And since we traveled a lot, we had access to all these different cuisines. In Arizona, we had a lot of Mexican food. Out on Long Island in the summer, we had sweet corn. My mum used to eat it raw. She loved it so much that she wouldn't even boil it or put butter on it.

Her family came from Ukraine, through Russia, to the United States. So I was exposed to borscht, coleslaw, pickles, things like that. My grandfather, Lee, became a lawyer and did very well for himself. He was an entertainment lawyer who loved creative people. He basically represented all of the abstract expressionists: de Kooning, Rothko, Kline, Motherwell, Albers, all of these incredible artists. So my mum was exposed to extraordinary creative talent.

She rebelled from her upbringing. Everyone else was kind of fancy, going to Harvard and Yale and Smith. It was all too much for her. She went to the U of A, and then she became a photographer. She shot Hendrix, Otis Redding, Aretha Franklin, the Mamas and the Papas. Then she met Dad, and the rest is history. She was just a beautiful, pure soul. I think the two of them meeting, and him surrendering into that relationship, meant that we as a family went into self-isolation at a very early age. We went up to Scotland, and it was just the six of us in a shed.

Everyone who cooks has one or two utensils in their kitchen that are so past their sell-by date that they're knackered and chipped, but you just can't throw them away. For us, it was the salad bowl. It was the sacred thing in the kitchen, this big salad bowl carved out of one piece of wood. Mum would never let anybody wash it. You'd just dry it out with a dishcloth or paper towels.

My mum made a wicked salad dressing. In England, they didn't really have salads when I was growing up, more like a blob of salad dressing on a leaf: the kiss of death in our house. Mum would always make these incredible salads. It was a big coming-together for us, because the salad would be tossed and we'd all be served out of the same bowl, and the last serving out was the best one, because it had the most dressing on it.

For my wedding, my aunt Louise, my mother's sister, got us as a present a salad bowl carved out of one piece of wood. I'm exactly the same with my kids as my mum was with us. If I see someone about to wash out the bowl with water, I have to run up and tell them that it's illegal. If the house was burning down, that salad bowl would be the one thing I'd save.

Growing up, it was already hard enough to walk into a room as the child of these legends. But then on top of that, I'd be at a dinner party and get served a special vegetarian entrée, like a grilled courgette. The person next to me would look on in horror and say, "*What* are you eating?" Almost as if they were saying, "What's *wrong* with you?" So I would already be apologizing for this life choice. And then, when I tried to explain it, I was often met with anger and defensiveness. Or I was the brunt of a joke. Every sitcom you'd watch on telly, if someone said, "Oh, I'm vegetarian," it was the setup for a joke.

I experienced the same kind of reactions in fashion as I did with food. Being a designer who has shunned fur and leather and never used animal products, I came at it thinking, "I don't understand why I'm not the coolest, most punk-rock person in the room. You're all using fur and leather and crocodiles. You're all eating meat. *You're* the ones that are boring and mainstream. *I'm* the one who's trying to push buttons and challenge convention."

It has since very much changed, largely because people associate animal agriculture with disease-ridden hotbeds and bird flu and mad cow and Covid-19. But I also think it's a conversation that more young people are having. A lot of them are vegetarian or vegan. Kids have been educated to see that the animal consumption is just not necessary. You can still eat really, really well. You can have great taste. You can still have a community around great food, great fashion, great everything.

I left home to go to college at St. Martin's, studying fashion design. When I came to London, I was lucky that I knew how to cook. I think watching Mum meant that I was a little ahead in that regard. I hosted my first dinner party when I was a bit older, and among the guests were Naomi Campbell and Donatella Versace! I had them to my house and I made globe artichokes. My mum would always steam a globe artichoke and make this amazing dip with olive oil, lemon juice, and Maggi, a liquid seasoning made from fermented wheat.

My guests came around and they were all like, "What's this, and how do we eat it?" And I thought, "Wait a minute. You're Donatella Versace. You don't know how to eat these?" I was so surprised. I've since come to think that when you're a vegetarian, you've already got a more heightened sense of things.

I was one of the first people to try the Impossible Burger. That's obviously a great success story for plant-based food versus conventional meat. When you look at things in terms of business, that's when I think we have a chance at solving these issues. As a businesswoman, I know that the minute that a plant-based meat company is growing faster on the stock exchange than a real-meat company, something exciting is happening.

I have been working closely with a company in San Francisco, a tech compny, that is growing leather from mushrooms and mycelium roots. That kind of thing is really fascinating, the crossover between food and fashion. I'm literally making handbags out of mushrooms.

*Stella, what is your comfort food?*
Probably a good bowl of pasta. With pasta, there are different levels of entry. Is it dried pasta? Is it with your three- or four-hour-simmering tomato sauce? Or is it with your quick one? Or is it homemade tagliatelle with truffles? I would probably go for the last option.

# VICTORIA BECKHAM

When Victoria comes to The River Cafe, there is no fuss. Sometimes she comes in with friends, at other times with her husband, David Beckham, and their children, Brooklyn, Romeo, Cruz, and Harper.

I'm always impressed that Victoria arrives early, to greet her guests and to discuss the menu and what she might like to eat. I was surprised to learn from Victoria—usually the one being observed—that she also likes to come to The River Cafe to people-watch.

She insists that her upbringing was "not as posh as people think." Her parents ran a successful wholesale electronics business. And though cooking was not a big part of the household, eating as a family was.

Victoria found the diet that worked best for her and sticks to it, rigorously. On the podcast, she read our recipe for Roasted Sea Bass.

You know what my mother used her oven for? A filing cabinet. This was the '80s, when I was growing up. If it didn't go in the microwave, Mrs. Adams wasn't interested in cooking it. She was a great mum and a great wife, but cooking was never really her thing. It was all about being super, super quick.

I was always darting in and out from dancing and singing lessons. Mum was so busy driving us around, running me and my brother and sister to all of our activities. That's part of the reason why she loved the microwave meals. But mealtime was important. We did always sit together, the five of us, in the kitchen. That's something we still do now with our kids, unless I'm traveling or David is.

We went out to dinner on Friday nights. My mum and dad loved Indian food and Chinese food. And my parents had a house in Spain, so we

were lucky enough to go there and also have a foreign holiday every year: Cyprus, America a couple of times.

I stopped eating red meat when I was about seven years old. I was at school, in a home economics lesson, and they were telling us about what goes into making sausages or hamburgers, something like that. I was absolutely horrified and haven't eaten meat since that day. My children eat meat, though. David does, too.

When I was sixteen, I moved to Surrey to take a place at Laine Theatre Arts college in Epsom. I ate very, very student-style food: Super Noodles (there we go again, the microwave), bowls and bowls of Frosties with skim milk, and those yogurts where you peel the wrapping off a corner of the container and dump a whole load of sugary God-knows-what into it. This was the '90s, when the phrase "fat-free" was rammed down our throats. We used to eat a lot of fat-free food without realizing how much sugar we were eating. Now it's quite the opposite. My diet includes lots of healthy fats from avocados, seeds, and nuts.

When I joined the Spice Girls, we lived in a house together and still ate like students, fighting over the food in the fridge. When we signed our record deal with Virgin, they took us to a lovely restaurant and opened a bottle of Cristal Champagne. I'd never had anything like that in my life. I was like, "Wow, that Champagne costs *how much*?" It was insanity. And I was supposed to be the posh one.

It was incredibly luxurious. We were going to wonderful restaurants and eating wonderful food, not just in England but all over the world. Initially, I was inclined to eat the entire contents of the bread basket. But very quickly, I came to the conclusion that I needed to adopt healthier ways.

So I became more conscious of what I was eating. I was demanding a lot of myself. I'd walk into the stadium in a pencil skirt and a blouse, carrying a Birkin, and then have to change into a PVC catsuit. I had to really try and eat in a clean way: lots of fresh vegetables, lots of fish. I don't have any dairy at all. I like things to be cooked in a very simple way. I don't like oils and butters and sauces.

Growing up, I had really bad skin. I went to see numerous dermatologists and no one could ever figure out what was wrong. But all of that cleared up when I started eating in this healthy, clean way.

I don't deny myself anything. If I want something, I'll have it. I like to have a drink with dinner. But I am the way I am: very, very disciplined.

*Victoria, what is your comfort food?*
Whole-grain toast with Stilton. I love salt. I'm a savory person as opposed to a sweet person.

# DAVID BECKHAM

David Beckham is close to being a professional chef. This is unfair. After all, I don't go around kicking balls into nets—how dare he make a brilliant risotto? His idea of a great evening is being home alone and cooking—impeccably, a three-course meal—for himself!

Growing up, David was always an adventurous eater—eating jellied eels and matzo ball soup with his grandfather in East London. When he was tranferred to AC Milan, he spent all the time between training taking cooking lessons, learning how to make the perfect risotto Milanese and rolling out the silkiest pasta sheets for ravioli.

Coming into The River Cafe to read the recipe for Tagliatelle with Fresh Girolles, Butter, and Parmesan for the podcast, he went straight to the kitchen and insisted on cooking it himself.

I love to cook. Along with wine, it's one of my biggest passions. I was in the kitchen the other day cooking for the kids, and Victoria was like, "Can I help? What can I do?"

I said, "Honestly, sit down. Have a vodka and tonic. Relax, be with the kids. This is what I love to do."

I had hardworking working-class parents. My dad, who installed boilers, was out from six in the morning 'til seven in the evening. My mum was, and still is, a hairdresser. She'd drop us at school in the mornings, then she'd do hairdressing throughout the day, then pick us up from school and bring us home. She cooked for me and my sisters every single night, and for every Sunday lunch.

She made the most amazing gammon and chips, served with a fried egg,

pineapple from a tin, and coleslaw: one of my favorite meals. Later, at around eight or nine in the evening, some old ladies would arrive and she would be doing their hair 'til eleven or twelve at night. I would make the cups of tea and bring the biscuits or the cake for all my mum's ladies. I loved doing that.

We spent weekends at my nan and granddad's house—my mum's mum and dad. Every Saturday morning, we'd turn up at their flat in London. My granddad was in the print trade. Because he had to go to work at about eleven o'clock in the morning, we'd arrive really early, around nine o'clock. The first thing I did when I walked through the door was open the fridge. In there, my nan always had fresh strawberries in a big pot of sugar.

My granddad was Jewish, so my gran also made this amazing chicken noodle soup with matzo meal dumplings, or what Americans call matzo balls. That's what I was brought up on. That and jellied eels, one of the delights of being from the East End of London. My nan and granddad liked to take us down to Chapel Market for pie and mash and jellied eels with liquor. The liquor is a green sauce made with parsley and the juices from the stewed eels.

Not many people I know like jellied eels. My gran liked them stewed. I like them in the gelatin. They come cut up in slices in this plastic pot, and I pour vinegar and pepper on it.

The filling in the pies was just ordinary mincemeat, but the pies were made with the most amazing pastry. I always asked them to turn mine upside down on my plate. On the side was a big dollop of mash with hardly any butter in it, just salt and potatoes. The jellied-eel liquor went well with the mash. I'd put some spicy vinegar on top, with a little bit of salt and lots of pepper.

I left home at fifteen to move up to Manchester. I was in lodgings for about four years before I bought my first house. I was excited to try cooking for myself, because I'd spent a lot of time in the kitchen with my mum.

I liked going out to dinner, but my favorite evenings were, and still are, cooking for friends. Or just for myself. Near the end of the pandemic, I had to be in isolation for five days because I'd been to Italy. On one of the last days, Victoria's parents had a party and I couldn't go to it. So everyone was out of the house. I secretly loved it. I had two amazing cuts of meat. One was a T-bone and the other was English Wagyu. I treated myself to some good red wine because I was on my own, feeling sorry for myself. I set the barbecue up and turned on the football.

I don't like to brag, but I cooked the meat to absolute perfection. I'd been watching the TV program *Chef's Table* that morning, and they had an Italian butcher on. I watched what he did. I put the T-bone on the grill—it was quite a thick piece—and cooked it for six or seven minutes on each side. I like my meat rare—medium at a push, but preferably rare. It came out perfect. And it was only me in the house, so I ate it all.

There's nothing better than when you have time to get everything right. I made a nice tomato-and-shallot salad and opened a bottle of Italian Masseto. Poured a couple of glasses for myself. It was the most amazing meal that I'd had for a long time.

When Victoria and I were first dating, we used to go to this restaurant in the Midland Hotel in Manchester called the French Restaurant. It was very fancy. We'd sit in the corner and order the most expensive bottle of Champagne and the most expensive bottle of red wine. We didn't know what we were drinking. We just wanted to have a nice night out and know that we were drinking something great. I want to say that I ordered a '62 or '67 Latour. I had no idea what it was but I knew I was tasting something special.

When I had to leave Manchester United, I was devastated. But living in different countries proved to be a real education—eating different foods, trying different things. In Manchester, I only drank a glass of wine every now and again. But when we moved to L.A., I really started loving wine. We would go up to Napa Valley and sit with winemakers like Bill Harlan and Ann Colgin. There's nothing better than sitting at a table with someone who really knows what they're talking about—what they're drinking, what they're smelling, what they're tasting. Annoyingly, Victoria has a better palate than I do. She'll never admit it. She'll say, "David's the expert." But then she'll say something like, "Ooh, that tastes of smoke and charcoal." And I'm like, "Uh . . . yeah. It really does."

When I first moved to Spain, I was twenty-seven years old. I lived there for four years. I tend to become obsessed with wherever I live, because in my head, I decide, "Okay, this is where I'm going to be for the rest of my life." I had to look at it like that, because I wanted to throw myself into the culture, the language, the food, everything about the country.

Spain has a big food-and-family culture. I couldn't believe how long the lunches went on for. We'd start at two in the afternoon and still be sat there at seven. Then they'd all go for a sleep, and then we'd all come back and have dinner at 11 o'clock, by which time I was falling asleep at the table.

I loved everything about the food in Spain: the *jamón*, the *lomo*, the *percebes*. Every time I go back to Madrid, I come back to London with a big leg of *jamón*. It goes in the middle of the kitchen island in our house. Every time one of the kids walks past, they slice a piece off.

When I was playing in Italy for eleven months, on loan to AC Milan, I decided to take a course in Italian cuisine. I'd train in the morning and learn to cook in the afternoon. I took private lessons at first, but then I joined a class. Everybody was so focused on what they were doing that they couldn't be bothered that I was there.

I did the culinary course because my kids' favorite food is Italian. I wanted to make the perfect ragù and the perfect risotto. I'd always had in my head that making a risotto was difficult, but actually, it's not so. The stock is the most important thing. Then you're literally stood there for twenty minutes, keeping an eye on everything, making sure that it's not going dry, that it's not got too much liquid in it. The ending is the part where everything comes together with the Parmesan. The thing I love about Italians and Italian culture is that it's all about family. And about food and wine, too, of course.

I was lucky that food never really affected my fitness. The dietary requirements for athletes, especially in football, have totally changed over the last twenty years. When I first joined Manchester United, after you finished training, the canteen was all about steak and chips and beans. And then you'd have a jam roly-poly or a slice of chocolate cake with custard.

Now, depending on the manager you're playing under, you have a more restricted diet. There were certain managers who only wanted us to eat boiled chicken, which was disgusting, but that's what we had to eat. In Milan, it was the opposite. I was concerned about staying fit while eating so much pasta and olive oil. But in fact, it was one of my fittest periods, because the produce is so clean and the quality of the ingredients is so incredible. I was also careful never to have so much as a glass of wine for days before a game, because I didn't want it to affect me.

That awareness is part of the culture now. It's what we try and do with our kids, to educate them that if they eat and drink the right things, and look after themselves starting now, at a young age, they'll continue it throughout their lives. Brooklyn, like me, loves to cook. He posts a lot of the things he's making on Instagram. All the kids love cooking, really. During lockdown, Harper and I built our own herb garden. We planted rocket, mint, and rosemary, and we got very excited when we saw it all come together. Now, every time Nana comes over and has a gin and tonic, Harper goes out into the herb garden, cuts off a sprig of rosemary, and puts it in her glass.

*David, what is your comfort food?*
A toastie, with Hovis bread and baked beans.

# SALMAN RUSHDIE

Food. Stories. Family. Tradition. These animate Salman's novels.

Salman and our family have been close friends from the day we met in the late '80s, traveling to Italy together, meeting for family dinners, just knowing we were there for each other. Wherever we were, there was a search for a Ping-Pong table for Salman, Richard, and Roo—Salman is proud of the fact he was one of the only people who could beat Richard.

Salman lives in New York City with his wife, the poet and novelist Rachel Eliza Griffiths. Raised in Mumbai, he was educated in Britain. Salman has always cared deeply about food. When I asked him to select a recipe to read aloud on the podcast, he immediately chose our Marinated Grilled Lamb, a dish that dates back to our earliest River Cafe times.

Salman was there on the first day of The River Cafe, and the lamb is still what he orders today.

I was born and raised in Bombay. My mother didn't like highly spiced food. She didn't like chilies, so the food in our house was always quite mild. My sister, Sameen, and I grew up on this food.

We had a cook. My mother trained the cook in the food of our household. In India, in middle-class kitchens that employ cooks, there is always what is known as a copy book, hanging on a hook. In those books are the recipes of the family. I've always thought that if somebody could just go and gather all the recipes in the copy books, that would be the greatest Indian cookbook of all.

My mother's mother was not a cook. She was a grumpy old lady who shouted at cooks. But my mother was a gentle person. I also had an *ayah*, a nanny from

South India. She came from Bangalore, which has its own very distinctive cooking. Mary Menezes, she was called. She spoke seven languages and was illiterate. She lived to 102. Her pickles and chutneys got into my novel *Midnight's Children* because I grew up on those. There was a particular green chutney, just a lot of green things chopped up with a lot of chilies: a very South Indian recipe that arrived in our house through her.

There's a line somewhere in *Midnight's Children* where the narrator talks about stirring feelings into food. I always believed that if you're in a good mood, the food tastes one way, and if you're in a bad mood, the food tastes another way. Your emotion goes into the cooking. My mother wasn't a great chef, but she enjoyed cooking, so her food was enjoyable.

I don't think my father ever so much as fried an egg. His family was originally from Delhi. My parents had moved to Bombay before I was born, but he still had a lot of connections and business in Delhi, so sometimes I would go with him, staying in a hotel and messing around while he did his work. Delhi is the heart of North Indian cuisine—Mughlai cooking, as it's called, the cooking left behind by the Mughal Empire. It's richer than South Indian food. It uses a lot of yogurt and ghee. The farther south in India you go, the more vegetarian the cuisine becomes. And the farther north, the more meat-oriented it becomes. That's the difference between the Muslim culture of the North and the Hindu culture of the South.

I was only thirteen when I left home to go to boarding school in England. The food there was dreadful. When we got overcooked beef patties, that was the highlight of the week.

I didn't like much about school. I felt quite isolated. The food was certainly part of what I didn't like. When I got my place at Cambridge, I didn't want to go. I asked my parents to let me go to university in India. But my father had been to King's College at Cambridge and was very keen that I follow him. In the end, I went, and I'm glad I went, because I had a much better time than I did in boarding school.

Five of us from Cambridge rented a place in London just off the New Kings Road: a five-bedroom house for £5 each. This was 1968. Those were the days. There was a kitchen there, so we would all pile in and make spaghetti.

Then I went to work in two or three advertising agencies. I was at Ogilvy & Mather for a long time. I never did the three-martini-lunch thing. In those days, Ogilvy's was more or less on Waterloo Bridge. There wasn't much in terms of food. You would walk to Covent Garden if you wanted to get something to eat, the fruit and vegetable market. Eventually I managed to get a job where I only had to be there two or three days a week, which gave me the other days of the week to stay home and write.

As a writer, my view about eating is work hungry, eat later. If I've had a nice meal, I can't write. I just get slow and sleepy.

In the morning, I have virtually nothing other than a cup of coffee. Sometimes I have some fruit juice with it, but not much more than that. And then I go to work. For how long depends on where I am in the writing process. In the early stages of writing a book, when it's making something out of nothing, after two or three hours, you're burned out and you start writing things that you know you're not going to use. But in the later part of a book, when you are writing a final version, I work all the time: twelve, thirteen, fourteen hours a day. Sometimes then, I'll have a bit of lunch.

I like to go out for dinner. In New York, the grand old restaurants just have a great feeling to them. If you walk into Indochine, Balthazar, or the Waverly Inn, you think, "This is a place I want to be." What I like about Indochine is that it's been there since the mid-'80s but the food has never dropped in quality. The restaurant is obviously not what it used to be, when it was the hottest ticket in town, but they've never allowed the food to become ordinary.

Food does a lot to tell you where you are. Just before the pandemic, I was able to go to a literary event in Oaxaca in Mexico, where I ate a whole plate of fried grasshoppers. One of the sensational things about Italy is that it's impossible to have a bad meal. The same is true of Paris—you don't have to go to a fancy restaurant, you can sit at a corner brasserie and have something delicious. My big hole, in terms of travel, is the Far East of Asia: Japan, Vietnam, Asia. They're all high on my list of places I'd like to go.

I remember that when I was looking for a U.S. literary agent, I was taken out to a very swanky lunch at the Russian Tea Room by a very powerful agent whose name I won't mention. She was so grand at me that it was actually off-putting. Meanwhile, there was this other agent wooing me who had an office that was one and a half rooms: him, a secretary, and a Xerox machine. But he was so dynamic and energetic, I thought, "I want that one, not the fat cat." That's how I came to appoint Andrew Wylie, and it's the best decision I've ever made.

My sister, Sameen, wrote a cookbook. She's all sorts of things—she's a very good lawyer, she's worked in community relations. She wanted to capture our home cooking in some way, and I egged her on because she is a very good cook. It took her a long time, but what came out of this agonized process, *Sameen Rushdie's Indian Cookery*, is something close to a classic. Not all of the recipes are memories of my mother's kitchen, but that's where she started. Then she added in stuff of her own. It turns out that Sameen is ridiculously talented.

*Salman, what is your comfort food?*
It's always going to be Indian food. I'm very happy with yellow dal and white rice. One of the bad habits I have is to have bread at the same time as rice. You're supposed to have either/or. So that's my bad-behaving comfort food.

# RACHEL ELIZA GRIFFITHS

There's nothing better than when someone you love finds love.

Eliza Griffiths is a poet and photographer whose black-and-white images evoke the work of Dorothea Lange. Her critically acclaimed debut novel, *Promise*, is about two sisters living in Maine at the dawn of the civil rights movement; food plays a major role in their story.

Eliza and Salman revel in each other's food heritages: African American in Eliza's case, Indian in Salman's. Eliza joined us in The River Cafe kitchen preparing Smashed Broad Beans with Mozzarella. And so did Salman. We only put this dish on the menu when the first broad beans of the season arrive, small and sweet.

I grew up in Wilmington, Delaware. Between Wilmington and Washington, DC, there's so much culture and so many kinds of food: Ethiopian, French, Italian, all different kinds of things. My mother experimented with cooking different types of food. I have a lot of vivid memories of shopping for food with her. She never did it all in one place. She had a certain butcher she went to, a certain place for flowers. Sometimes we'd go as far as Philadelphia just for a certain spice.

  Our home was a place where, in our community, if people knew that my mother was cooking, they were not declining that invitation. I'd have to iron and starch the tablecloths and help with the flowers and polish the silver. It was a whole stage that she set, even down to the music that might be on. There was so much joy about it. She had her tasting spoons. She wouldn't give up on a recipe until she really got it, until she didn't have to look at the cookbook anymore. I think some of that ethic is involved in my process as a writer. You can fail at your sentences, but you just keep pushing language until it gives, and you think, "I hear it now!"

I'm the eldest of four children, so I would be my mother's sous-chef quite often. It's made me a better person. Cooking was serious business for her. She was very meticulous about her equipment and materials. She actually taught classes sometimes. She had a chef's uniform she would put on, and she won prizes for her bread pudding recipe. I've been spoiled by her version. Whenever I see bread pudding on a menu, I immediately see her face and hear her say, "No one's is as good as mine!" She put a special ingredient in it that only me and my three siblings can ever know.

My mother's kitchen was a place where I learned a lot of lessons. My hands were always busy and I loved that. To me, she was a real artist—how she worked with color, how the dishes were composed, the flowers she chose. It was a whole event. Even if you were making a grilled cheese, I'd be like, "How is this grilled cheese so amazing?"

When I was eleven or twelve, my mother was diagnosed with kidney failure. Her ability to work a more traditional job changed, because she was trying to raise four children while living with this chronic illness. One of the most beautiful things was that cooking was like a cure for her. She would spend part of the day in bed on her medications, but then she would rally and make things for her children and her family and her friends. She'd put on Smokey Robinson and Diana Ross and the Supremes and dance around in the kitchen. Suddenly, she wasn't a sick mother.

I went to the University of Delaware, and then, for graduate school, Sarah Lawrence College in New York. In college, I was the person doing dinner parties. I commandeered the dormitory kitchen. Pots of pasta, garlic bread. I would drape scarves over the awful fluorescent dormitory lights. And I would have candles everywhere. I wanted to make people feel like it was a home away from home. I do not like doing dishes, so other students would volunteer to do that part.

I'm used to cooking for six people or more, so I love making large pots of things. Sometimes my husband is like, "Don't make so much, just cook for two. We're going to eat this for five or six days."

In 2003, I had that moment that I think many writers have, where I just thought, "I need to live in New York. I want to see what I'm made of. Can I make it?" I worked every kind of job. I was a nanny at one point. I was a waitress for about an hour.

I loved finding little places to eat. It was just wonderful to have these discoveries, and also to go to restaurants that you read about when you're dreaming of becoming a writer. Suddenly you're going to them. I loved Caffe Dante in the West Village, the Hungarian pastry shop up by Columbia University, and Noho Star. The diner situation in New York was great for me—to just sit in a diner and write.

Now that I *am* a writer in New York, I don't really have that much food in the morning. For wellness's sake, I'll have my green mucky drink. Or I'll have some poached eggs, which I like with a little spinach.

It depends on what I'm doing. If I'm out in the field working on photographs, then I don't eat. I'll just have some fresh-squeezed juice and then I'm out, because I need to follow the light very carefully. If I'm writing, I can write for long periods of time on just a lot of tea. Salman and I both have a deep appreciation for wonderful cooking. So we'll work all day, and then perhaps we'll go out to a restaurant and meet a friend. We love to have Indian food delivered.

One of the things I love to do when we come to London is to sit at Salman's sister's table. Sameen usually cooks when we come to visit. It's such a treat. She'll have the chutney and the sauce and the samosas. She says, "Oh, I just put something together," and it's like the best thing you've ever tasted. When I've flipped through her cookbook and looked at the spices and things involved, I've felt overwhelmed. But I know that sooner or later, I'll need to get a proper curry in my skill set.

In novels, I love seeing how food is introduced to the reader. When no one's eating, you kind of notice. I do, anyway. What were they eating? What exactly are they drinking? What's in season?

In *Promise*, the two Black sisters who are the central characters of the novel are coming of age in 1957 in a remote sea village in Maine. In that space, which is very spare and bleak and suddenly becomes hostile to them, the shelter of their home is one of the things most important to them, along with their relationship to their mother as a nurturer. How does she feed her children? What's in season in a place like that?

In the space of that kitchen, with a mother who has her rules and her recipes, they're safe. Whereas outside of their home, things are beginning to become quite unsafe for them. Their mother cooks them a special "first day of school" meal that's almost as important as Christmas dinner for them. There are moments in the book in which certain things about each character are revealed by how they feel about the kitchen, or what they're eating, or the comfort that food offers them in a place that is starting to change as things are happening elsewhere in America.

If I were to expand outward and think about Black American families and their food trajectories and storylines—how food is important to joy and survival, how foods are invented, how recipes are handed down—I find all of that lovely and magical. It's a delicious lineage.

*Eliza, what is your comfort food?*
I'd probably make something my mother made me. She had some wonderful soups. When I was young, there was nothing like coming into the house on one of those days where I was a little bit blue and I could immediately smell that my mother was making a soup.

# KERI RUSSELL
# MATTHEW RHYS

Looking out in The River Cafe, I'm always happy to see couples having a great time. But I also know that every table has a story. A change of jobs, a marriage proposal, or a separation.

I first met this couple, Keri Russell and Matthew Rhys, as stars of one of my favorite television series of all time, *The Americans*, when they were playing a couple—but were not yet a couple. I watched their tempestuous relationship on screen through thick and thin for six years.

It was therefore a big moment for me when I finally met them officially, sitting at a table in The River Cafe, as guests of Jane Hartley, a friend and the U.S. ambassador to the United Kingdom. Much to Jane's amusement, Keri acts this very same role in the Netflix series *The Diplomat*.

Keri grew up in southern California, Matthew in Wales, and they now live in Brooklyn with their three children. I caught up with them when visiting New York. "Sage and butter are big in our house," Matthew declared—perhaps this is why they chose to read The River Cafe recipe for Tagliatelle with Porcini and Sage.

**Matthew**

I grew up in Cardiff, Wales. My parents were teachers and then my father became the principal of a Welsh-speaking school. Like a lot of the Celts, the Welsh are very culturally minded, in the cause of keeping their culture alive.

At school, English lessons were in English, but that was it. Everything else was taught in Welsh. I remember learning English when I was four. It was this new phenomenon. I used to call it "Yes-No Language" because those words were all I could say for a while. I speak only Welsh to our youngest, Sam.

It wasn't a particularly conscious choice, it was just something I did instinctively when he was born. But then, I speak to dogs in Welsh. I don't know what that tells you.

Welsh food, like that of the Irish and the Scots, comes very much from a peasant culture. The off cuts are primary. The great dish of Wales is what we call *cawl*, which is a lamb's neck soup, usually made with potatoes, leeks, and carrots. Everything is simmered and you add a little bit of milk in, and some thyme and salt.

The other big one we ate was laverbread, which has nothing to do with bread. It's triple-cooked seaweed made into a patty with oatmeal and then fried in bacon fat and usually eaten with cockles. The majority of Wales is surrounded by the sea, so, again, it's peasant-influenced, by what could be scavenged from the shoreline.

The culmination of the week was always the Sunday roast. That was everything. We'd go into the dining room for that. A lot of lamb and beef. A number of people in my father's family are sheep farmers. We are now obsessed with Yorkshire pudding, which I've terrified Keri with. The kids obsess on it now. They call it "those bread things."

Restaurants for me growing up were very special. On Mother's Day, we always went out. There was one place, still going, called the Walnut Tree in Abergavenny. My parents took us there when we finished our big A-level exams. That, for me, was the dizzying height of cuisine. The first time we went, for my older sister, I saw the seafood platter and said, "What's that?" When it was my turn, that's what I ordered.

**Keri**

My dad was a suit for a car company. He would get in a car and drive to multiple places for work. So four nights a week, it was just my mom and three kids. I am the middle child, with an older brother and a younger sister.

My mom wasn't the best cook, but what she was great at was asking things like, "Do you want pancakes tonight?" There were no rules. The magic of that was really nice to grow up with.

That being said, I really noticed when there was good cooking at a friend's house. No disrespect to my mom, but I loved watching mothers who really spent time cooking. My grandmothers were great cooks. They were raised in completely different places, but they both made incredible chicken noodle soup. My dad's mom was a bit more into elaborate meals. There were rules and people dressed nice.

**Matthew**

You said you always remembered the clink of ice because the cocktails were always big. Highballs.

**Keri**

Yes, the tumblers and the ladies with painted nails wearing nice slacks. My mom was more of a hippie, so that was also exotic to me. We always ate together, and it was a loving, fun, imaginative time. She was a really good mom in that way.

Now in our family, though our teenager doesn't really love it, we eat dinner really early, like 5:30 or 6 p.m. I like that when everyone comes home, you have to sit down and eat. You can do anything you want after.

**Matthew**

My mother loved to cook and entertain. We certainly grew up instilled with the idea that everyone sat around the table for dinner. I've become the stickler in our house for table etiquette. I'm a little too crazy about the correct holding of the knife and fork. My big thing is, "It's not a pen. Are you writing with that knife?" Also, napkins on laps. Then we're into the second phase, which is conversation: "Can you please ask one of your siblings a question?"

**Keri**

River, he's the eldest. By the time we come around to him, he's just like, "Willa. How was your day?"

**Matthew**

He's like, "What's the bare minimum I can say that will get me away from this table as quickly as possible?"

**Keri**

I started working when I was fifteen. I love everything that I've been able to do because of this strange circus upbringing that I've had. But there was a point in my young twenties, when I was doing a television show called *Felicity* and working crazy long hours, that I had heartache and romantic nostalgia for normal stuff like family dinners and birthday parties.

I was working at such a pace for so long. The wonderful thing about our lives now is that we work hard, crazy long hours when we're shooting a show or a movie, but then that affords us six months off where I get to do nothing but do laundry, organize birthday parties, walk the kids to school, and cook dinners. When I had one kid, I was more involved in cooking and I would bake a lot. Now that we have three kids, it's more like survival. I know I'll get back to it. But to be a good cook, it's just the highest art.

**Matthew**

She's being modest. She's got a very good baking game. She makes a ginger scone, and every birthday, she makes me a pear cake with cream cheese frosting.

Pasta is an absolute staple of our household, as I'm sure it is for many people with young children. I've been out for beautiful dinners with Keri and she'll come home and make a bowl of pasta with butter and sage. With genuine wonderment, I'll ask, "Where and how?"

**Keri**

Yeah, I love the restaurant food when I eat it. But if miraculously I'm still awake past 9 p.m., by 10:30 or so, I need more food.

I think my upbringing informed my longing for family dinners in my younger twenties. I consistently sought out boyfriends who had big families and moms who cooked. I realized, "Oh, I'm dating you for your mom!"

**Matthew**

I left home when I was eighteen, to go to the Royal Academy in London to study acting. But I always headed home for Christmas and all the big holidays. I have such visceral memories of running to Paddington and grabbing a four-pack of Stella Artois for the train. And sometimes, Mum would do a slightly earlier Sunday roast so I could get one of the last trains back to London.

**Keri**

When I'm on a set, I think we can both confirm that I mostly eat donuts.

**Matthew**

Donut fiend. She can inhale them.

**Keri**

Not so much anymore. But when we were doing *The Americans*, it was often winter, shooting outside in New York at night. They became my fuel. I'm sure that was really good for my health.

**Matthew**

The meal scenes in *The Americans* were pandemonium because you're in that one concentrated area for so long. Everyone is trying to figure out how to eat without eating.

**Keri**

Because you shoot a scene that will last five minutes. But you have to shoot it for six hours to get everyone's coverage of it. One of the fun things about *The Diplomat* is the writer who created the show, Deborah Kahn, wants the character to eat really messily—just constantly shoving food in her face, which is really fun. But it's gross, too, because you have to continually eat.

**Matthew**

Actors talk about those who really do eat onscreen and those who are just nibbling. Noah Emmerich and I had this one scene in *The Americans* where our director said, "Listen, I really want to *see* you eat. I want to see you swallow. I don't want chewing and then we cut away and you spit into a bucket." We really had to map out the length of the scene and how to shoot it coverage-wise. I had so much dough in my stomach at the end. I didn't feel well at all.

*Keri and Matthew, what are your comfort foods?*

**Keri**

Something I cook myself. Matthew joked about when we go out and I still make pasta before going to bed. It's a simple pasta with butter and whatever I have. I might add rosemary to it, but sage would be ideal. That's what feels good.

**Matthew**

I'm certainly with you on that pasta. But if I'm talking pure comfort, it would always be that cawl my mother made. I used to play soccer, and I'd come in on a winter's morning feeling so cold. The cawl was on the stove and it would be served with a huge piece of bread and some cheese. That was everything.

# ELTON JOHN
# DAVID FURNISH

The River Cafe's open kitchen gives me the chance to observe people having dinner with their children. When I see Elton John and David Furnish with their sons, Zachary and Elijah, they are particularly focused—listening, laughing, the four of them together in their own private world. They take the food seriously, spending quite a long time over the menu, deciding what to order.

Elton, one of the greatest musicians of our time, and David, a producer, director, and actor, are committed activists and philanthropists. They founded the Elton John AIDS Foundation in 1992. Together since 1993, they registered their civil partnership in 2005, the first day it was legal to do so in the U.K., leading the way for others to follow suit with confidence and pride.

I met with them at what Elton describes as "the hub," their country house near Windsor Castle. They read our recipe for Risotto with Porcini and Girolles.

**David**

We met here, in this house. Our first meal together was at this table. Elton had just come back from touring. He was single and had a friend staying with him. He said, "I don't want to sit around the house like a widow. Let's just have a dinner party and invite some people down."

**Elton**

I was in AA , so I hadn't really met anybody except AA people for three years. I had thrown myself into getting well as much as I had thrown myself into getting unwell. I did what I was told and had a great time. But I had lost touch with people.

**David**

So Elton's friend rang my friend Malcolm. I was supposed to go to Malcolm's house that night. He was having a dinner party. Elton's friend said, "Why don't you bring your dinner party down to Windsor?" Elton didn't know me. I had no connection at all. It was very random.

I was vegetarian then. I came through the door and everyone was having spaghetti Bolognese. Elton's housekeeper made me a pasta bake with cheese. Honestly, I wasn't thinking much about the food. I was so overwhelmed by meeting *Elton John*.

He asked for my number that evening. The next morning he called me and said, "I'm coming into London today. Would you want to come around and have dinner with me at my house? We'll have a Chinese takeaway."

I arrived at the house and there were four giant cardboard boxes on the kitchen counter, with the table set for two. I said, "Who else is coming?" It was all from Mr. Chow. Elton didn't know what I liked, so he ordered the entire menu.

**Elton**

I grew up in the aftermath of World War II. I lived in a council house in Pinner with my mother and grandmother, because my father was away in the air force in Aden. I didn't really see much of him. It was a women's household. My aunt, my mum's sister, was always there as well. So I grew up with a bunch of women who knew how to cook, which was great.

My grandmother was wonderful. She could cook anything and make it taste incredible. Basic ingredients were hard to get back then. We were rationed, so bacon was usually a no-no. We'd be given a tiny bottle of orange juice, which you diluted and poured into everyone's glasses. But I never remember a bad meal or going hungry, and everything that was left over, my grandmother made into something else the next day.

What I loved about her, because I have the biggest sweet tooth, was her bread puddings and apple pies, her scones and Victoria sponges.

The coal cellar was in the kitchen. Can you believe it? The laundry was done on the stove in a boiler. We toasted our toes by the fire. It was a very basic upbringing, but the smell of cooking was always wonderful.

I fell in love with very basic, simple English food. Sometimes I'll walk into a restaurant in, say, Yorkshire, and they have things like that on the menu, and for me, it's just a sheer delight. Or if you go to St. John in London, for instance, they have Eccles cakes that they serve with cheese, and it's just like, "Wow, man, this is from heaven." Nowadays, unfortunately, I can't eat things like that because I'm semi-diabetic. But I do love those English stalwarts.

**David**

I grew up in Canada, in Toronto. I was the middle of three boys, and we were very lucky. My mum was a stay-at-home mum, who could make almost anything happen instantly. She had a deep freeze in the basement. Sometimes we'd come back from school or a sports match and we'd bring two friends along. She'd say, "No problem!" She'd go downstairs and thaw out some pastry, some meat, and a tomato sauce or something else she'd prepared in advance. Our dinner could expand or change with just thirty minutes' notice.

My grandparents on my mother's side were from the north and the south of Ireland, and my grandparents on my father's side were from England and Wales. So a lot of those traditions came across to Canada: the Sunday roast with Yorkshire pudding, roast potatoes, roast beef, brussels sprouts, beans, carrots, a really good gravy, and then always a baked pie or cake for dessert. My British grandmother was an amazing baker.

**Elton**

The thing about my grandmother was, because we had a garden, we grew all our own produce—because it was so much cheaper. My grandmother had a green thumb, so we always had fresh vegetables. I hardly ever had canned or processed peas. The great advantage of those days was that food wasn't really instant. No instant whips, no instant mashed potato. It was all genuinely from the garden, which was delicious.

Like it was for David, Sunday roast was very important for our family gathering. So I would shell the peas and peel the potatoes on Sunday morning.

My mother worked really hard. She worked in a shop, at a dairy, for the air force. But she always came home and cooked. The first time I remember going to a restaurant is when we went to a Chinese restaurant in Harrow. Chinese restaurants suddenly became the rage. Coffee bars had been the rage before that. It was just so delicious and exotic. "Wow, bean sprouts!"

**Elton**

When I met Bernie Taupin, my songwriting partner, I was nineteen or twenty and we shared a flat in Islington. It had a kitchen, but I am incapable of cooking anything, and Bernie is, too. So we just ate out. Fish and chips, stuff like that. We couldn't afford expensive things.

The first real exciting restaurant I went to was when Dick James took me to a restaurant off of Tottenham Court Road. He was my manager and music publisher. He had also published the Beatles. He was very famous. We went to this restaurant called La Maisonette. I had a prawn cocktail. I'd never seen anything like it and didn't know how to eat it. That was the first "posh"—in inverted commas—restaurant that I ever went to. And the bread was lovely, too. I thought, "This is a step up. It's not the Aberdeen Steak House, this one. This is a proper restaurant." I'm sorry, Aberdeen Steak House.

When I became successful, it was a different kettle of fish. I met people who were more sophisticated than I was, who knew the London restaurant scene. I started going to better places with them. It's all part of the same journey: playing better venues, earning more money, living in a better place, eating at better restaurants. Step by step, you get introduced to different things. I never collected art until I suddenly became wealthy enough to buy some prints. It goes hand in hand with going to lovely restaurants. There were two restaurants in Covent Garden I used to go to all the time, The Garden and Inigo Jones.

**David**

In the '90s, Gianni Versace was a big part of our lives. We used to go to Gianni's house in Milan. He lived above his offices on Via Gesù in a beautiful apartment that had been decorated by Renzo Mongiardino. Spectacular. The meals were theater. He had white-coated butlers with white gloves and white jackets. You sat down and there was a beautiful piece of antique porcelain, and then whoosh, it was cleared away, and then a plate went down with a starter, and then whoosh, it was cleared away. And then another antique porcelain plate came down to be cleared away for the second course, and then taken away again for the main course.

**Elton**

The risotto at Gianni's was like nectar. Just so delicious. And the presentation went a long way, because he got me into collecting china and tablecloths. And napkin rings. It's his fault.

Gianni introduced us to the tablecloths at Jesurum in Venice, which is now closed, but it was the most beautiful shop. Then, on the island of Burano, we went to Merletti dalla Olga, which is the most incredible shop and has tablecloths of every size. We spent so much money one weekend on tablecloths that I couldn't believe it.

**Elton**

I like the restaurants we go to for their staff. I know a lot of people in my business who talk down to the serving staff. That's one thing I hate the most. The seductiveness is part of the experience.

Da Ivo, a place we go to in Venice, is the simplest restaurant, but it's beautiful because the maître d' comes to the table with this little chalkboard. You arrive there by boat and never look at a physical menu. They give you all of the specials for the day, and it's never the same meal twice.

The simplicity of it is so sexy and fun. I hate pretentious restaurants. I can't bear them. That's why The River Cafe is always enjoyable, because you come in and it's like the greatest canteen in the world, where you mix with a lot of people you know and everyone just seems to be having the best time. The service is great. The atmosphere is fantastic whether you're inside or outside. There's not an ounce of pretentiousness to it. And if there is, I'm off.

*David and Elton, what are your comfort foods?*

**David**

A really simple pasta with butter and Parmesan.

**Elton**

Bacon sandwich. On whole wheat bread with butter. Proper English bacon, not Danish, not streaky. Luscious bacon with the fat cut off and cooked well, so it's quite crackly.

# MICHAEL ELIAS

Michael is an actor (Living Theatre), a director (*Lush Life*), a novelist (*You Can Go Home Now*), a screenwriter (*The Jerk*), and a passionate cook. He is also my brother.

I am told that I fell in love with him the moment I met him: he was eight, I was a few hours old.

In the earliest days of The River Cafe, Michael surprised us with T-shirts and baseball caps with our logo. He was an early investor—"emotionally," he says—in everything we did.

My brother has vivid memories of our grandmothers and aunts cooking. Our sister, the artist Susan Elias, is also a great cook—when she lived in Paris, she did pâtisserie tours for American arts students.

Ricotta al Forno is the recipe Michael read, as he remembers me cooking it at home, long before The River Cafe opened.

We grew up in the Catskill Mountains and had family in New York City. Our grandparents kept kosher and cooked Eastern European food.

Our father's parents, Rose and Sam, were Hungarian. Rose made beautiful stuffed cabbage and roast chicken. She ground the meat herself for whatever she was making. And if she was visiting us, she brought her own rolling pin to roll out the strudel.

My father had six sisters, and they all cooked. They made Grandma's recipes, and everybody loved to eat. We always had big family dinners in their backyard in Brooklyn, under the trees. It was wonderful.

As family lore has it, the first time that our grandmother came to visit

after I was born, Mom asked, "Would you like to come and see the baby?" Grandma's response was, "Let's eat first."

One thing that set us apart from other families is that our father, Fred, who had gone to medical school in Germany and Switzerland, was rather sophisticated in terms of food. He came back to America with European tastes. I'm not saying that he taught our mother European recipes—he could barely boil water. But we were exposed to different things. We had sauerbrate. We had kippers and eggs for Sunday breakfast. We had eggplant Parmesan. We had interesting food growing up and we demanded it for the rest of our lives. I think he was an influence in that regard.

In the summers in Woodstock, we had fresh corn. Tomatoes and farm stands were a huge part of our lives. People would put a pot of water on the stove before they left the house so that by the time they returned from the corn stand, they could immediately tear off the husks and throw the corn in. It was almost like a contest: who could serve the freshest corn?

I went to college in Maryland, the home of the crab and the oyster. You could go down to the docks and get them fresh. Then I moved to New York to be an actor, and I couldn't afford any of those things. I was working in off-off-Broadway theater. I depended on the kindness of friends who were in the publishing business. They had expense accounts, and they took me to lunch, and that was wonderful.

In 1969, I moved to Los Angeles. It was very different. First of all, there were enormous supermarkets open twenty-four hours a day. They were like giant warehouses, brightly lit. I had never seen so many fruits and vegetables. And then there were Mexican restaurants. I met my first taco at a Mexican restaurant at the Farmers Market. And that became my love: Mexican food. I took Ruthie and Richard to La Super-Rica Taqueria, a roadside place in Santa Barbara that had become famous when Julia Child said, "This is the best Mexican restaurant on the West Coast." She was right. Sometimes, with friends we would drive down to Tijuana, then further south to Rosarita Beach, where there was a little restaurant that served broiled quail and the most exquisite baked potatoes. There was also a good Basque restaurant in Tijuana and Caesar's, where they invented the Caesar salad.

In L.A., I followed Wolfgang Puck from Ma Maison to Spago. I think he changed the world, opening a first-class restaurant that served pizza. It was revolutionary. He was also the first European-born chef in America to say, "I'm going to use Pacific influences in the food." All of a sudden, you saw Japanese and Chinese influences, very subtly, in what was basically an Italian restaurant.

I worked as a comedy writer. I wrote for the variety shows of Glen Campbell, the Smothers Brothers, and Leslie Uggams, and was at the same time writing scripts for *All in the Family* and *The Mary Tyler Moore Show*. Then I got into the movies. The first one was called *The Frisco Kid* and starred Gene Wilder as a young rabbi who comes from Poland to America during the Gold Rush and makes his way to San Francisco. Harrison Ford was also in it. Then I teamed up with Steve Martin and we wrote *The Jerk*. My passion project was *Lush Life*, which I wrote and, at my insistence, directed. It starred Jeff Goldblum and Forest Whitaker as jazz musicians. From that point onward, I could afford to eat well.

L.A. has so many ethnic restaurants now: Cambodian, Laotian, Chinese, Japanese, Mexican food of every region—all good stuff that I can't make at home and wouldn't even try to. That's the fun of going out in Los Angeles.

At a certain point, I told myself I was finished with movies and television and decided to write novels. My most recent book is *You Can Go Home Now* about a homicide detective in Queens. I like to write about what my characters eat. I feel it's as important as describing someone's nature or their physical appearance. I write about the lousy food my detective eats when she's on a stakeout, a foot-long meatball submarine sandwich and a lousy soda that's bubbling in her stomach.

That information is important to me. I don't like it when I read a novel and they say, "We stopped for dinner and then moved on." What did you *have* for dinner?

*Michael, what is your comfort food?*
Our aunt Florence's cheese blintzes. A blintz is a thin pancake stuffed with sweetened cottage cheese, and then folded over and fried in butter. You put sour cream on it or applesauce. I'm a sour cream guy.

Aunt Florence would periodically send me boxes of frozen cheese blintzes from Stockton. They would come on a Greyhound bus to downtown Los Angeles. She sent her last box just before she died—I ate them slowly, each one a reminder of her, keeping her alive. Now when I need something that really connects me to my family and our heritage, and to the generosity of the women who cooked in our family, I find a deli where I can get cheese blintzes and remember our lovely aunt Florence.

# ROO ROGERS

It's not an exaggeration to say that I know Roo Rogers intimately. We met for the first time when I gave birth to him in Paris, his father, Richard, and I having had a sensational dinner the night before in our favorite restaurant, L'Ami Louis.

He grew up in Paris, the best city for a young mother to expose her child to a culture of food. On the way home from the hospital, when he was five days old, we stopped at Les Deux Magots for a coffee, and the waiter thought his Moses basket was full of market produce rather than a sleeping infant.

Roo is a seriously good cook. I hope he learned from me. I'm continually learning from him.

My earliest memories are of walking into restaurants in Paris. I remember going into Benoit and hearing stories from Dad about how it was the place where he and Renzo Piano designed the Pompidou Center in its earliest stages. I learned quite quickly not only to have a passion for food but also to understand that you should book the restaurant first and *then* figure out who you're going to invite along. Growing up, I always felt that going out to eat was an exploration. Not a convenience or a necessity, but an exploration.

I also remember the markets—walking through the market on Boulevard Raspail with Mum and Dad. Dad would buy a roast chicken, which they put in one of those silver foil bags. There were no knives and forks. So the three of us would find ourselves just eating chunks of chicken as we pulled them off. It was the most delicious thing. When we needed dessert, Mum bought some raspberries and we ate them straight out of the carton. That was lunch back then.

In a way, we all love food in the Rogers family because Richard Rogers was a great eater. I think being a great eater is a fundamental skill. It can be frustrating, because you're analyzing everything all the time. But it's also beautiful, in that you are constantly searching for new tastes and new experiences. Dad had a Michelin guide with yellow Post-it notes and his scribblings all over it. He would walk into a bookstore to ask, "We just found this restaurant but we haven't been—do you recommend it?" That's the amount of due diligence we did just because Dad wanted to have a great lunch.

Dad was not much of a cook. Once, when he went on a skiing trip with Bo, they bought asparagus and had to figure out how to cook it. Dad looked at it from an engineering or architectural point of view. He noted that the tops of the asparagus stalks were narrower while the bottoms of the stalks were wider. So he cut them up into pieces because the wider bottom pieces would need more time in the water than the top pieces. A very pragmatic view.

My brothers, Ben, Zad, and Ab, are all amazing cooks, yet very different in approach. Ben is very precise and conscientious in terms of the planet—what he's cooking, how much of it he's cooking. But it always tastes perfect. My standing image of Zad—and probably of my entire lifetime of food—is of going to stay at his house and watching him hang up a duck and blow it with a hair dryer, drying it for Christmas. Ab is an explorer and you never quite know what to expect. I do not like surf and turf; meat and fish together seem wrong to me. But when I go to Ab's house, not only am I going to have scallops with blood sausage, I also know it's going to be delicious. He is the king of surprise.

My mother is American, so every summer we'd go to the States to visit her family. There are four things we all really loved eating in America: hot pastrami sandwiches, corn on the cob, steak, and lobster. There were also mussels that we used to harvest at the beach. The lobsters came right out of the sea and we just boiled and ate them plain. The steak in America—

we simply didn't have anything like it in London. And in New York, we always went to the Carnegie Deli to have hot pastrami sandwiches with strong mustard.

All that said, I think the real American influence on my feelings about food is my mother. Her idea is that food makes people feel at home—that if, for example, food comes to the table, you instinctively want to serve it to other people, even if you're not in your own house. Food can be such a source of generosity and warmth. That's what makes The River Cafe so extraordinary. Ruthie only ever says "Yes." *Yes* is such a beautiful word.

I went to college in New York, at Columbia University. The most important thing I learned as a Columbia student was the value of a slice of pizza. New York pizza is delicious, and we lived on it. It can be a snack or it can be a meal. It has to be eaten the correct way. The first time I ate a slice of New York pizza, I didn't fold it and held it angled down, the result being that I dripped grease all over my clothes.

I also cooked for my friends all the time. I learned about New York ingredients and where to buy what. My favorite meal to cook was mussels with spicy tomato sauce.

A useful thing I learned early on was that when we had parties, it was good to have a dish that you could make quickly and easily, to help soak up the alcohol in everyone's system. So I would make pasta with tomato sauce. Now I serve the same version to my kids.

The other thing I loved about New York is that people are never self-conscious eating on their own. It's normal behavior. You see a person in a diner reading a book and that's a really beautiful thing.

I have always used restaurants as public spaces. I need to be around other people when I think, and there's nowhere better to be around other people, and be surprised by them, than a restaurant. There's a certain level of discomfort to it, in a good way. You're putting yourself in somebody else's hands. You don't know if they're going to cook something the way you want it prepared or not. You're surrounded by people you've never met before, and you don't know what conversations might arise. You're taking a risk. That risk can really pay off when you've had a meal that surprises you.

I like serendipity. You get serendipity when you walk down an unfamiliar alley and find a restaurant you've never heard of. You walk in. Only one time in ten will it turn out to be amazing. But when it does, that risk is truly rewarding. That's what I'm always looking for.

Everywhere I travel, I seek out local restaurants, the most authentic food. When I went to Ethiopia a couple of years ago, the taxi driver who picked me up at the airport stayed with me for three days. The best meals I had were in his family home. He also took me to the meat market in Addis Ababa, where they have enormous carcasses of meat hanging and people shooing flies away from them.

We walked in, and the taxi driver said, "Choose your meat." So I chose a couple of cuts of meat. I even chose some sweetbreads to be adventurous. They took it away and we went to sit down in the back. The food came to us literally ninety seconds later. I was thinking, "God, they cook it quick here." No. It was raw. They serve all those meats raw, with a spicy chili sauce or nut sauce. It was all amazing, and we drank really good Ethiopian coffee.

When I cook at home, we pretty much eat Western-style food. I would rather eat out and have somebody who knows what they're doing prepare dishes from other cultures. That said, my wife, Bernie, is Chinese American and makes incredible dumplings and wontons, which we all cherish.

What's interesting is that there are very few things in Western cuisine that are completely original. Everyone is influenced by everyone else. An amazing wonton is actually like an amazing raviolo. Bernie would correct me and say that it's the other way around: an amazing raviolo is like an amazing wonton, because China and its food have existed for quite a bit longer. Whether it's wontons or ravioli, it's all about the quality of the pasta, or the wrapper, as they say: how light and thin you can get it, how fresh the ingredients are. If the chives are good, that makes the wonton.

I fell in love with Bernie over an order of Dover sole. We were at dinner at Chez Georges in Paris and had only just properly met. I ordered the Dover sole. It was served on the bone. While she and I were talking, I filleted the fish and ate it, without any break in the conversation. Little did I know that this really impressed her. Bernie told me later that she found my knife-and-fork skills with the fish sexy and alluring.

I'm very interested in the subject of food security. We talk a lot about overpopulation, but what we should really be talking about is food security. There are more than enough resources in the world to feed the people on this planet. But we choose politically not to feed those people. We choose not to send grain to places where it's needed. We choose to have cows and dairy where we don't need more milk. We choose not to provide loans to small farmers in Africa and India. We make choices every day around food security that have nothing to do with whether or not we have the ability as a people to sustainably feed everyone. We can. I passionately believe this, that, should we choose to, we can feed everybody in a healthy, equitable way that's good for the planet. It's a choice.

*Roo, what is your comfort food?*
I am very, very privileged, because it's not a question of what I eat—it's a question of where do I go? I go home to see my mum and eat anything she cooks.

# EMILY MORTIMER

Emily Mortimer is family to me. I have known her since she was tiny. Her parents, John Mortimer, the playwright and barrister, and Penny, her throaty-voiced, charismatic mother, were close friends—and Emily has been coming to our house for Thanksgiving since she was six.

This year, Emily returned after time away living in New York. Looking out over a table of forty people while singing, as is traditional, "You Are My Sunshine," our eyes met and stayed there for all four verses. Memories flooded back of Emily and the happy times spent with her parents, including games of tennis in which Penny managed the not-small feat of playing while smoking.

Emily is an actor, writer, and director. She acted in *Notting Hill*, *The Pursuit of Love*, *The Newsroom*, *Match Point*, *The New Look*, and *Paddington 3*, and has just written a screenplay with Noah Baumbach.

When I see Emily, our conversations are mostly about what she did rather than what she's doing—she was one of the first employees of The River Cafe, back in 1989, when being seventeen and totally inexperienced was no obstacle to being a waiter. Emily likes to go around saying she was one of the worst waiters we had. Someone once asked for lemon to go with their fish, and Emily simply took the wedge of lemon off another customer's dish. But I think she was a wonderful waiter. Though defining what makes a wonderful waiter might be open to debate.

Emily read the recipe for our Pear and Almond Tart.

I started working at The River Cafe at the beginning of my gap year. I knew I was going to go to university, and I knew I was going to go to Russia before I went to university. I think my parents just said, "You need to make a bit of money. Why don't you be a waitress?" And Ruthie Rogers very kindly agreed to have this completely callow, demented seventeen-year-old work for her.

It was really the beginning of my life, because I was very, very shy. Believe it or not, I still am. Cooking, I have found, has been the greatest way of counteracting being shy. Because you can have people over and have parties and friends, but you can also hide behind the business of getting something ready. Having people for dinner in your own home is like putting on a show in a way. You make the place nice, put the music on, light the fire, and create this stage set. But it is all kind of an illusion. Behind the scenes, you're going, "Aaaaagh!" and shouting.

Coming to The River Cafe and being a waitress was really the first time that I had been *in life*, having hardly ever kissed a boy, having never got drunk, having really lived a very secluded life. Basically, I learned how to cook. At The River Cafe, you have to get in earlier than most waiters do when they come to their job at a restaurant. You grate the Parmesan and chop up the basil and parsley, things like that. My mum says, "Ruthie always says, 'Just get a good smell going.'" And that's true. You know everything's going to be okay in the kitchen if you've just got a good smell going.

I really was a very bad waitress. I broke everything over everyone. I remember the dry-cleaning bills that had to be paid on my behalf to people who had red wine dropped in their laps. I've come to the conclusion that being a waiter is a very difficult job. There's so much going on in your head. You can get from the starter to main course, that's okay. But then you take the main course plates away and forget about the table for hours. You forget totally to bring them their pudding menus. And then, once they've had their pudding, you totally forget to bring them the bill.

That was always the bit that undid me: remembering. There was this awful thing I still feel guilty about. There was a man—I think his name was Dougal McDougal—and he was eating his lunch. Everybody was going bananas because it was almost Christmas and all the people from all the offices were having their big Christmas lunches. The phone was going off the hook. It kept ringing, and no one had time to pick it up.

Finally, I picked it up and said hello. It was a woman who said, "You've got a Mr. Dougal McDougal dining with you today and he's urgently required to come to the telephone." I put the phone down and I thought, "How do I find Dougal McDougal among all these people?"

Then I looked around and I saw this man and thought, "I think you are Dougal McDougal." He had a sort of mullet hairdo and a suit that was slightly ill-fitting. But he looked really lovely. I went over and said, "Are you, by any chance, Mr. Dougal McDougal?" The man said, "Yes, I am."

I felt so victorious. He took his phone call and it was all good. All lunch long, I was so happy, laughing about this story to myself. At the end of lunch, I told all the other staff and the waitresses and the chefs all about it. I described his mullet and his badly fitting suit. Everybody was laughing uproariously. I said, "I saw this man and I just knew out of everybody in this restaurant full of people, *he* had to be Dougal McDougal!"

Then this little voice went, "I'm still here, you know." It was Dougal McDougal. He'd gone to the loo.

I still, to this day, wake up in the night feeling bad about this.

My dad could really cook and loved food. He always said his idea of good food is food you don't need teeth to eat. Mashed potatoes and kedgeree were his favorite things. When I was a little girl, my dad cooked me boiled eggs and toast soldiers. I used to say, "Get my eggs, you bugger!" I was a very shy child, but I was not shy with my dad. I would send back the eggs if they weren't cooked to a certain specificity. If the toast soldiers weren't perfectly lightly toasted, I was very annoyed.

My family, as all families are, was quite dysfunctional in lots of wonderful ways. But the one thing that they always got right, my mum and dad, was meals. We always ate together, whether it was dinner at home, with Mum normally cooking, or in a restaurant. My sister, Rosie, and I have inherited a love of restaurants. Dad's attitude to restaurants was that there was no problem so great that it couldn't be made slightly better by a delicious meal in a restaurant, with a white tablecloth and a glass or three of Champagne. Rosie and I still have that. We're addicted to restaurants.

Dad loved young people. He thought children were the best type of people, and he was always so sympathetic about being a young person: "Life will never be as hard as it is when you are young and school is awful. These terrible hours, the unpaid labor, the terrible food at lunchtime." He was very inclusive. Lunches, dinners, whatever it was, we were never expected not to be part of it. So I think that no matter how much life is falling apart at the seams—which it always is, of course—if you can manage to corral the people who you love for lunch or dinner, it does make a difference.

I went to Russia in my gap year. This was '89, '90. I was in Moscow. I love Russian food because I associate it with that time. It was quite stodgy: pelmeni, little dumplings with cream and lots of dill. They put dill on everything. I still cook lots with dill. Somehow that really brings me back to being there.

And I cooked my first and last goose in Moscow. I was going to try and cook a roast chicken. Then I went to the market and they didn't have any chicken, but they did have a goose. I called up my mum. You couldn't really make phone calls back and forth to England at that time. I had to go to this hotel and pay with a credit card for a phone call that cost about fifty pounds for five minutes.

Mum looked up the recipe for goose and kept saying, "A goose is very different from a chicken, darling." I spent all day long with this goose. You had to take the wings and the breasts off and then prick it and primp it.

I remember putting the goose in the oven and saying, "I'm so sorry. I feel like I've really got to know you so well over this time. I feel terrible."

In Russia, I'd get invited to someone's home for dinner and it would last a whole day. Generally, the people were living in tiny apartments on the outskirts of the city. They would make a table out of a bit of wood and put some chairs together in the middle of the only living space. It was feast: all these crazy, mismatched things, just dish upon dish upon dish. It was such an act of love. I'm writing a film, which I hope to direct, about my time in Russia.

I went to Lincoln College at Oxford, which was famous for its food, but I don't really remember eating much. I just went to lots of parties and slept and did plays. It was about a forty-five-minute drive back home, so I would go home at the weekends. I'd take my washing and get a good Sunday lunch. The smell of Sunday lunch cooking and the sound of my dad listening to Radio 4 is something that I really miss. When I come back to England and have Sunday lunch, I'm just immediately full of nostalgia and happiness.

In my late twenties, I moved to America, where they don't really have Sunday lunch. I try to do it sometimes, a roast or something, but it's hard to keep up that tradition when the culture isn't doing it. I don't really know how to do an American brunch, so I go really over the top and then it's sort of "brunch at the Four Seasons": quiches and just too much. If you do a Sunday lunch in America, you have to make a thing of it. Because people don't really carve out time on a Sunday to just sit around doing nothing.

*Emily, what is your comfort food?*
Ravioli. If I wanted to treat myself or I was feeling really sad, I'd order a plate of ravioli. They're quite delicious. Just putting the fork in and something oozing out. It goes back to my dad: food you don't really need your teeth to eat.

# Food Is Tradition

In telling their stories, guests often speak more emotionally about the cooking of their grandmothers than of their mothers.

Perhaps released from the pressures of parenthood, there is simply more time. But there is also more investment in continuing traditions.

In families who have emigrated from other countries, the mother will often adapt her cooking to her new country's culture, while the grandmother keeps her identity rooted in the food culture she grew up with.

Quite a few of the guests on *Ruthie's Table 4*, such as Tom Hollander, have brought in recipe books that were given to them by their parents and grandparents: notebooks crammed with family recipes; tattered, kitchen-stained cookbooks that have served more than one generation; primers offering advice on where to find hard-to-find ingredients.

There's pride in the way the families' culinary and entertaining traditions are described. In many of the interviews, stories are told of growing up in homes where privilege was not a given. Linda Evangelista's family came from Pignataro Interamna, in the hills of Southern Italy. Trudie Styler's family lived under Britain's postwar austerity and rationing.

All of these families prioritized good cooking and healthy food, and made the most of what they had.

# GRETA GERWIG
# NOAH BAUMBACH

When Greta Gerwig and Noah Baumbach wrote to say they were moving to London for a year, we decided to meet for Sunday lunch at The River Cafe.

After that first lunch, we made a date for the following Sunday. After the second one, we agreed to meet for the one after that.

On the third Sunday, Harold, their five-year-old son, turned to me and said, "Ruthie, is this the meaning of tradition?" From that moment, our Sunday lunches became known among the four of us as "tradition."

As in—
"What time are we meeting for tradition?"
"Will you be here next week for tradition?"
And even, "That was a delicious tradition, wasn't it?"

It's Sunday. So Greta, Noah, and I are here in The River Cafe to talk about life, how food brought us together, and the beautiful movies they've made. And when we're done, Harold will join us and I will have lunch with three people I adore.

That's tradition.

**Noah**

You know *Defending Your Life*, the Albert Brooks movie? He and Meryl Streep are in a kind of limbo where they're being judged, to figure out if they're gonna go up or down. While they're there, they can eat anything they want because there's no consequences. So there's a lot of good eating in that movie. And *The Adventures of Robin Hood*, with Errol Flynn. There's a scene where he comes into the king's banquet hall and takes a big turkey leg, sits back in his chair, and eats it really confidently. I loved that movie, and I loved Robin Hood, but I thought the turkey leg looked especially delicious.

**Greta**

When I made *Little Women*, our producer was Amy Pascal, who loves food in movies. We did all this research about the food of the time, with American cookbooks from the nineteenth century. Food was actually a big part of the Alcott family's life in the 1850s because their father was one of the first vegans, and he moved them to a vegan commune called Fruitlands, in Massachusetts. It was fine in the summer because things grew, but they basically starved in the winter because it was just root vegetables and whatever they could store.

This was one of the movies that I was pregnant on. The woman who did the food styling made all these samples of the kinds of breads that were around, the kinds of cake. There's a scene where the Laurences send Christmas dinner to the Marches, and peppermint ice cream. The food stylist made cakes and different things for me, ostensibly just to look at, for me to say yes or no. But she realized that I was so hungry, so she started giving me cakes. And then I would be eating nineteenth-century cakes all weekend. Gradually, I was getting bigger and bigger. I wore these big coats, and no one knew I was pregnant. They thought I just liked the cakes.

**Noah**

We watched this Yasujirō Ozu movie from the 1950s called *The Flavor of Green Tea over Rice*. It's about a marriage, and you discover over the course of the movie that they're from different class backgrounds. He likes green tea over rice and eats it very fast. She doesn't approve. But the movie ends with them making green tea over rice together in their kitchen. They're used to having the help prepare food for them, so they don't know where everything is and they're figuring it out as they go. It's a beautiful, quiet scene.

**Greta**

In the Bergman series *Scenes from a Marriage*, they're always eating. Their kids are never there, and she's like, "Can I make you a sandwich while we're talking about our marriage disintegrating?" It's, like, eleven at night and he sits there eating a sandwich.

**Noah**

With a beer.

**Greta**

With a beer. Why is he always eating sandwiches while everything is falling apart? I also remember the scene in *Spanglish* where Adam Sandler makes a sandwich. They do a close shot of him cutting the sandwich, and the egg yolk drips out. It looks like a really good sandwich.

**Greta**

I like having a big cast-and-crew dinner before I start directing a film. Because once you're going, it's hard to get everyone on the same page. One of the reasons I love making movies is the communities that spring up, the sense of common purpose. The idea of eating with your community, your makeshift temporary merry band, is so great. You're all doing something kind of outrageously vulnerable together, so it's like, "Let's all have a meal."

**Noah**

But I don't like that we have to stop for lunch. It's hard to come back afterward equally strong.

**Greta**

The one version that works, and I got this from David Lynch, is that if you meditate during lunch, if you just take twenty minutes, it gives you a second morning.

I also find that on movie sets, I revert to juvenile food habits. Cheetos and Diet Coke in astonishing quantities. It's almost like part of what I need to be doing in order to make the film. I don't eat Cheetos or drink Diet Coke in the rest of my life. I think it connects to childhood. I direct movies from a place of childhood, incorporating people and ideas from it. There are different versions of Barbie, and the logo has gone through several changes since 1959. But the Barbie from my childhood—I was born in 1983—is the one with the big bubble letters. So for *Barbie*, the movie, I wanted the logo that meant something to me. And I'll have it with Cheetos and candy. I don't even have a sweet tooth as an adult, but on a set, I'll eat candy. Skittles and Sour Patch Kids and Starbursts.

**Noah**

It's also aspirational, because when you were a kid, you thought, "I can only dream of maybe making movies someday." And also dream that maybe one day, you could eat any candy you like.

**Greta**

Right, those were things I was not allowed to have as a kid most of the time. I have always seen writing, directing, and acting as slightly doing something I'm not supposed to be doing. I'm somehow misbehaving by just doing it. And that taps into the idea of "as long as you're being bad by making a movie, you might as well have candy."

**Noah**

In *The Squid and the Whale*, I put things from my childhood in the movie. I had Jeff Daniels literally wearing my dad's clothes. There's a scene where he and Laura Linney are discussing the failure of their marriage, and she says he never even cooked dinner, and he says, "I made burgers that time you had pneumonia."

Post-divorce, my dad had a few things he felt he could handle. He made blueberry pancakes. He was very proud of those. And he would do a veal cutlet and hamburgers, for sure. A friend of mine keeps threatening to do a divorced dad cookbook.

**Greta**
There's a meal he does that he calls "special meal."

**Noah**
Oh, yeah, I put that in *Marriage Story*, actually, the special meal. It's kind of like a hash.

**Greta**
Potatoes, ground beef, onions, and peas. We were with this friend when there was a big hurricane in New York. We ended up walking to his place in Brooklyn because we didn't have power. He made special meal for all of us and we loved it. We ate so much special meal. It would definitely be a featured item in the cookbook.

**Noah**
My dad was not much of a cook when I was growing up. My mom was more the cook.

**Greta**
My mother was more of the sous-chef. She would prepare and chop. My dad did the cooking. He was better at making things like omelets. He'd do the flip and everything.

**Noah**
And your mom cleans up while you're still eating.

**Greta**

Yeah, she's like, if you put a glass down, you're done. It's already been washed. Mealtimes expanded and contracted over time in our family, because I have a brother and sister who are older. At times it was just me. Then at times it was also them and their friends, and we always had an extra person living with us. Like, we had a woman who was dancing in the Sacramento Ballet who lived with us for a while. So there was a lot of cooking for volume.

Everyone had activities at night, between sports and clubs and things, so my memory of the together meals is mostly of breakfasts. My mom always had me eat eggs. She was concerned that no one was getting enough protein. All I ever wanted growing up was dry cereal with milk, and I wasn't allowed to have it. I could have muesli if I put yogurt on it. When I finally got to college, all I ate for a solid year was plain Cheerios with milk. For breakfast, lunch, and dinner.

**Noah**

I was always a little self-conscious about my mom's cooking even though I liked it. She would do, like, bean curd things. I'd go to friends' houses and eat very basic things that I craved and didn't eat at home. Like macaroni and cheese and double-decker sandwiches. Things I'd see pictures of in magazines.

One thing I got from my grandfather, my mom's dad, was to have a big salad for dinner. He was in World War II, a decorated soldier. My mom found an old telegram where he is coming back from the war, and he's arrived in America but isn't home yet. And he says, "Hey, I'll be there Thursday. Can you make me a big salad?" So at home, I like to have a big salad.

*Greta and Noah, what are your comfort foods?*

**Greta**

My friend Sarah makes a great macaroni and cheese casserole. She makes it just perfect, with a roux and a crust that's just right. My birthday is in August.

When we were in our early twenties, we lived together in this tiny apartment that had no air-conditioning, and she made me a macaroni and cheese casserole for my birthday in the August heat. I was like, "She must love me, because who does that?" Then, during the pandemic, she made one for my birthday and got it to me. The food in itself is comforting, but it's also the fact that she made it.

**Noah**
My dinner salad is a comfort food for me. I don't have to make a decision. I know what it is.

# LINDA EVANGELISTA

One night at a dinner in London, Jony Ive pulled me over and said, "Ruthie, come meet my great friend Linda Evangelista." Of course, I already knew exactly who she was.

Linda is warm, engaging, and curious. She grew up in a large and loving Italian Canadian family where cooking and eating were central to their very identity. Her work as a model required restraint around food, an issue Linda has been vocal about in recent years. Like me, she considers food central to her life. She loves to eat and she loves to cook, especially with her son.

Linda read the recipe for Gnocchi with Slow-Cooked Tomato Sauce, originally published in *The River Cafe Look Book*, our cookbook for children. This felt right, as in her childhood Linda loved making gnocchi at her grandmother's side.

My family comes from a town called Pignataro Interamna, which is near Cassino and Montecassino, where a big battle of World War II took place. My father was born in 1940 and he came over in 1956. My mother was born in '43 and she came over in 1950.

Both of my grandfathers had been in the war. One had been a prisoner of war. My grandparents left Italy in search of a better life. They lost everything—not that they ever had much.

They were headed to the United States when the country closed its doors, saying it was not receiving any more immigrants. Somebody in the United States found a sponsor for my father's father in Canada. Similar story for my other grandparents. They settled in St. Catherines, Ontario, across Lake Ontario from Toronto, right near Niagara Falls and the U.S. border. Our neighborhood was very Polish and Italian, with some Ukrainians.

I have the two handmade hammered copper pots that my mother's mother came over with, the ones she made her Sunday tomato sauce in. Those are my precious heirlooms. There are no paintings or jewelry.

My grandmother was a peasant who didn't know how to read or write. She never learned to speak English. She didn't really need to. She went to Italian mass, shopped at the Italian store, and worked picking fruit on a farm with other Italian ladies. I remember how excited they all got, that generation, when Canada went metric. I was about ten years old. They were so happy, saying, "Oh, *this* is how many grams of meat I'm buying!"

I have two brothers. My parents spoke English to us growing up. Only when they were arguing did they speak to each other in Italian. So I can tell you where to go in Italian, but I can't ask you if you are having a nice day. My mom also spoke the dialect of the region she came from. It got even more complicated because then these things took on a life of their own in Canada. Not quite as badly as in America, where they've totally butchered the language. I don't like the way they cut off the ends of words, calling mozzarella mozza-*rell*.

We ate a lot of homemade food, which I appreciate now. But growing up, I wanted the TV dinners with the little compartment in the corner for apple pie. My father took us out for dinner every Friday because my mother, who had a job in retail, worked late. He let us choose the restaurant, and by "restaurant," I mean fast food: McDonald's, Denny's, or the pizzeria. We were very spoiled with that. As for fresh food, we had homemade pasta on Wednesdays and Sundays. We had roast beef once a week and steak or barbecue once a week. My father got a good job at General Motors and that put food on the table. I think he spent so much money on food because he didn't have much growing up. They might have had chicken or a rabbit once a week.

My father liked to serve us dinner. He put this mound of food on your plate and you had to eat it all. For him, the most important thing was you weren't hungry, that you were nourished. He also didn't want a lot of talk at the table, because his workplace was so noisy. So there wasn't a lot of conversation. It was, "Dive into your food and finish it, because you're not leaving the table until you do."

Everybody in our neighborhood devoted their whole backyard to a garden. We never played in our yards, we played in the street or in a parking lot. What they produced in these gardens was unbelievable: tomatoes, cucumbers, broccoli rabe, onions, herbs, different kinds of radicchio. The basil leaves were bigger than my hand. The seeds were a whole thing, a network. Whoever had the best tomatoes that year would save their seeds and hand them out. Now you see all these expensive heirloom tomatoes, and I'm like, "Those are the tomatoes I grew up with!"

Then there were the fruit trees. My father had a green thumb and he would graft things together. He did these sensational things. The apricot tree had plums growing on it and the red apple tree had a branch with yellow apples. He also made his own grappa. For years, it was just awful. Then suddenly, it kicked in and was amazing. He would make it from pears, plums, and peaches. And all the Italians made homemade wine in their basements. Totally illegal.

I think my father would have been happy as a farmer, because he was so good at it. He didn't get an education as a child, because he had to work the land. I know he had a donkey, and whenever he talked about Italy, he referred to it as "the good old days." We kept some chickens and rabbits, even though we lived in a suburb, in zoning that didn't allow for farm animals. It was embarrassing to me at the time. The roosters, when they would go off at 5 a.m.? Oh my God.

When the harvest came to an end, we had to pickle everything or put it in a jar or cure it for the winter. We also made sausages. Don't ask me how it got divided up or who did what, but our extended family—uncles, cousins, etc.—would buy a whole animal. Then they would make sausages, prosciutto, and capicola. The sausages were a lot of work. That's one job I didn't like, washing the casings.

We made our own tomato sauce. Sometimes we bought more tomatoes than we'd grown because we wanted to make enough to get us through the winter. We'd start with a passata, the tomato paste. My father took a motor off of a washing machine and rigged it up to a machine that separates the seeds and peels from the tomatoes and purees them into a passata. So we didn't have to do that work by hand.

We still make the tomato sauce every year as a family. My father is no longer with us, but the machine still runs, making a lot of noise. I don't know how many bushels we do per day, but we go through bushels and bushels and bushels of tomatoes. You need multiple people to come over, because it's so much work.

I ate really simply when I started living on my own as a model. I was in New York for a month or so, but the agency shipped me off to Paris because I wasn't doing so well. I was nineteen. I was first in the Hotel Saint-André des Arts, but I got bedbugs there. So I went to the Hotel La Louisiane. I would go to the market on Rue de Buci and I would get a baguette and a piece of Brie and a piece of fruit. That's how I ate on a budget.

Back in the day, I could eat anything. I had a crazy metabolism. It started to slow down when I was closer to thirty. I started working out when I was twenty-seven, twenty-eight, because I noticed that things were getting a little different. Back then, if I overindulged for too long, I could cut back on everything for three days and drop five pounds. Now it's very easy for me to gain five pounds in a weekend.

There was a time, when I was flying every other day, running around and jet setting, that I had to work to keep the weight *on*. And then there began a period when I had to really watch myself. I started doing cleanses all the time. I loved doing them, but I think they were harmful to me.

I did the Master Cleanse quite a few times. I would do medicinal cleanses where it's a powdered drink with a rice base, like Metagenics. Or I would go to We Care once or twice a year for a week. We Care is a spa out in Palm Desert, California, and you just do liquids: mostly teas and waters with lemon and mint. You get a glass of juice a day, and then you get a very diluted, watered-down vegetable solution they call a soup. It's basically a starvation diet.

It's been quite the journey. I'll never do the deprivation thing again, though there is something to be said for a nice twenty-four-hour fast with celery juice. I still enjoy doing something like that. I find it refreshing. You kick-start your mind into a new place of, "Okay, I'm going to get on this healthy track." And eating healthy can be very, very delicious, especially for someone who happens to love vegetables.

My son loves my soups. The other day, I made a mixed vegetable soup. I pureed it and passed it through a sieve to make it super, super smooth. I also make lots of minestras, soups with greens and beans. I made one last week, and he said, "Oh, it's *that* season again." If I give him a crunchy baguette to dip in his soup with some Parmesan, he's as happy as can be.

*Linda, what is your comfort food?*
My mom's eggplant parmigiana. She makes it for me on Canadian Thanksgiving. It's the second Monday of October. We make regular Thanksgiving food, too, all the traditional things. But if you're Italian, the Italian food makes its way in. My stepfather farms with his son, so last Thanksgiving we had beets and Swiss chard. Those are not Thanksgiving foods, but they were on the table. It was a mishmash. It was not cohesive, but it was delicious.

# EDWARD ENNINFUL

Edward Enninful's debut issue of British *Vogue* was published in December 2017. On the day it came out, Condé Nast hosted a party at The River Cafe to celebrate him and his team.

Born in Ghana and raised in Ladbroke Grove in London, Edward worked as a stylist for American *Vogue* and as editor-in-chief of *W* magazine. But it was at British *Vogue* where the world learned his name. In his seven triumphant, influential years there, he advocated for and helped shape a more diverse fashion world. His memoir, *A Visible Man*, tells the story of his extraordinary life and his drive to change the way the world sees beauty.

Edward read the recipe for one of his favorite River Cafe dishes, Slow-Cooked Veal Shin with Barolo and Sage.

Historically, the idea was that to be fashionable, you shouldn't eat. But when you look at *Vogue*—at least my *Vogue*, anyway—everybody is welcome, all shapes, all sizes, all colors. What I love is that by the time I was three years into the job, when you looked in all the other magazines, everybody else had become equally welcoming. Designers now know that they've missed out on a whole market from sizes 14 to 16. Why would you want to miss out on a section of a population that can make your business even better?

That strict thing of not being able to be a certain size, that being a size 0 is the perfect—that doesn't exist anymore. Even the idea of being a model has changed. You can be short, you can be curvy, you can be disabled. To watch the industry change, for me, was one of the great things about my job. We dealt with topics that real women are passionate about.

I spent the first twelve years of my life in Ghana. Everything was spicy and peppery. A lot of carbohydrates and soups. Ghanaian soups have a lot of meat in them, like a chicken soup or a lamb soup. I remember chewing through bones and skin. It's a comforting memory for me.

My grandmother lived with us, and she always cooked. My mother was a seamstress and was busy working, making clothes. Pretty much what I do now. My grandmother cooked in these huge pots. She'd never cook just for the family. It would be aunts and uncles popping in. There's something about Ghana: the minute the food is ready to go, all of a sudden, your aunts and uncles appear out of nowhere. So, food for me, as a very, very shy kid, became a way of socializing. To this day, going out to restaurants fills me with happiness.

My father was in the Ghanaian army, so we lived on the military base, which was called Burma Camp. It was a surreal upbringing, living on the base but not really living in the city. Then we moved to London. First, we lived in Victoria for a few months, opposite the Chelsea Barracks. Then we moved to Ladbroke Grove. That's when my life really began. Oh my God, Jamaican food! Rice and peas, jerk chicken.

I always say that I felt as if I lived in two countries. Anybody who has been an immigrant will attest to this. When I was at home, I felt Ghanaian, with my parents speaking Ghanaian and the family eating the flavors of Ghana—having things like fufu, which is a pounded dough made from cassava, served with soups. But the minute I left the house, I was in England, where you have sausage rolls and chips and pork pie. I just love that duality. The person I am today is made from that duality, in every aspect of my life. And it started with food.

My grandmother didn't move with us to England. So when we got there, my brother took over the cooking duties. Sometimes my sisters took turns. My father never cooked. I don't, either. Somehow I missed out on the cooking gene. But I can really eat.

I would bring friends home to dinner, but Ghanaian food is very specific, and you either take to it or you don't. Again, it's very meaty. I'm definitely a carnivore. Meat reminds me of my grandmother.

My friends always loved the jollof rice. It's a rice made with tomatoes and spices, and the color is sort of orange. It's very famous. There is a competition between Ghanaians and Nigerians called the Jollof Wars, over who makes the best rice. Nigerians think theirs tastes better than the Ghanaians'.

I also remember lots of okra in everything. I never ate salads growing up. Ghanaian vegetables are always cooked and stirred and beaten within an inch of their lives.

Every Saturday, my mother took me to Brixton Market. It was basically an African market where you could buy meat, fish, clothes. I'd hear the music of Bob Marley and Peter Tosh while my mom was looking through the meat, trying to find the best cuts. That really defined my early teenage years.

We never went to restaurants, by the way. There were six of us kids in the family. The first time I went to a restaurant was when I started modeling. I was about sixteen. It was a Chinese restaurant next to the Ladbroke Grove tube station. It wasn't really a proper restaurant, maybe three tables and takeaway. But it felt so glamorous. I remember thinking, "Oh, God, what do I do here?"

Then I started traveling for modeling, making new friends. My whole life changed. The first place I went to was New York. I went out for lunch, dinner, and sometimes breakfast. Burgers! Oh my God. And milkshakes. Then I went to Paris. French cuisine was incredible, but I always found it a little too heavy. But I loved the food in Italy. When I went to Milan, I discovered Italian food and loved everything about it.

Going out to a restaurant is still very special for me. It's one of the few times in the day that I get to completely enjoy myself. I always dress up. When I was growing up, my dad told me, "To get on a plane, you have to dress up. To go to a restaurant, you have to dress up." So you'll never see me in a restaurant not dressed up.

I really love going out. I love looking at people, seeing what they're wearing, just seeing people having fun and enjoying themselves. It's almost like therapy for me.

*Edward, what is your comfort food?*
Something very simple. Rice and beans with chicken. It's what my grandmother would make whenever I wasn't feeling well.

# MEL BROOKS

Mel Brooks, born in 1926, has made people laugh over ten different decades—from his boyhood years in the Williamsburg section of Brooklyn through a career as a writer, director, and performer.

Mel is part of The River Cafe family, having first visited us with his late wife, Anne Bancroft, in the 1990s. He really knows his food and is a serious collector of fine wines.

Mel being Mel, he asked me to hold off on my questions about food until he had demonstrated one of his special skills for our listeners. "I would like to do my imitation of a cat," he said. "Because not a lot of people know that I make the best cat sound in the world. I used it in *Young Frankenstein*," he said. "There's a dart-throwing contest and one of the darts hits a cat. And you hear, 'Rrrreeeyow!'"

When my mother cooked, she wasn't making food. She was making something that passed for food. Mostly it was chicken. Chicken, chicken soup, brisket, brown potatoes. It was standard Williamsburg, Brooklyn, Jewish tenement food. Breakfast in the winter was always hot cereal. Cream of Wheat or Ralston, which was a kind of brown porridge. In the summer, cornflakes or Rice Krispies or Wheaties.

   I hardly ever ate fish as a kid. I don't think I liked fish until I was seventy or eighty and had the Dover sole at The River Cafe. Sometimes my mother would get a live fish, a carp, and keep it in the bathtub. My brother Bernie and I fell in love with one of them. We called him Artie. We fed him breadcrumbs and chased him around the bathtub. And then . . . it was unspeakable. I can't even describe it. My oldest brothers, Irving and Lenny, held us back. We

were screaming, "Don't kill him!" My mother said, "We've got to eat supper." She killed Artie and served him to us. We cried but we ate him.

Every once in a while, on a Sunday night, my mother would make spaghetti. She would buy a box of Mueller's noodles. They were flat. And she'd cook them until they were dead. Then she'd put them in a baking pan and empty a bottle of Heinz ketchup over them. She'd bake it all for thirty or forty minutes, until the pan was dead, until everything was dead. Then she'd cut it up into squares and serve it to us. She'd say, "Spaghetti!"

Until I was about thirteen or fourteen, that was spaghetti. And it was okay. Then I joined a club called the Balsa Bugs. We made model airplanes. I think we enjoyed smelling the glue more than we liked making the planes. The Balsa Bugs were Bernie Steinberg, Flappy Rothman, and a kid named Tony Galliani, an Italian. One day, a Sunday, Tony said, "I'm going home to have spaghetti." I said, "We have spaghetti on Sunday, too." He said, "Come on over, try our spaghetti." So I walked over to his apartment, which was in Greenpoint, on the edge of Williamsburg. As I walked in, I was assaulted by these smells, the aroma of garlic—I mean, it was just incredible.

Then I sat down and they served this warm, squiggly spaghetti: real spaghetti, not dead. It fought back a little bit in the mouth. And the sauce! This thick, red, beautiful sauce with meatballs in it. Sprinkled on top of it was this white stuff, like snow: Parmesan cheese. I took one bite and I started to cry. I wept. I said, "Tony, this is spaghetti. *This* is spaghetti."

When I came home, I said, "Mom, you are not making spaghetti. I don't know what that stuff is, that cardboard, but it's not spaghetti."

Once in a while, we went out to restaurants. Mostly Jewish restaurants, what were called dairy restaurants, where they'd serve stuff like blintzes with sour cream. You never mixed meat and dairy. It was some religious nonsense.

We went to a Chinese restaurant in Williamsburg where the whole meal cost twenty-five cents. You got egg drop soup first. Then you got chow mein. And then a yellow ball with a little piece of ice in it. That was the ice cream dessert. And some fortune cookies with paper in them. I ate the paper, I ate everything.

One of the most delicious things I liked was very simple. We liked to play ball in the street, and when we took a break, we all had lunch. My friends brought their lunch in bags and sat down on the curb. We lived five stories up in our tenement. I was not going to go upstairs for lunch. So my mother would throw down, in a brown paper bag, a Kaiser roll smeared with a lot of butter and almost a whole tomato sliced and salted.

I'd always catch it. But one time, I missed it, and *splat!* The bag was crammed with wet. So I very carefully peeled what used to be the bag away from the sandwich. I began eating the sandwich. Once again, I cried. It was so great. It was the closest thing I ate to pizza. I never had a real pizza until I was sixteen or seventeen.

When I was nine years old, my uncle Joe, the shortest Jew on earth, took me to see *Anything Goes*. He was a cabbie and he stood about four foot four. When you saw a big Checker taxicab rolling down the streets and there was no driver, that was Joe. Because his friend Al was the doorman of the Alvin Theater on 52nd Street, where *Anything Goes* was playing, Uncle Joe took me. I couldn't believe it. Even though we were in the second balcony, as far away from the stage as you could get, Ethel Merman was too loud. No mics. And Victor Moore was the gangster. At the end, I nearly clapped my hands off. I just couldn't stop clapping and screaming and shouting.

When I got back into Uncle Joe's cab, I said to him, "Uncle Joe, I'm not going into the garment center." Everybody at 365 South 3rd Street in Williamsburg, between Hooper and Hewes, worked in the garment center. They were shipping clerks, cutters, designers, salesmen. Everybody on the whole street—361, 363, 365, all tenements—everybody was in the garment center. And I screamed at my uncle Joe, "I'm not going into the garment center! I'm not. I'm going to go into show business!" And I did.

We had some favorite restaurants that Uncle Joe would take me to. One was Gallaghers Steakhouse. They had, like, half a cow hanging in the window. The steak was incredible. Sometimes we'd go to Jack Dempsey's restaurant. Also great. Always meat, no fish.

When I was seventeen, I was sent to the Virginia Military Institute. There was a guy who came to my high school, Eastern District High School, when we were about to graduate. The guy said, "If you can pass a test, you'll be in the Army Specialized Training Reserve program. It will stand you in good stead, because later, when you're drafted or taken into the regular Army, you'll already have had some background in military and you might be able to choose your branch of service."

Great! So I took the test. It was not hard. It was like, "How much is two and two?" They sent me to VMI, the West Point of the South. I'd go to restaurants in Lexington, Virginia. Whenever the waitress took your order, she'd say, "You want grits with that?" I'd say, "What?" I didn't know what grits were.

In June '44, I was transferred from VMI to Fort Dix in New Jersey. Now I was in the regular Army. I went into the mess hall at Fort Dix and was shocked by what I saw. On a great big griddle, maybe twelve feet by twelve feet, I saw a thousand eggs, sunny side up. You'd say, "Give me two, give me three, give me four." And then there was a giant barrel full of oatmeal.

At the tables where the cooks were, there was a big, round bowl with stuff in it. The cooks had big spoons to slop the stuff onto toast. The guys next to me ate it. I said to them, "What is that?" They said, "Shit on a shingle." It turned out to be creamed chipped beef on toast. I tried it and it wasn't so bad.

Then, when we were on bivouac—bivouac means you're on a campsite and you sleep on the ground—we'd go through a mess line with this stuff to eat with. It was all aluminum, with a tray that had indentations for food in it. They always did the same thing. They put the beef stew in the deepest spot in the tray. Then you ask for, let's say, the mashed potatoes. You figure, "Well, there's a big spot next to the beef stew, they'll use that." No, they put the mashed potatoes on the meat. And to top it off, they put sliced peaches on top of the mashed potatoes.

In the Army, they call it a mess hall. In the movie studios, they call it a commissary. Fox, where I worked, had good food. At Fox you could get an omelet. Other studios didn't know what an omelet was.

When I was young and not yet a filmmaker, I was on the Universal lot, writing a movie for a guy named Marvin Schwartz. I looked across the way and saw a building with a sign that says GRANART. I said, "Marvin, what the hell is Granart?" He said, "That's Cary Grant's production company." It was only thirty feet away.

So I started watching the building, to see if I could spot him. Sure enough, a Rolls-Royce pulled in, a chauffeur got out and opened the back door, and, bounding two steps at a time up the stairs, in a dark gray double-breasted suit with chalk stripes, it was him! Cary Grant! I said, "Holy shit!" I couldn't believe it. One day soon after that, I was walking to the commissary at Universal. I heard a little *click-clack, click-clack* behind me and turned around. "Mel Brooks! I don't believe it. You're Mel Brooks." It was Cary Grant. I said, "How do you know me?" He said, "I got your *2000 Year Old Man* record. You cost me a thousand dollars, I bought so many records." Then he said, "Wait, where are you going?" I said, "To the commissary." He said, "Well, let's go together." So wow, I had lunch with Cary Grant. I called my brothers Bernie, Lenny, Irving—everybody in Williamsburg. They wanted to know what he ate. I said, "He had two poached eggs on toast. I had tuna fish."

Next day, the phone rings. "It's Cary, Mel! Come to lunch." Boom. Me and Cary Grant, we walked out. Wednesday, me and Cary Grant. Thursday, me and Cary Grant. We're really talking. He says, "What's your favorite color?" I say blue, he says yellow. "What's your favorite car?" I say a Buick, he says a Rolls. Come Friday, I don't know what to ask him. I've run out of dialogue.

The phone rings, and I say to Marvin, "If it's Cary Grant, I'm not in." That last part is not true, but it makes for a great story.

I had never cared for wine when I was young, because it was always Manichewitz and Mount Carmel, sweet Jewish wines.

Gene Wilder, I could cry thinking of him. He was so sweet. He invited Anne and me to dinner at his house in the Village and served a Saint-Estèphe. I said, "What is this?" He said, "It's wine." I said, "So *this* is wine!"

He got me hooked. From that day—I was twenty-something—if I have wine, it's always a good wine. A good Italian or French or Napa Valley wine.

I got a few wine books. I started visiting the chateaus of Bordeaux. The owner of Cheval Blanc invited me, and I spent the weekend there. I learned about Italian wines. I love a Barolo. Italian wines can be soft and wonderful or they can be rough and beautiful.

Up until *Blazing Saddles*, I was hanging on in show business by the skin of my teeth, not making any money. The first movie I made was *The Producers*. Good movie. I won the Academy Award for the screenplay, but it just about broke even. And then the next one was *The 12 Chairs*, which was one of my best movies, but it didn't make a penny. I was thinking of going back to television when *Blazing Saddles* happened. That was an explosion. It busted open the doors and windows. It gave me enough money to buy a house and good wine and finally pay for dinner. Anne didn't have to slip me money under the table.

*Mel, what is your comfort food?*
The spaghetti that you, Ruthie, made for my son, Max. We came in and Max was hungry and you said, "I'll make him spaghetti." And it was the most delicious spaghetti in the world. When food is really good, it serves more than just the belly and the hunger. It serves the soul. And I'm not talking about Dover sole.

# WYCLEF JEAN

You never know what's going to happen at The River Cafe. One evening, while I was having dinner with friends in the garden, I received a message that Wyclef Jean was sitting at Table 4—the real one—and wanted to say hello. *The* Wyclef Jean, who, with Lauryn Hill and Pras Michel, formed the transformational musical trio the Fugees in the 1990s. An hour later, Wyclef, all smiles, joined us at our table. Late into the night, we were still there, talking about music, politics, and, of course, food.

Wyclef emigrated from Haiti at age nine, moving into a Brooklyn housing project. He played fourteen instruments by the time he was thirteen. He speaks seven languages. He has won three Grammys. What a man. I knew I wanted him on the podcast, but given his packed schedule, I suspected that I would have to be patient.

A few days later, out of the blue, I received a phone call. It was Wyclef. "Ruthie, I've delayed my flight. Let's record tonight," he said. We recorded so much more than a conversation. Instead of reading our recipe for Bruschetta with Grilled Red Peppers, Anchovies, and Capers, Wyclef started beatboxing and drumming his hands, insisting that I speak while he interpolated the recipe musically—echoing my lines, freestyling melodies, and offering commentary. And throughout our talk, he broke into song: gospel tunes, hip-hop, Enya, French chanson. As I said, what a man.

I grew up in Haiti in extreme poverty. My father left when I was one year old—he got a work visa to preach in the United States. So I was raised mostly by my grandmother. One of my bandmates from the Fugees, Ms. Hill, she was like, "Yo, Clef, remember back in the day when you used to tell us you used to eat dirt? Man, we thought you was, like, beyond exaggerating. Until we went back and did our research and realized mud pie was a real thing." Me and my brother were eating dirt from the floor!

But when you are in extreme poverty, you don't feel it. Because you're living inside of it. So my level of wealth was, "Man, no matter how much we can't eat, I know one thing about Grandma. She just got two chickens, and once them chickens lay some eggs, and then we go to the main city and she sells some of them eggs, we're going to come back and we going to have the biggest meal."

She'd go to the market in Port-au-Prince and sell what she grew. No matter what we was going through, it didn't matter, because we know at the end of the day, Grandma is going to make us *diri*, which is rice; *sos pwa*, which is black beans; and callaloo, which is okra.

Yo, let me tell you about my daddy. He's the original Aquaman—this dude can hold his breath for a day. When he going underwater to get that fish, oh, he's coming up with that fish. My grandma, my daddy's mother, later on when we lived in Brooklyn, she would make us laugh by telling us how he would just jump in the water and get that fish. That side of the family was the fishermen. But the thing is, once he left us, we wasn't on that side. We was more on the side of depending on, "Is it going to rain today?"

My mom was pregnant when my dad left. She joined him right after she had the baby, my brother Samuel. So my grandma and my aunt raised us.

My grandma knew my musical abilities at a very young age because I would just make songs up. There was these women in the village every Sunday that would sing these church hymns, and I would just be part of that. The hymns were saying, "We're blessed and we should acknowledge that basically every day of our lives."

After church, there was something we called Lucky Sunday. It didn't happen often. But on Lucky Sunday, everything came out. The meal was big. A lot of meat. Goat cooked very interestingly, fried. It's called *tasso*. They would put it out in a big aluminum pan. Traditionally, how they cook in Haiti, they use *charbon*, charcoal. They would make *pwason gros sel*, which was salted white fish.

One day, when I was five, I was in the village and a Jeep pulled up. Keep in mind, I'd never seen no Jeep before, so it looked like a UFO to us. We all stood next to my grandmother. And then *le blanc* gets out. This is my first time seeing a white man. He's got this robe thing on and long hair. He goes in the back of the Jeep and gets these bags of rice. I was like, "Grandma, who's this?" My grandma looked me dead in my eyes and said, "That's Jesus Christ."

Jesus brings this rice to my grandma and says a prayer. He's actually a missionary. And then, as he's leaving, I'm saying to my grandma, "Why ain't Jesus leave the seeds? Why ain't he bring no fertilizers?" Even at a very young age, I'm screaming, "Bring back the rice mills. Is there a way where we can just start producing in the country?" I say that to show you that what the kids want in these villages is an opportunity.

When I was nine, the immigration laws worked out and my parents were going to get us from Haiti. Me and my brother were going to see them for the first time since we were born. My grandma gets this dress, she takes our bags, she brings us to the airport. I've never seen an airport before. So when their airplane is landing, you can imagine what it looks like to me: another UFO.

The airplane lands and I'll never forget, my mother had a yellow outfit on. She looked like Jackie O. She had the sunglasses. She looked like Miss America. I'm like, "Yo, that's my mama right there!" My dad had a long beard looking like he Moses. They come and hold my brother and me in a hug. I can still feel that hug.

In Brooklyn, my mama had a thing that you could only eat in the house. I didn't know what it was like to go to a fast-food restaurant. A lot of what was cooked in Brooklyn was something called *legume*, which is similar to gumbo. A lot of vegetables: eggplants, watercress, yam, sweet potatoes. A lot of fish.

My father, who was also an amazing cook, he used to cook liver for iron. He would dip the liver in beaten egg whites and batter it so it wasn't rough. Everything was very tender.

There was a juice we had called *korosòl*, soursop juice, that my mother made us drink. We naturally grew up in an environment where the food wasn't processed. For chicken, she would always go to the butcher. There was no such thing as going to the supermarket to get chicken. She would make *poul di*, seasoned and stewed chicken. It was pretty amazing.

My mother said to me, "You're going to be real successful." I said, "Why?" She said, "Every time we cooking, all you do is come in the kitchen and sing. And while you sing, you stay here and wait so you're the first one to eat."

When she would cook rice, she would have me work on the seasonings with her. There's a seasoning that comes in a cube called Maggi that they put in everything. She was like, "Yo, give me two Maggis." The rice game is crazy in Haiti. She'd be like, "Okay, put this amount of water in the pot. Put in this amount of oil."

And one of the things she used to have me do was wash the rice. Cleaning was very, very important to her. I'd be like, "But the rice is already in the pot. Just—"

"No!" she'd say, "You've got to put the rice in the water." So literally for five minutes she has me cleaning this rice out. I would sit back and watch the water boil. And while the water was boiling, I would sing my mother's favorite French song, "Ne Me Quitte Pas" by Jacques Brel. Marianne Faithfull did it. Sting did it. I have a version of it. I put the hipness into it. I put that sauce, the Maggi, into it.

We grew up in Marlboro Projects, one of the roughest projects in Coney Island. But as far as me and my brother was concerned, we came from a hut. Now we're living in a building, so we are rich. We're like the Jeffersons: movin' on up to the East Side.

What was amazing about Coney Island was that we lived in one of the most dangerous projects, but when we went on the roof, we could see the entire amusement park on the beach. We literally could go from the projects to the beach. In Haiti, in the village, we played in a cemetery. Our Walt Disney World and our playground was this cemetery. So in our head, there was this transformation from the cemetery to this amazing amusement park. What that did for us was make us think, "We are in the land of opportunity. There's nothing that's going to set us back."

But being that I was the oldest, I would get in a lot of fights. Cousins of mine ended up getting killed in Brooklyn. I mean, I still have a stab mark on my left leg. It was rough, it was real, and my parents saw that I was headed in the wrong direction. People ask, "Why are you so sensitive to prison reform? Why do you connect with the youth so much?" I said, "I remember me and my cousin going into a bodega and thinking we're going to rob it." It was just a natural thing at the time that we felt like we had to do—this false sense of reality becomes reality within the environment you're in, if you don't have the right mentors. And your parents ain't going to be with you all the time.

My dad moved us from Brooklyn to New Jersey after the craziness. He started a small church at 1108 South Orange Avenue in Newark, New Jersey. It was an old, burnt-down funeral home. He said, "God has given me a vision." He's going to create the first bilingual church, where he's going to push the faith in English, Creole, and French. On the right side is an Irish pub. On the left side is a Sicilian crew that's running numbers, doing what they're doing.

One night, my dad looks outside and it's nothing but Cadillac Eldorados in the back of the funeral home. In his Haitian shorts and sandals, he knocks on the door of the Sicilian crew. He goes [*Haitan accent*], "Who park these Eldorados? I call da police now."

The dude goes [*Italian American accent*], "Vinny! Vinny! Ay, it's the ministah! Come talk to the ministah!" Vinny comes and he goes, "Ministah, I'm Catholic, you can't call the police! Every Sunday I'm going to come and contribute something to the church."

And guess what? Every Sunday they came and contributed to the church. The Irish pub folks came. It wasn't until a year later I realized, "Holy shit, my father bought that funeral home because of the big parking lot." He was able to rent out that parking lot to different communities, and that's how he was able to raise money to actually build the church.

In seeing that, I just started seeing things completely different. We were his church band, like the same way you see the Jackson Five. That was us. We was prodigies in the church, me and my brothers and sisters.

The way that the Fugees happened is amazing. Pras comes to my high school. Lauryn Hill is at Columbia, another high school. Pras was working in the studio with Ms. Hill and another girl called Marcy. I'm in my dad's church and Pras gives me a call. He goes, "Yo, man, I'm out here doing this recording and I have these two girls. I need a reggae hook, man. Could you come sing a reggae hook?"

I get to the studio and I see Lauryn and Marcy. I go into the booth and sing this reggae hook. The producer, Aswad Ayinde, was like, "There's magic here. There's something going on here." And that is how it started. My whole thing was the consciousness of the village of where we came from. Fugees is short for "refugees." Fugees wanted to speak for the less fortunate.

When the Fugees got signed, things were good, you feel me? The product manager brought me and Pras to an Italian restaurant in New York City. But keep in mind, we ain't never eat out. So we get there, the table looks nice, the glasses look nice, the wine. This dude brings this amazing bread out. Me and Pras ate at least three hundred pieces of bread. This ain't no regular bread, this is a different type of bread because we're used to Wonder Bread.

After the three hundred breads, the waiter comes out like, "Yo, do you want to order?" I looked at Pras and said, "I thought that was the whole meal."

By the time that we could afford the lifestyle, we started to talk about, "Yo what restaurant you want to go to? What type of food do you want?" Then you start to read about, "What kind of wine do you like? What year did this wine come out?" You start to look at different fishes, "Okay, what kind of fishes is going to work?" Then you'd be like, "Oh, I got to do a movie this week, we've got to do all lean meats." And then you're like, "Okay, which restaurant is all grass-fed?"

I have a lot of energy, so I go very light before I go onstage. I might have soup or a conch salad. But when I get off that stage, I promise you, if it's Steak Day, we'll have the best steak. If it's Poultry Day, we'll have the best poultry.

You wouldn't be able to do this without money. At the end of the day, that changed for us, too.

*Wyclef, what is your comfort food?*
Red snapper, white rice, cabbage, and gravy.

# TINA FEY

"I believe that food is the only reward in life," Tina Fey announced on our podcast. "Money? Sure. But food . . ."

Tina makes us laugh with or without food—in the "Sandwich Day" episode of *30 Rock*; cuddling a life-size brownie husband in a satirical *Saturday Night Live* commercial; and the legendary cafeteria scenes in the movie *Mean Girls*.

When we first met, Tina and I bonded immediately over our mutual love of food. I invited her to our house for dinner and made slow-cooked tomato sauce. She ate two portions. (Actually, three.)

Another time, she joined the Rogers family for our Italian-style Thanksgiving, for which we served our turkey with puntarelle, cavolo nero, and the new season's olive oil. Best of all was a dinner at The River Cafe when Tina came with her composer husband, Jeff Richmond, and their daughters, Alice and Penelope. They ordered every dessert on the menu.

Tina joined Sian Wyn Owen in The River Cafe kitchen to prepare Tagliarini with Slow-Cooked Tomato Sauce and Butter. "If I could marry a nonhuman entity," said Tina, "I would marry this pasta."

I grew up outside of Philadelphia in a very Greek neighborhood. I'm half Greek, on my mom's side. So we had a mix of Philly food, '70s food, American food, and Greek food. I grew up watching my mom make spanakopita, and we'd go every year to the festival at the church down the street, St. Demetrius.

That was the only time we could get *lukumades*. They're deep-fried dough balls that you get with hot honey and cinnamon poured on them. They're the best. But they're a real pain to make. There's a Greek restaurant in New York that I won't name, but they often have *lukumades* on the menu.

But if you order them, they'll say, "We don't have them tonight." Because they're such a pain to make.

I don't have firsthand memories of any of my grandparents. My mother's mother passed away when I was still quite small. But for sure she cooked certain foods like avgolemono, the Greek chicken soup with lemon, and with orzo instead of rice. I think that Greek American food is to Greek food what Italian American food is to Italian food. The real stuff is lighter and fresher than what you might know. It's not some heavy, cheese-laden moussaka. One thing my mom always made for us on special occasions, for our birthday or something, was pastitsio. That's the Greeks' version of lasagna. It's a brown beef and tomatoey pasta with béchamel baked on top. As a kid, it's all you ever want.

My mom cooked just by virtue of the fact that it was expected of her. She was a woman who liked to work. The norm at the time was that you didn't work when you had kids. She had worked for a brokerage firm in her youth, and once I was in high school, she went back to work.

She did well in the kitchen. She cooked in that '70s rotation of, like, "Okay, one night is hot dogs and beans, then it's shrimp pilaf." I do remember, in the part of the '70s where the American economy was not great, that only every two weeks, we all shared one steak. You'd take the grocery-store white bread to soak up all the A1 sauce on the plate. And once a month, on payday, we'd go out to have hamburgers.

When it was Christmastime, getting ready for the holidays, there would be Greek specialties. My mom would make baklava and *koulourakia*. Those are little twists. They look like the AIDS ribbon and they're not very sweet. You have them with coffee.

A lot of times we would go to restaurants that Greek family friends owned, little coffee shops and dinery restaurants. For a long time, the son of my godparents owned a huge diner in Wildwood, New Jersey, called the

Vegas Diner. The Jersey shore area is full of these gorgeous 1950s diners, places where the menu is fourteen pages long and you can get shrimp scampi or an omelet or whatever. When those places are good, they're *so* good.

So I grew up with this Greek cooking culture. I still love to cook dandelion greens in the spring in New York. My mom's aunt came to visit from Greece once, and she kept saying to my mom in Greek, which I can't speak, that she wanted to pick the dandelion greens out of the cracked sidewalk. My mom was like, "No, no, no, Thea, you can't eat those. Cats pee on them." Because in Thea's mind, it was, "Oh, there's dandelions, we should cook them."

My husband, Jeff, is originally from West Virginia. Then his family moved to Ohio, where they would go out into the woods behind their house and pick ramps in the spring. Ramps are a very garlicky green, some kind of cross between strong garlic and a scallion. Jeff's family cooked them with potatoes. He was blown away one day, a couple of years ago, when we were at some New York City farmers' market and the ramps cost $16 a bunch. He took a picture and sent it to his mother. She couldn't stop laughing. "Po' folks food," she called it.

The other thing I have a really fond memory of is Saturdays. I think this is a Philadelphia thing. We'd get up and I'd go run some Saturday-morning errands with my dad, which always included going to the good Italian deli near our house and getting what we would call lunch meat. It was pretty legit stuff, like sliced provolone, mortadella, and capicola, which in Philly they called *gabagool*. And we'd buy fresh rolls. The reward when you got home was that you'd make a big-ass sandwich with all that stuff.

Having grown up with that real Italian stuff, I was in for a rude awakening when I got to the University of Virginia and it was just regular bologna. I was like, "This is not it. Velveeta is not it." Within my first couple of weeks in Virginia, I went to the cafeteria and picked up what I thought was a breaded chicken cutlet. I was actually biting into a chicken-fried steak.

I thought, "What the hell is this? This is disgusting." They take a steak and bread it and deep-fry it like chicken, and it is gross. But believe me, wherever you put me, I'll find what there is to eat. The way to play it in Virginia was to go to a chain called Morrison's Cafeteria and just get the vegetarian plate, which was biscuits, black-eyed peas, collard greens, and grits with butter and salt. These were all foods I had never had before.

I'll tell you exactly what I used to eat when I first cooked for myself, and you can imagine what I looked like from that. I used to get a box of Kraft macaroni and cheese, make it, and then add to it a drained can of tuna fish and some lightly cooked frozen peas. I'd stir that all together and eat it, and then eat a pint of ice cream. I also had a side of applesauce for nutrition. Honestly, it's a miracle I didn't gain more weight.

My husband, Jeff, is a natural cook. He's someone who really did learn from his grandmother. His grandma Pearline taught him all these things. The previous generations of his family were coal miners in West Virginia, and in the coal camps were the Irishy and Englishy families, and also a lot of Italians. The women of the coal camps all cooked together. So Jeff's grandma would sometimes make what she referred to as "two fingers," which were gnocchi.

I'm the kind of the person where if I cook, I have to read the recipe a hundred times and I measure everything. Whenever there's anything that's instinct-related, like, "Is the steak done?" my instincts are terrible and Jeff's instincts are good. I'm getting better. I can cook a steak for myself. But I had to really learn, and he's just a natural. I tried to sell my kids on old '70s-style tuna casserole, but they were like, "No, this is terrible. We have yellow-tail sushi." Lorne Michaels said to me once, and I think it's so smart, "You can't make them have your childhood. You can't explain. They don't have your childhood."

I went to Chicago to study improv and comedy. I worked at a place called

The Second City and another place called the ImprovOlympic. That's where I met Jeff. He was the piano player for the ImprovOlympic and he also worked at The Second City eventually. That's where I met my dear friend Amy Poehler.

Again, it was a diner culture. We would do two shows on Friday and Saturday and then go have a giant breakfast of eggs and waffles, at around 1 or 2 a.m. Your adrenaline is high. It's the end of your workday and you want to go out and have your evening. Your evening just happens to be at one o'clock in the morning.

At *Saturday Night Live*, Saturday was the most fun day because it was the day where it was finally all happening. You spend the week being worried and then on Saturday, you just have to go down the slide. You'd rehearse from 1 to 5:30 p.m. and then you'd go down to the NBC cafeteria and have dinner with everybody. That's one of my favorite memories of working there.

At *30 Rock*, we had a wonderful lady, Angel, who is no longer with us. She was in charge of craft services. There was a catering truck that did breakfast and lunch, but the food that people eat all day, the craft-services food, was on a table in the hallway. Angel had so much passion about her job. She was an Italian American from Staten Island and she would show up with special things. Alec Baldwin, who loves to eat, was in love with her, because she would bring him beautiful balls of mozzarella, rolled-up artichoke bread, all this stuff. It was so much more than what you normally get, which is a bowl of apples and some candy.

There's an episode of *30 Rock* where Liz Lemon is chasing a guy she loves through the airport. Liz's love interest is played by Jason Sudeikis, who you may also know as Ted Lasso. The other part of the story is that Liz has been trying to get the Teamsters, the union drivers, to tell her where they get these great sandwiches.

So in the climactic scene, I've got my special sandwich, which comes with a container of dipping sauce, and the security guard at the airport says, "You have to leave the sandwich behind. You can't take it through."

I say, "No, I believe women can have it all! I'm going to eat this sandwich in one bite before I go through security and I'm still going to catch my man."

As an actor, perhaps my only specialty is on-camera eating. I commit to it. It all came down to Angel. I said, "Angel, this is a special assignment for you. I need you to make me the perfect sandwich." Normally, it would've been the props department, but I said, "Angel, you're going to make the sandwich and I need to be able to eat it in one bite."

She went to these bakers she knew in Staten Island and had them custom-bake . . . I don't know what it was, but it was the softest, most delicious bread. It was an Italian sub, so it had some *gabagool*, salami, and cheese. I ate it in one take. The director said, "We got it." I was like, "Did we? Because if you need me to do it again, I am willing to." The sandwich was that good. The credit goes to Angel.

*Tina, what is your comfort food?*
I have so many. Obviously, The River Cafe tomato pasta would be top of the list. I also think back to New York diner food: a grilled cheese with tomato, with the big steak fries. You open the grilled cheese and put a few fries into the sandwich. And to drink, a fountain Coke. Not Pepsi. The other thing would be yellow cake with white icing.

# ALFONSO CUARÓN

I admired the film director Alfonso Cuarón long before we met. *Harry Potter and the Prisoner of Azkaban*, *Gravity*, and *Roma* are three of my favorite films.

Alfonso is from Mexico, a country I have visited since the architect Ricardo Legorreta brought us there in 1991. Meeting Alfonso, I realized we had far more in common than a passion for his country—our children are the center of our lives, food is the focus of our days, and for both of us, Italy is a second home.

Alfonso read the recipe for Orecchiette with Tomato and Ricotta. Why? "It sounds so simple," he said. "That's what makes it universal. It is one of those recipes that allows every single flavor to come through."

I belong to a middle-class family in Mexico City, where the mentality was always about making things last. The kitchen was very old, with a refrigerator—probably from the early '50s—that rattled a lot. The TV set was black-and-white, also very old, and it constantly crackled.

The dichotomy of this situation was that, although we didn't live opulently because of the horrible social structure of Mexico, almost every middle-class family employed domestic workers for household chores—many of whom lived on the premises. The running of the kitchen usually fell into the hands of these workers. In my home, one worker oversaw the kitchen and another was in charge of all the other chores around the house.

I have three siblings: one sister and two brothers. Our household was pretty much the way it's described in *Roma*. I remember that when I was very young, there was a cook named Benita. She was of Zapotec origin, from southern Mexico—a region that spans Oaxaca, Veracruz, Guerrero, and Puebla. Benita

was very old. My memory of her is a face filled with wrinkles, kneeling in front of the *metate* [grinding stone], rhythmically grinding corn kernels.

Benita cooked traditional Oaxacan dishes, but since we were a middle-class family in Mexico, there was also an array of dishes inspired by Spanish and French culinary traditions, along with the recent influence of the U.S—like hot dogs and burgers. Benita could cook them all.

She usually decided what to cook, except on special occasions like family gatherings and celebrations. On those days, my grandmother would arrive with a fat, ancient notebook filled with handwritten recipes from different women—her mother, her grandmother who had lived on a hacienda, and many others before them. Who knows how far back in time it went. As I was a kid, I wasn't that interested in the recipes, but I was amazed by the handwriting, which looked antique, and the dried flowers pressed between the pages.

I've always loved going to the markets, but as a kid, I loved it even more. Getting lost through the maze of the stalls displaying the freshest fruits and vegetables, hoping for a free slice of mamey, mango, or chico, always avoiding the meat and the fish sections because of the smell. I delighted in the cacophony of sounds: vendors chanting their products, always extending a vocal "*Mameeeeeeee-y! Mangoooooo! Zapoteeeeee!*" the chopping of the butcher's knife; distant music playing; and the sad metallic wail of the *tortilladora*, the tortilla machine, which announced the most beautiful smell of all: the smell of the tortillas.

The combination of sounds and smells was fantastic, but as delicious as the tortillas rolling out of the *tortilladora* can be, they're no comparison to handmade tortillas. Their perfect thickness and softness, and their smell—as if you're holding a cornfield in your hand. Laura Esquivel claims it is because those handmade tortillas are infused with the energy of the *tortillera*'s hands.

Growing up, going to a restaurant was a big treat for my family because it was expensive. My grandmother and my mother would always say, "Why eat out when we—meaning Benita—can cook at home and it's cheaper?" But once I started being independent, I pretty much lived in restaurants. A *comida*, or lunchtime in Mexico, can be dangerous because it can very easily extend until dinner, all punctuated by shots of tequila or mezcal.

*Alfonso, what is your comfort food?*
Definitely quesadillas.

# BOB PITTMAN

> Bob Pittman is a visionary. In the early 1980s, he co-founded MTV, which changed the way we experience music. More recently, he created iHeartMedia, which has revolutionized the way we listen to podcasts and radio.
>
> Bob is a storyteller. The first time we met, he told me about growing up in southern Mississippi, the winding path he took to success—and the food he ate along the way. It was always my dream to have him share these stories on the podcast.
>
> Bob read our recipe for Lemon Ice Cream, which requires no churning—a change of pace from the ice cream he remembered making as a child.

When I grew up, I didn't know we were poor. My dad was a Methodist minister in the town of Brookhaven, Mississippi. The church gave us a house and the local country club let ministers join for free. So we had a decent lifestyle, if little money. My dad was very well-educated. He had an undergraduate degree from the University of Southern Mississippi and a graduate degree from Emory in Atlanta. My mother was also a college graduate, which was unusual for two parents of that era. Our family really valued smarts. My brother and I often talk about how we won the parent lottery.

My mother worked as a schoolteacher for some of my childhood and later on was a stay-at-home mom. Most of our meals were cooked and eaten at home: eggs, a piece of meat, a piece of fish, peas, beans, some rice—wholesome eating. We also ate squirrel. Either I'd hunt them or somebody would bring some over because they'd been hunting. People often say of an unusual meat, "It tastes like chicken," but I always think, "It tastes like squirrel." Squirrel is my reference meat.

My mother was from northern Mississippi, originally a farm girl. Her cooking was more hearty. Every time she went up to visit her family and came back home, she'd bring bushels of butter beans and Crowder peas, which are sort of like black-eyed peas. My brother and I hated when this happened because we had to shell them all, so she could freeze them for the winter.

We visited my paternal grandparents often. They had a little house on the Gulf Coast in a place called Bay St. Louis. We called it the camp. My grandmother was from New Orleans and a proper Cajun cook, so when we went to the camp, we had all this fabulous Southern and Cajun food. She would start a gumbo at 9 a.m. My brother and I would catch crabs all day, and she would throw them in around five in the afternoon.

My grandmother had a churn for making ice cream. It looked like a wooden tub. You'd put the ingredients in a metal container that hooked onto the crank at the top. Then you'd put ice around the sides and kosher salt on top of the ice. You'd churn and churn and churn until it hardened up. I hated churning. I'd call over my brother and say, "You churn it some!" When the ice cream was ready, my grandmother packed it with more ice and put a towel over it while we ate the gumbo.

We would also gig for flounders. A gig is like a trident, a stick with nails or prongs on the end. Flounders are flatfish that burrow into the sand, so you can just pick them up with the gig. My grandmother coated them in cornmeal and threw them in the deep fryer, and we had this spectacular fried fish. Everything in southern Mississippi was deep-fried. I had an uncle who said, "I like ham any way you fix it, as long as you fry it last."

My favorite was fried okra: cut up the okra, roll it around in some cornmeal, get a cast-iron skillet really hot, put in some oil, and fry it up. By the time the okra came out, it was crispy, like popcorn.

Early in my career I worked at a radio station in Chicago. I loved the South Side because soul food is the food I grew up with. But when I started school in Mississippi, in 1959, the system was completely segregated: white schools and Black schools. Water fountains had signs that said WHITE ONLY and COLORED ONLY. Yet over the twelve years I went to school, everything changed. By my senior year in high school, my graduating class was about fifty-fifty white and Black. My dad was one of the people supportive of this change and worked very hard for it.

When I was fifteen, I needed money for flying lessons. My grandfather worked for a man in Picayune, Mississippi, who had a big lumber mill. My grandfather ran it for him. This man had a plane and my dad's cousin, my grandfather's nephew, was the pilot for it. So when I was little, whenever I got to go to Picayune, my grandfather would let me crawl all over the plane. I was just eaten up by airplanes, no idea why. There was just something about flying.

I walked into a radio station and asked the man who owned it if I could have a job. He said, "Do you get in trouble?" "Not really." "You get good grades?" "Yeah, I get good grades." He said, "Come into this room." He took me to a little studio with a reel-to-reel tape recorder. He turned it on. He tore some wire copy off the teletype machine that printed the news constantly. "Read this," he said. I read it. He listened to my tape and said, "That's good enough. Go to New Orleans and get your third-class radio-telephone operator's license," which would permit me to control the transmitter. So I went to New Orleans, got the license, and that began my radio career.

As a result, I also became a pilot. For years, if I was flying anywhere near Memphis, I would stop and land there. I would call my cousins ahead of time, get one of them to bring me some catfish and barbecue, get some fuel, and take off. I got to eat Rendezvous and Corkys BBQ ribs all the time.

I've always found that I when I get in that cockpit, whatever I'm worrying about goes away. On my cross-country trips, I used to look down at the ground and stop in these little towns to get fuel. I would often borrow a crew car, and while they were refueling the plane, I'd go into town and find a restaurant.

I stopped in North Carolina once and ordered some barbecue. They brought out this meat with vinegar on it. I said, "I'm sorry, I ordered barbecue." They said, "This is barbecue." I was like, "Boy, I don't know what this stuff is, but it's nasty." To them it was perfect barbecue.

Later on, I was introduced by a mutual friend to a guy from North Carolina. I said to him, "I don't know what that stuff you have is, but it's not barbecue." So he organized a party that summer and invited all of his friends from the South to bring barbecue from their home state. It was great fun. We did it for a couple of years. You realize that South Carolina has this mustard-based barbecue. Texas has barbecue that looks like Mississippi's because it's red, but there's nothing sweet about it—the red is from chili powder. Then you get up to Missouri and the barbecue is not pork but beef.

In my younger days I was so ambitious that I put all my efforts into working. I ate like a college student. I'd eat stuff out of a can. Bags of potato chips and candy. I had a ravenous appetite for junk.

But in my travels I discovered regional foods. Milwaukee was the first place I ever saw a submarine sandwich. I ate my first pizza in Detroit. I liked it. It was not what I expected.

In Chicago, my girlfriend at the time introduced me to the artichoke. She had to explain to me, as if I was a simpleton, how to eat it. I thought, "Wow, this is so advanced. I can't wait to go back to Mississippi and tell them about the artichoke."

I have three grown kids. I don't know whether it was the busy New York life or particular to our family, but everybody ate when they wanted to eat. If I was going out, it was often at something like nine o'clock, not at all on the kids' timetable. But I would sit with them while they ate dinner.

My oldest son is now a really good cook, very interested in food. He has great knife skills and knows how to use them. My daughter has always been a great baker. I was off sugar for about three years. For my sixtieth birthday, she said, "Daddy, if I make you a cake, will you eat a piece?" I said, "Sure." I ate that piece of cake and it triggered me. Now I eat cookies, ice cream, everything. Ten years later, I'm still not able to get off sugar for any more than a month or so.

*Bob, what is your comfort food?*
Ice cream. I'll say, "I'm not going to have any." Then I'll walk up to the refrigerator, literally look at the freezer, and walk away. Then I'll get closer to it. Then I'll open it up and look at the ice cream. Then I'll go, "I'll have one spoonful." Suddenly I've eaten the entire container.

# J.J. ABRAMS

When J.J. was directing *Star Wars: The Force Awakens* about a dozen years ago, he would often stop in The River Cafe on the way home from Pinewood Studios, always sitting at the table closest to the kitchen, either with someone from the film or just by himself, with work to do. This is how our friendship began.

There are many stories to tell about J.J. and the presents he has made for me over the years, including a Lego model of The River Cafe, and a perfect lightsaber with my name on it.

But the one I always talk about is the one hundred fresh tamales sent to my room in Mexico City to get me through a difficult time. There is no one like J.J.

We moved from New York to Los Angeles when I was five. I was a chubby kid, and I was never athletic. I conflated that feeling of being chubby and not a good athlete with being a bit of a fat slob. But I loved food. I was always making things, sometimes by myself, sometimes with my mother. It was L.A. in the '70s, so she cooked things very much of that era, like stuffed zucchini. She made an amazing Caesar salad. I don't know what her secret was, but it was great.

My mother was always talking about what we were going to eat, to a point where it was insane. We'd be sitting at lunch and the conversation would be about what we were going to have for dinner. I've inherited that from her. I tend to look forward to eating in a way that is probably not right. I literally get sad when I'm halfway through a meal. I'm like, "Wait a minute—this is going to be over soon." There's probably a strong analogy somewhere in there to how I think about life itself.

Growing up in L.A., there was a handful of very '70s and early-'80s West Coast restaurants that we went to. The Sizzler was a big deal—a chain that served steak, seafood, and salads. Hamburger Hamlet was another one. We lived in Westwood, which is where UCLA is, and there was a restaurant there called The Chatam, kind of a fancy place, that my mother sometimes took me to.

She was loving to a fault—so loving that I remember thinking, "Whatever it is that I've done, it's not as good as you think it is." But what I really admired about her was how she never let herself be limited or defined by any one label. When we moved from New York, she started working as a real estate agent. Then she got interested in art and took classes to become a painter. Then, when she was approaching forty, she thought she wanted to be a lawyer. She asked someone, "Is it crazy to start law school when you're in your thirties?" The response she got was, "In two years, you're going to be forty either way." So she went to law school and graduated at the top of her class. For a while, she worked as a law professor.

In Los Angeles in the '70s, there was a bit of carelessness. It was a freewheeling, odd place to grow up, and I had a lot of friends whose parents were kind of off the rails. But I certainly felt safe. It was never like, "Oh my God, my parents are crazy!"

My mom was always so careful about everything and wanted us to be so careful. I have that, too. For whatever reason, when I look at a professional kitchen and see how crazy it is, I feel the nervousness that she used to feel. I think, "Dear God, please put an oven mitt on!" The idea of reaching into an oven bare-handed and grabbing a pan of mozzarella marinara is a nightmare.

To understand where that came from: my mother's father was Harry Kelvin, who was one of my favorite people. He had a company called Kelvin Electronics, which is still around. We would do these little projects together where we'd mount a motor on a plank of wood and then hook it up to a battery and a switch, so he could show me how a circuit works.

But he was also petrified of his grandchildren getting hurt. Every corner in his house, whether it was a table or a counter, was padded. He'd take tissue, roll it up, and put electrical tape on it. His company had some really cool designs of his in its catalogs. One of them was a circuit that looked like a letter *K*. Years later, I set up a little in-house visual effects company that we called Kelvin Optical. I said to our graphic designer, "Why don't we use the logo that he used to use?" She looked at it and came back to me and said, "This is a circuit that actually exists. It's called a bipolar circuit."

My mom had passed away by that point. What I really wanted to do was call her and say, "You're not going to believe this, but your dad's *logo* was bipolar."

My father only cooked sometimes. Fairly simple stuff, like the soft-boiled egg that he put in a little cup and tapped with a spoon so he could take the top off and dip the toast in. Never in my life will I understand the appeal of that. But if you said to my dad, "You can have a giant pile of gold or some eggs," he would choose the eggs. He loves eggs in a way that I don't think is healthy. Not in the sense of the cholesterol being unhealthy—I think *mentally* unhealthy.

I was obsessed, for some reason, with omelets. It looks so easy, making an omelet. You think, "Come on? What? Eggs in a pan?" But it's deceptively difficult. First of all, one of the key things is not keeping the pan on the fire. You actually have to take it off, as soon as the eggs start to congeal. And I'm not good at flipping. It's fascinating to watch someone at a hotel who makes ten thousand omelets a day, flipping one after another—it's like watching an Olympic jumper. It scares the hell out of me. As for fillings, I have very simple preferences. A little bit of sautéed onions and maybe some diced tomato.

I was a host at a Mexican restaurant in L.A., and I worked at a few different ice cream stores. I learned that feeling of doing your job, doing well by someone, and sometimes not getting any acknowledgment. The value you have socially as a kid is often connected to how well you play sports or what your grades are. My grades were never particularly great, and I was never any good at sports. So, weirdly, I had nothing of value as a kid. I remember that feeling of "I'm not seen as anyone of note or importance." It's one of the reasons why, in terms of stories, I tend to love underdogs.

And look, no one is crying for the little white boy who couldn't throw a ball. We all have insecurities and experiences that shape us. In service jobs, it's so easy to be overlooked or treated badly. Sometimes people go out of their way to berate you because it makes them feel better to use you as a punching bag. A waiter is a prime example of someone who is doing you this sort of beautiful service—even if the waiter's not particularly great, they're still *serving* you. On that level, to not acknowledge that person, to not have gratitude for them, says a lot about who that customer is. My takeaway is: "Don't continue a relationship with a person who treats waiters that way."

I go to restaurants to write all the time. I like the energy of the space, the noise of it. When you're at a restaurant or a coffee shop, it modulates between the most extreme, dramatic breakup that might be happening two tables over to a first date. Or a parent having lunch with a child. Everywhere you look, there is a window into personal drama. It fuels me in a way that being in a room alone doesn't. It's hugely inspiring.

I start out a script by writing longhand, until what I'm writing turns into something—until it starts to become more congealed and solid, like an omelet. Then I will carry it over to the laptop.

*J.J., what is your comfort food?*

I just took my dad to dinner at Dan Tana's, the old Italian restaurant in West Hollywood. We were talking about how it's such comfort food. Comfort food feels like it's got to be a bit Italian. There's something about pasta that feels so good. It might be the carb-y, starchy thing. But really, it's hard to imagine any food that on some level doesn't provide some kind of comfort: a really great sushi dinner, a great pizza. Food in general is a comfort.

# TRUDIE STYLER

Trudie Styler and I share a love of food, wine (she has her own vineyard), and family. In Tuscany in the summer, we both fill our houses with our children, our children's friends, and our friends' children, occupying every bed. There is always space for another chair around the crowded table.

Trudie, who is married to the musician Sting, grew up in the West Midlands, her father a factory worker, her mother a school cook. Trudie's was anything but an easy childhood, but to her family, mealtimes were an important part of their day.

The day we recorded the podcast, Trudie brought a special gift: a package of The Original Atora Shredded Beef Suet—according to the label, perfect "for fluffy dumplings, pastries, puddings, and pies"—an essential ingredient of her youth.

Trudie chose the recipe for Roast Grouse, which we cook in Chianti in our wood-burning oven.

I was born in the mid-1950s in a little village called Stoke Prior. We were brought up on a council-house estate in the county of Worcestershire, where, being sort of postwar, there was still this feeling of people having to conserve and preserve. My mum could go to the butcher's just once a week, for the Sunday roast. And then the Sunday roast was made to stretch through the week.

She was very inventive with how she could stretch it. In fact, I became a lover of offal, which I preferred over the Sunday roast because it was very flavorful. We would have liver and onions and kidneys that she'd sauté with mushrooms. Lamb's liver was sort of the posh one. Pig's liver was the cheapest one.

And then we would have faggots, or savory ducks as they were known, because my mother was from the north. It was cooking up the rest of the joint that hadn't been used on Sunday, and if you hadn't got enough to stretch—in our case because it was three kids and a mum and a dad—she'd buy some sausages and raw onions. I got the job of being her apprentice, to mince everything up. She would buy a pig's bladder, and then she'd wrap up the cooked meats, the raw sausage meat, and the onions, with salt and pepper, in the bladder, and into the oven it went. And it was utterly delicious.

At that time, living in rural England, nothing was ever wasted. Now I live in New York and we have so-called superfoods like "bone broth." But we were having bone broth then because my mum made stock from big animal bones, and then she made soups from her stock.

I don't think my mom had it in her to open cans of things to make pies. Sting talks about his mum making pies from cans of Fray Bentos beef cubes. My mother was a scratch cook. She would begin at the beginning, with the stock. At the end, we would sit down together at a table with an embroidered tablecloth that she had embroidered herself. Even in a council house. It was important to her.

We didn't go out to restaurants. My first memory of being in one was when I was six or seven, and my nana brought us to a Lyons teahouse in Cheshire. I saw somebody eating what looked to me like a plate of worms. There were these long, long strands and I could not believe my eyes. It was like, "Are they eating worms? What is all that red sauce? Is that the worms' blood?"

It was spaghetti. I declared to myself that I would never eat it in my life. Only to now say that spaghetti aglio e olio or spaghetti peperoncino is actually my favorite thing. I could eat it all day long.

When I was only two and a half, I was in a serious accident. I'd toddled out of the house while my mum was bathing my younger sister. I went down the stairs and the little girl from across the street called me to see if I could come over to her place, and did I want to have a sweetie? I said yes. She was only about five herself, I think. She took me over to her house. She got me a sweet, and I think her mother thought that I was going to be escorted back to our house. But I wasn't.

I was crossing the road when a fifteen-year-old kid jumped into a baker's van. While the baker was delivering his bread, the kid jumped in and knocked it from neutral into first and took the hand brake off. The van started to roll down the hill. Luckily the wheels missed me, otherwise I wouldn't be telling the story now. But the exhaust pipe caught me at the back of my head and dragged me along the street, taking off quite a lot of the left-hand side of my face.

Growing up, kids can be a bit cruel to children who look a bit different, and I did look a bit different as a youngster: I had very livid marks on my face. But Mum got a job as the school dinners lady, and she was a very formidable-looking woman. She was about fifteen and a half stone, and nobody was going to mess with Pauline Styler. She protected me from a lot of unfair remarks that were being made.

My dad worked in a lampshade factory and was also the school caretaker. I was co-opted to help him, which was always much more fun than helping mum, because she gave me the washing-up jobs. With Dad, I got to change into my overalls and sweep the playground with him.

In the summer, we were given permission from the headmistress to go into the orchard, which was part of our playing-ground fields. It was full of plums and apples. We would put ladders up against the trees and take home literally boxes of apples. As we both rode bikes, we'd have to make multiple journeys to get the apples back. We'd wrap up the apples in newspaper or brown paper, usually newspaper, because we had the *Daily Express* every day.

So under my bed I would have, throughout the winter, my little piles of apples. My room smelled like an apple. We used them through winter, bit by bit. In March, they were still going strong. Having them in a dark place, they didn't go off, but they did get a little bit wrinkled. That didn't stop Mum from making baked apples. She made so many apples. For November 5, Bonfire Night, she made all the kids in our street toffee apples from the purloined-with-permission apples from under my bed.

Things weren't so good between my dad and me when I decided to be an actor. He was very fearful: "What is that? Nobody in Walls Road has become an actor." He wanted me to have a safe job that guaranteed a paycheck, in the typing pool at the paintbrush factory.

It was an upsetting time, because I was a headstrong seventeen-year-old who had been to a grammar school and loved literature and everything to do with the performing arts. After all those years of not knowing who I was, the performing arts were a way to express myself.

Suddenly my life changed profoundly, being a student actor going to Bristol, going to Manchester, exploring areas in England, and eventually acting with the Royal Shakespeare Company in London. I had a season at the Donmar Warehouse, when it, rather than the Aldwych, was the RSC's London home.

My horizons just opened and opened and opened. When I was eighteen, I hitchhiked through Morocco with my boyfriend and stayed there for three months. It was the first time I'd had Middle Eastern food. The sights and sounds and smells were so evocative. You begin to be inclusive in your own diet of so many different flavors and tastes that you acquire with the years that go by.

When Sting and I bought Lake House, a farm we've had in Wiltshire for over thirty years, I found my dad again. He came and visited. He was a man of the country. We would walk through the grounds and I'd say, "Harry, what shall we do?" After we fell out, I never called him Dad again. He was Harry to me. I'm proud to say I've got a beautiful grandson who's named after him.

We became pals, and that was important. I didn't need him as my dad anymore because I'd sort of found my place in life without my parents.

Even in our very modest garden in the Midlands, because we were a middle house, we had this sort of double lot. So we grew a fantastic amount of veggies. Dad was very proficient with that and didn't use any fertilizers. We were always rapturous when we saw so many worms in the garden. He became a really important component of steering me through the process of creating a really good organic farm at Lake House. The Soil Association were fantastically helpful, and Dad was always coming over and giving me his ten cents' worth of "Just plant different varietals of apples and potatoes."

Taking on Palagio was a whole different animal than Lake House. After two years of just having vegetable gardens, I decided I should learn a bit about the vineyard on the property. And so I started to get my hands in the soil again.

The vineyard was very broken down, not tended to that well. The wine was being sold into the community at that point. I was having my neck adjusted at a chiropractor and saw a picture of a marvelous vineyard on the wall. I said, "Where is that picture?" The chiropractor said, "Oh, that's my vineyard." I went to see it and asked him how he did it. He said, "There's this guy called Alan York and he does biodynamic wine. Would you like to meet him?"

Cut to Alan York coming to Palagio. I had the great pleasure of learning a lot from Alan. In 2002, we planted a lot of varietals. In 2007, we had our first vintage, for Sister Moon and When We Dance. A lot of the wines are named for Sting songs.

My favorite is a white Vermentino called Baci Sulla Bocca. We made it in 2020, when we were in full-on pandemic and wearing masks. Nobody seemed to be kissing anybody. I thought, "Let's call this 'Kisses on the Mouth' and hope for the day to come back that we can."

*Trudie, what is your comfort food?*

I brought you my ultimate comfort food. Atora Shredded Beef Suet, to make the most fluffy dumplings!

Fluffy dumplings were one of the first things that my mum taught me to make. They couldn't be simpler to make, because it's three ingredients. You have, say, eight ounces of Atora beef suet—which is sort of lard made from a cow—eight ounces of self-rising flour, and water. Combine the lot and add a pinch of salt.

And then, as your chicken casserole or chicken stew is bubbling away nicely, you form little balls and put them in for the last twenty minutes. The gravies go into the dumplings, but the dumplings rise because of the self-rising flour. They actually provided much-needed carbs for kids growing up in the late '50s and '60s. If you couldn't afford potatoes at the time, this was a very sort of cheap fare.

# TOM HOLLANDER

I like spending time with Tom Hollander.

He is passionate about what he cooks and cares about the food that he and Fran feed their son, and upholding his family's Czech-Austrian culinary traditions.

When he came on the podcast, he brought the small handwritten cookbook his mother made for him when he went off to college, something he is so proud of and has updated to be his own. The recipe for his chosen comfort food is from that book.

Tom is funny and smart, one of Britain's best actors—*Pride and Prejudice*, *The White Lotus*, and in the title role of *Feud: Capote vs. The Swans*.

A few months after the recording, he came back to The River Cafe bringing his mother's cookbook again so he could show it to our chefs. Then he made fresh pasta with Joseph Trivelli.

Again, there are many reasons to like Tom Hollander.

We lived in Oxford, my family. My grandparents were in Devon. In 1939, they came to England from Czechoslovakia with my dad, who was three years old.

They made this epic journey across Central Europe and landed at Harwich, I think. They had something like twenty-five suitcases at the beginning of the journey. The suitcases were thrown off one by one, reduced to about three by the time they got to the end. The only money they had left was in my father's shoe, a toddler's shoe. But they knew some people. My grandfather was in charge of the classical music at a radio station in Czechoslovakia. A BBC producer had sent him a letter inviting him to give a talk about the Czech composer Leoš Janáček. My grandfather was a friend of Janáček's and had written about him. That was what allowed them to get through, because people were suspicious of them. They spoke with German accents.

My parents were teachers. I have very happy memories of our family suppers, in which the day would be downloaded and we'd all share our experience of school. We used to say our life was bohemian, but technically, it was Moravian.

I've brought with me a book that my mother made for me in 1985, when I was going off to Cambridge. She put in a few of the favorite things that she'd cooked for us, just to start me off.

She wrote "Bon appétit!" and sectioned it into Soup, Fish, Meat, and Miscellaneous. Under "Miscellaneous" is tomato chutney. My mother grew up in Africa until she was six and then she was in England. But these are the sorts of things we used to eat as children: *tiroler gröstl*, a sort of peasant Alpine dish. Potato and garlic sausage. You let the potatoes fry, add the meat and other ingredients, and cook for ten minutes. It was a good recipe for a college student and then a bad recipe for an out-of-work young actor who didn't have enough to do and would think, "Well, I can fill the day with the buying of the ingredients, the cooking of lunch, the overeating, and then the falling asleep. That'll get me to the *PM Programme*." I remember making *tiroler gröstl* in Peckham in 1989.

What's fascinating is that Dad is an Englishman now, but when we talk about food, it reveals your origins. He loves Wiener schnitzel and he loves *apfelstrudel*, which he now makes. Mum used to cook goulash regularly, which I've recently learned to make. I just made a goulash with mushrooms because Fran, my wife, is a vegetarian. If Fran's not at home, I secretly make it sometimes with venison. We live in the country, which is infested with deer, and people are always giving each other piles of venison out of the deep freeze.

I was a child actor in the Children's Music Theatre, now called the National

Youth Music Theatre. We did a show called *Captain Sturrock*. It was a brilliant dark ballad opera. We were all ragged children, Dickensian beggar children. Captain Sturrock was the young kid who was our leader. It wasn't *Oliver Twist*. It was actually darker, and Captain Sturrock went mad.

I was thirteen, fourteen, and we did it on the stage of the National Theatre. We had sausages that we didn't really cook, but we acted as if we were cooking them and then we got to eat them. It was quite fun to have something to eat halfway through the second half.

I got picked up for a TV film, a BBC Dickensian drama called *John Diamond*, an adaptation of a Leon Garfield book. That was so exciting. I had a term off school, I was driven around in a car, and I got to stay in a hotel and eat. I remember eating duck à l'orange on my own, thinking, "Wow, this is the life." That rather rewired my brain in a way that is either helpful or unhelpful, because it meant the end of imagination. I thought, "Well, I must repeat this for the rest of my life and become an actor." Then I went back to school, went to university, and I was waiting to start acting.

On the last play I did, on days with a matinee and an evening performance, I always had a falafel salad in the dressing room without leaving between shows. I would buy it beforehand, put it in the fridge, eat it, and go to sleep between performances. That was my ritual and it was very good.

I never drink before going onstage. I tried all of those things in my twenties and it's a mess. It affects your timing and your memory and your speed and your reactivity. It ruins it. But I remember the actor Oliver Cotton telling me that if you were on a stage with Paul Scofield and you were downstage center, you would expect to smell whiskey on his breath. They were just used to it. I think they drank so much more in those days that it just didn't affect them in the same way.

But a small amount of alcohol or of any intoxicant releases your imaginative stuff and makes you relax. When I played the violin at school, I found concerts very tense-making. I discovered that having half a glass of beer allowed me to play better in a concert situation, just because I was so racked with nerves otherwise. But the association between being artistically brilliant and being intoxicated has got an awful lot of people into terrible trouble over the years. Not least of whom, Truman Capote.

His swans didn't really eat. They drank and smoked and died young. Perhaps they were celebrating being in the "in crowd" and being at the best table in the best restaurant. But they restrained themselves. He couldn't stop. He couldn't control his appetite. And he loved cooking. He loved his own kitchen.

The Black and White Ball he threw in 1966, on the back of *In Cold Blood*, brought together his obsession with high society and his own celebrity in one glorious moment. Aristocrats flew from Europe, all the film stars, Frank Sinatra, Mia Farrow, the Agnellis. They all turned up at the Plaza Hotel and he gave them corned-beef hash, which he remembered fondly from Monroeville, Alabama, where he'd grown up. But they all complained about the catering. His budget for it was very small. It was more about getting them in. They were the decoration, they were the party. I think the party ended relatively early and a whole bunch of them went gambling.

We think, those of us who made that show, that Truman Capote threw that ball for his mother. His mother had abandoned him when he was four and married a man called Joe Capote, who gave him his name. Truman's mother had nearly made it into Upper East Side society when Joe Capote was revealed as being sort of bankrupt and hopeless. It all fell apart and she killed herself. Truman had this ball to say, "Look, Mom, I've done it! I've done it for us!" In our version of it, his mother comes to him as a ghost in the ball. What Lee Radziwill, played by Calista Flockhart, sees is Truman dancing drunkenly on his own. She's thinking, "Poor sod. He's just a drunk." The final scene of the episode goes from black-and-white to color, and he's not dancing on his own but with his mom.

Truman was addictive and compulsive. He went up and down. In our version, we pretty much did Fat Truman because, given the schedule, I couldn't go up and down. Ryan Murphy said, "You need to put on some weight." I did, which was very enjoyable. I've done this a couple of times for work. Basically, you eat all the obvious things like pizza and ice cream and Cornish pasties and chips. Then you get fat very quickly.

It was marvelous in the moment. But then I started to find it hard to put my socks on, and I got breathless doing ordinary things. Also, I'm a bit old to be messing around with my weight like that. I have spent most of my professional life going slightly up between jobs and then having to diet before a job. I'm trying to stay more disciplined, like my father, who weighs himself every day. If he ever goes over eleven stone, he has a light breakfast. He says, "I know whether I can have a heavy or light breakfast depending on what the scales are telling me." He sounds like one of the swans with his level of obsession, but he's still going strong.

To be at war with food is not good. I do have a sense of that, because being an actor, you inevitably become obsessed with your appearance. It has a tendency to make you think, "I mustn't eat, I mustn't eat, I mustn't eat, so I'm beautiful, beautiful, beautiful."

It's never really made any difference. I met an actor once in Italy who was long retired. He'd been a famous 1960s heartthrob, but he said, "I had to retire because I was sick of being thin and I wanted to eat." He lived in the hills near Cortona and he loved food and he ate it. He was living the life.

Anyway, I can't do that. I now need to live as long as I can. We have a child. The family-dinner thing, it's suddenly becoming exciting. The home-cooked food thing, that's suddenly becoming the new aspiration. I'm looking forward to cooking our child fish fingers and peas.

*Tom, what is your comfort food?*
In a sort of *Desert Island Disc*–y way, if I was allowed one food, I would take my mother's chutney recipe, which is actually my grandmother's.

# FRANCIS FORD COPPOLA

For me, a great movie is like a great menu. You can pick any scene, as you would pick any dish, and find it compelling. Francis Ford Coppola has made great movies—the *Godfather* trilogy, *The Conversation*, and *Apocalypse Now*.

His most recent film, the ambitious *Megalopolis*, ends with this thought: "The human being shall rightly be called a great miracle." It's a message of hope and resilience in turbulent times, and one that Francis and I have taken to heart. We have both survived the deaths of our sons in their twenties, and, just as I lost Richard not too long ago, Francis recently lost his wife of over sixty years, Eleanor.

There is much more that bonds us: a love of Italy, a love of food and wine. Francis is not only a filmmaker but a winemaker, and he generously brought some of his favorite bottles for us to share. Though we had never met before, by the end of this episode, we were friends.

Francis read our recipe for Puntarelle Salad with Anchovies.

My mother's side of the family was from Naples. My father's side was from Lucania, which is today called Basilicata. If you look on a map, it's the arch of the boot. Bernalda is the town we're from, near the Ionian sea. When he came to America, my paternal grandfather still wanted to eat the food of Lucania. His wife, my paternal grandmother, didn't know how to cook it because although her family came from Southern Italy, she was actually born in Tunis, the capital of Tunisia, which was built by Italians. That's why her father was there. But because Tunisia was a French protectorate, he had to be in cahoots with a French business partner. Then his French partner double-crossed him. He got mad and took his three daughters to New York.

So in America, my wonderful grandmother, who was born in Tunis, married my Lucanian grandfather. In those days, the husband called the shots on what type of food his wife cooked. It turned out that there was a *paisan* in New York, an immigrant, who had cooked at a railway station in Lucania. His son taught my grandmother how to cook all these strange dishes.

There was one called *gnummarieddhi*. It's lamb innards, like lungs, sweetbreads, and intestines, that are packed into a casing and then cooked on the grill. And there was *fegatelli*, where you take the caul fat from the stomach, which looks like lace, and wrap it around a pork liver and add a bay leaf before you roast it. It's delicious.

We also had an item called *capuzzelle*, which is literally half of a lamb's head, with the eye and everything. It was stuffed and baked *oreganata*-style, with seasonings and breadcrumbs. The big dare was to eat the eye, but I never saw anyone, not my grandfather or even my daring big brother, do it. But I did eat the brain. I thought that if I ate a lamb's brain, I would become smart.

When I was growing up, each immigrant group was bullied by the one that came before it. Before the Italians came the Irish, so the Irish, who were mostly the policemen, used to beat up on the Italians. But it was a wonderful mix of cultures. We used to get Chinese take-out food, and every street corner had a German delicatessen, where you would buy cheesecake, and a candy store with a soda fountain. A Coke cost five cents. It was made fresh, with syrup, not sold in a bottle.

In our neighborhood there were also a lot of Poles. Because both Italians and the Polish were Catholic, I went to a lot of Italian-Polish weddings and knew what Polish food was like. They had kielbasa, whereas we had *salsicce*.

I spent all of sixth grade, an entire year, in bed with polio. There was an epidemic among children in 1949. I went on a Cub Scout camping trip. One night it was raining. The next morning, I had the symptoms. The fever only affects you for that one night, but there is lasting damage to your spinal cord.

I woke up in a ward with hundreds of kids. There were rows of kids in iron lungs, because they couldn't breathe and needed a machine to do it for them. It was a nightmare. I felt so sad for those kids. Then I tried to get out of bed and fell on the floor. I realized I couldn't walk. I stayed in that ward for another week, and then they took me home. A French doctor gave me a big speech about how I was a going to be a good soldier. The prognosis, he told me, was that I would be able to do everything a normal person could do—but in a wheelchair. I hadn't realized it was that serious. We all went out for Chinese food, my favorite, and I was crying into my moo goo gai pan. But my father heard about the Sister Kenny method. Sister Elizabeth Kenny was an Australian nurse who thought that, rather than keeping a paralyzed patient immobilized so as not to cause further damage, you do the opposite, putting the patient through physical therapy. My father got the National Foundation for Infantile Paralysis to pay for a Sister Kenny therapist, a wonderful lady named Miss Wilson.

The exercises were very gentle but effective. Otherwise, I lived in my room, playing with puppets and watching television. There was a variety show sponsored by the Automat chain Horn & Hardart, *The Horn & Hardart Children's Hour*. It was all these talented kids singing and dancing, and I wanted to be part of that.

Eventually, many years later of course, I went to the film school at UCLA. I was very poor. My father was not going to help me because I had run away from the New York Military Academy, the same military school President Trump went to. He never forgave me for that because he still had to pay for it, so when I went to UCLA, I had about $1.25 a day to live on: 25 cents for breakfast, 50 cents for lunch, and 50 cents for dinner. I pretty much ate 19-cent Kraft Macaroni and Cheese dinners every night. I just got fatter and fatter and fatter and fatter, and I was very depressed.

I had no money, no car, and no girlfriend, and there was a time when I thought I would quit. But I had a wonderful directing teacher named Dorothy Arzner—Miss Arzner, we called her, out of great respect—who had been the only woman director working in Hollywood in the 1930s. At my lowest point, she said, "You'll make it. I've been around, and I know." I stayed on, and ultimately I won the Goldwyn Prize, a writing award, which came with $2,000 and changed my life.

I founded my company American Zoetrope in San Francisco, where Dolby, the great sound company, was also based. Picture and sound contribute equally to a movie being good, but sound is much cheaper. So we made a big investment in sound.

You want to know why I bought a vineyard? I'm an Italian American, which means I never saw a dining table that didn't have wine on it. There was a rule during Prohibition that very few people know about. If you were from a wine-drinking culture, you were allowed to buy wine grapes. As long as you made your wine at home, you could make and keep two barrels a year. So most Italians continued drinking wine during Prohibition, making it themselves.

I had many uncles, and they told me stories of how when the grapes came, they would steal them. They otherwise ate very little fruit. A poor family like mine would have a single orange, and each kid would get one segment. The stories of the grapes and how Grandpa made wine sounded like fun. So when I made money from *The Godfather*, I said to my wife, "Let's buy a small house in the Napa Valley. We'll have an acre of grapes and we'll make wine to give it as gifts to our family."

Our real estate agent said, "This isn't for you, but they're going to auction off the most beautiful wine property in Napa Valley, the Inglenook estate. It's much more money than you want to spend, but it's a chance to see it." So we went to see this place. It had two things I liked most: It had a mountain, with a nascent lake and a huge oak in front of the house with a swing for my little Sofia. And it had a hundred acres of grapes. My wife thought I was crazy, but I made an offer for it.

We didn't get it. But everything we looked at seemed ridiculous compared to this gorgeous property. Then I heard that the people who did buy it were running into trouble. They were financed by a group intending to build sixty homes on the mountain, but that would have violated the county's agricultural zoning. So, right before I was going to make *Apocalypse Now*, I went back to the seller and said, "I heard that your buyers can't build these sixty homes. Would be you be interested in selling to me?"

They said yes. The price was about $1.5 million, which was a lot of money for me. But I had a percentage of *The Godfather*, so I got a loan. The 1978 Niebaum-Coppola was our first vintage.

The key thing to understand about me and cooking is that I love to eat. It's the most wonderful thing in the world. I was very poor when I was starting out, so, rather than going to a restaurant I couldn't afford, I would call my mother and say, "Mom, how do you make spaghetti with clams?" And she would tell me.

Since then, I've developed a habit of, every time I love something I've eaten, whether at a restaurant or in someone's home, I ask, "How do you make this?" So if I've recently been to a Moroccan restaurant and had *pastilla*, when you next come to my house, you will have a *pastilla*.

*Francis, what is your comfort food?*
Halvah. It's a Middle Eastern sweet made of ground sesame seeds and honey. I always loved it as a little kid. If I were ever to take my own life, I would infuse some halvah with arsenic and eat all I want.

# Food Is Discovery

Though many of the guests on *Ruthie's Table 4* are knowledgeable about cooking, they didn't necessarily begin that way. They started life exposed only to the culture of food within their own homes and, like everything else, their horizons expanded as life unfurled outward. Many of them view their exposure to food and wine as a measure of their success.

Food plays a major part in the films of Wes Anderson today, but even bagels were exotic to him growing up in Houston.

Sarah Jessica Parker had never been to Ireland until she met her husband, Matthew Broderick. Now she is rapturous on the delights of Kerrygold butter and County Donegal lamb.

Tastes and experiences may be discovered through the person you fall in love with. Meeting Richard's Italian family and spending time with them in Florence opened up the world of Italian cooking for me.

# MICHAEL CAINE

I often say that the main reason I have a restaurant is that once a week, after Michael Caine has finished his dinner at The River Cafe, I get to walk him from his table to his car and kiss him goodnight.

Michael revolutionized acting in Britain, unapologetically speaking in his natural Cockney accent when he ascended to film stardom in the 1960s. Though he was raised in a working-class household, he never wanted for food. Indeed, he grew up around it. His mother, Ellen, worked at a branch of Lyons' Corner House, a chain of London brasseries and tea shops that flourished in the mid-twentieth century. His father, Maurice, was a porter at a fish market. For a time, Michael was a restaurateur himself, a founding partner of Langan's Brasserie in Mayfair.

Michael knew instantly which recipe he was going to read on the podcast. "The River Cafe has a dessert that is my favorite: Panna Cotta with Grappa."

I was born in Bermondsey, which is South London. But I'm a Cockney, because I was born in a part of Bermondsey which is opposite Bow Bells. If you're born within earshot of Bow Bells [the bells in the ancient Church of St Mary-le-Bow], you're a Cockney. My father was a Billingsgate Fish Market porter and a big gambler. So he never brought home steak, it was too dear. But he used to nick a lot of fish. So for fifteen years, I ate fish, every kind of fish you could imagine. I later realized it was a very healthy thing.

Another accidental healthy thing for me was the Second World War. Because of rationing, you couldn't get any sugar. Then we were evacuated into the country and I lived on a farm for six years. So I went from the smog, which was terrible in Bermondsey because everyone had coal fires, to fresh air.

The food in the country was wonderful. I caught some of it myself, because I could outrun a rabbit. I used to catch a rabbit with a stick and give it to my mother to cook for dinner. We used to go and nick a cabbage. Pheasant, partridge, fresh vegetables—we had all those things. And on top of all that, my mother insisted that I have porridge for breakfast for fifteen years! So, thinking back on it, health-wise I was very lucky.

Eventually we came back to London, and the council gave us a prefabricated house. They were made with asbestos and put up in a few weeks. People sympathized with families like ours who had to live in these little prefab houses. What they didn't know was what life was like for us before. In the flat we lived in when I was a little boy, there was no toilet, for a start. You had to go down to the garden. We used to have a bath in the kitchen with hot water that my mother poured from a kettle.

When my brother Stanley and I walked into the prefab for the first time, we were stunned. We were in a place that had electric light and an indoor toilet. And it had a little garden. The kitchen was lovely. It had an electric stove and a refrigerator. We'd never seen one. It was fabulous for my mother because it cut out masses of work. She was so happy and her food got even better.

I like to cook. I don't do desserts, because I'm afraid I'll eat them. I'm the one in the house responsible for Sunday lunch, so I do roast beef, roast lamb, a roast turkey for Christmas. I make what are allegedly the best roast potatoes that anybody who has come over has ever eaten. The trick is, when they're cooked, mash them just a little bit—just crack them open and put oil on them. Then bake them again, so the oil gets baked inside.

My mother was a cook in a Lyons' Corner House. That was the first sort of brasserie in England that I ever saw. But there were no true brasseries. I learned this later when I went to France. I *loved* the brasseries in France and came back to England and met the restaurateur Peter Langan. And we both said, "There isn't a proper brasserie in London." So we opened Langan's Brasserie together.

I loved the idea of having a restaurant right from the start: designing it and then getting drunk for nothing. I said to Peter, "How are we going to design this?" He said, "We've got masses of walls. We'll cover them with paintings." I said, "*Paintings?* I'm the money!" He said, "No, no, we'll get paintings for very little money because I have the perfect partner who's gonna help me choose them: David Hockney." David even designed our menu.

When I was starting out as an actor, I used to go to the cheapest restaurant I could find. I found an Italian restaurant in Soho that served a three-course meal for half a crown.

When my dad died, he left me a bit of money, about £100. I was seventeen and so sad. I thought, "I'm gonna get on a train and go to Paris." I got on a train on my own to Paris and I stayed there for about seven months. I adored the food there. I didn't do it all on the £100. I worked. I used to sell frites for a franc on the street. And I had a French mate who had a café, so I ate there. Then I had an American friend who worked in the air terminal. So I used to go in there, and I could get free food from him. I'd also bring an empty suitcase. If I didn't have enough money to stay somewhere, I'd sleep on a sofa in the terminal as if I was waiting for a plane. And I learned to speak French.

The first luxury food I had was at the White Elephant in Curson Street, in London. Harry Saltzman had given me the part in *The Ipcress File* and he took me there. There was caviar all over the place. I'd never eaten caviar. I obviously couldn't afford it. It was wonderful. And of course, I was under contract and I could have anything I liked. And I suddenly realized, "This is what my life is going to be": having enough money to have great food.

I had a wonderful time in Italy on *The Italian Job*. A great restaurant every evening. We didn't bother much with lunch because a movie is a hard thing to make, especially one with all those cars and crowds. I'd wind up having a sandwich or a bowl of spaghetti for lunch. I generally avoid food on a set—I don't want to go to sleep in the afternoon when I'm supposed to be doing ten pages of dialogue. But we'd always have a great meal in the evening.

In Hollywood, when you're having a meal with executives, it's always quite serious. But it's never dinner, it's always lunch. I will never discuss business at dinner. You've got to come to lunch for that, 'cause I'm not wasting a dinner doing that. Chasen's was my place in L.A. I used to go there every Friday. You'd look around and Alfred Hitchcock was always over here, Cary Grant was over there. It was one of those incredible restaurants that was like a club. But everyone only ever went to the same restaurant on the same day. If you went to Chasen's on Tuesday, there would be no stars there—only on Friday night. Spago was another one: Thursday, everyone was in Spago. The great thing is, it was all the stars I'd been seeing in movies all my life. My grandfather actually knew Hitchcock. He was born in South London, too. His father had a grocery store next door to my great-grandfather. When I was at Universal, making a picture called *Gambit* with Shirley MacLaine, I was given a temporary dressing-room bungalow next door to Hitchcock's. His was a permanent one. I got to know Hitchcock very well. I said to him one day, "I saw *Strangers on a Train*, and there wasn't one shot of a train in the entire movie!" He said, "Whose viewpoint on the train would *that* have been?" And there, in one line, he summed up directing movies.

My life is spent with one hundred fifty people all day. And when I go home, I love to write, I love to garden, and I love to cook. All on my own. And that's why I chose those things. I didn't know I'd chosen them for that reason, but from my point of view as an actor, I realized that's why.

*Michael, what is your comfort food?*
Years ago, it was sausage and mash. Now it's caviar.

# JAKE GYLLENHAAL

When we had the idea for *Ruthie's Table 4*, my first call was to Jake Gyllenhaal. He's one of the most food-obsessed people I know. On any given day, we will call or text each other with the news of what we ate, where we ate, and who we ate with.

Jake and I have known each other for a long time, and he stayed at our house for a couple of months when filming *Spider-Man* in London. One of my fondest memories is of him being taught how to prepare slow-cooked tomato sauce by our then ten-year-old granddaughter Ruby.

Last summer, while rehearsing his lines for the Broadway production of *Othello*, he made me one of the best pizzas I've ever had.

I chose the tomato sauce because I think simple is the most difficult. When you take just a few ingredients and you cook with them, what comes through is the person cooking them.

Whenever I'm slicing the canned tomatoes for this sauce, I think of that time when Ruby was instructing me. It was her favorite part, because it's essential to the recipe. When you empty those tomatoes into the colander, you have to slice them to get the first juices out of them. Over time, as they simmer, they turn into a sugary glaze. And then, how they stick onto the pasta is like nothing else.

I would say, rather honestly, that meals were the only thing that really worked in my family. By that I mean they were the only thing without some sort of drama or tumult—though it *was* full of wonderful drama, us all being sort of competitive and partial control freaks in the kitchen. There was a lot of nudging and bumping around and, "Don't do it like this, do it like that."

When I was very young, my parents took us to the Hollywood Farmers' Market in Los Angeles. That was an experience in itself. I remember my mom holding my hand and taking me to the woman who grew Japanese tomatoes and Japanese cucumbers. We'd always get shiso and then move over to the lettuce she loved, and then citrus. We were always tasting things.

In America, that's not so common, that experience: buying the food from local farmers, knowing the beautiful thing you've bought, and then cooking it in the kitchen. Sitting down to the table, my parents were always trying to tell stories of different kinds. They were really beautiful artists in their own ways. My sister and I were performing at a very young age. I mean that not only as actors, but just generally, in our personalities. But the thing that was pure, that was clear, at least to me, was always the meal.

Both of our parents cooked. My mother was more of a salads and antipasti person, not much transference of heat. My dad was more of a burn-it, roast-it kind of guy. He would always get lots of root vegetables, carrots and potatoes. And mushrooms. He was very close to the mushroom man at the market. I remember going to the mushroom man and getting all these funky little mushrooms, and my dad would roast them with olive oil, salt, and herbs.

They both loved food. And they always said to me, "You know, if and when you make your own money, if you're going to spend money on anything, it should be a great meal."

I worked in a few restaurants as a busboy for a while. When I was sixteen or seventeen, I started working for Marco Canora, who runs the restaurant Hearth in New York. He had a restaurant in Edgartown in Martha's Vineyard, and I was, for a while, a prep chef for him. I did buckets of lemon confit for months. That was quite an experience.

I also worked with one of my oldest friends from childhood. He cooked in New York for a number of years, and sometimes I actually joined him in the kitchen when they needed an extra pair of hands here or there.

Food professionals don't have any time. It's all taken up from 10 a.m. until midnight. It was hard to have a friendship only on his days off. So when I was in college at Columbia, sometimes I'd just join the line with him.

If you were to ask people closest to me, they'd probably tell you I'm not always the most fun person to be with in the kitchen. I had my stint learning from professionals, and it's a very tough place, a kitchen. It requires a particular type of focus and a sense of geography, knowing small spaces and how to move hot things. I might take it all a bit too seriously. It's a general note for myself. But my sister likes it when I cook for her. I love cooking for my nieces. I love asking them what they want. "I'm coming over. What is your favorite thing? I'm going to bring you anything that you want and we're going to cook it together." The satisfaction of that—there's nothing like it to me.

I think a lot of actors would tell you that they worked in restaurants. There is a theater to it. The special thing about The River Cafe is that your experience is never what you expect, because the menu always changes. You have your consistencies, certain desserts that will always be there. You have certain things you know you can always ask for. But then there's the unexpected. I love that part of the experience.

What I love so much about the theater is going to the same place nightly. When you have a matinee, it's like having a lunch service. On Broadway in particular, I love coming through the front of the house. You see all of the ushers preparing the *Playbill*s. If there's a bar, they're prepping the drinks and making sure everything is in order. You're walking through people who are picking up their tickets. You get a sense of the majesty of it all.

It gives me, as a performer, an appreciation for every single night, because sometimes, when you're doing 200 or 250 performances, it can start to feel monotonous. You have to remember to honor the audience that arrives every night. Every audience is different. The energy from them is different. It is a wild ride. Some are very steady, some have their own personalities. Oh man, that excitement!

I did this film *Nightcrawler*, where I lost close to thirty pounds. I was doing it safely, supplementing it with running a lot, but I didn't really have all the knowledge. I've learned more about that over the years. For someone who loves food, you're taking not only the food out of your life, you're taking away the experience of being with people. You're missing out on that more than anything. And it helped form the character, because he was a very lonely man. I had a space to use my feelings in.

But the only thing that matters to me is food. I legitimately have no other interests. I'll be honest. When I'm going to a city, the first thing I always think is, "Where do we go to eat?" As insufferable as my friends say that I am, the one thing they cannot deny is that they will always go to a great meal with me, whichever city we're in.

In Venice, there's this small restaurant that serves this incredible black radicchio pasta. I've had a few films that have gotten into the Venice Film Festival. As exciting as that is, it's not as exciting as knowing that I'll be able to eat that pasta.

*Jake, what is your comfort food?*
Pomodoro.

# SARAH JESSICA PARKER

The first time Sarah Jessica Parker and I spoke, she was on the phone in The River Cafe kitchen, and I was on a beach in Mexico. She was in London for a West End production of Neil Simon's *Plaza Suite*, costarring opposite her husband, Matthew Broderick; I was on holiday with family and friends.

The phone connection was poor, but Sarah Jessica's warmth traveled the six thousand miles separating us.

A short time later, I was back in The River Cafe and so was she, with Matthew and their three children. They were sitting at Table 1, just a few feet from our wood-burning oven. "How does all this work, Ruthie?" she asked. "How do you make sure that Matthew's ravioli comes out the same time as my asparagus bagna cauda?"

This sense of wonderment encapsulates Sarah Jessica's attitude toward food.

She chose our recipe for Puntarelle alla Romana, a bitter-green salad she and Matthew discovered in New York in their early years together. "For anybody who lives in New York, puntarelle is like contraband," she said. "It's very hard to find, and when it is finally in season, you have four days to enjoy it. To have it here at your whim is pure decadence."

I'm one of eight children. My mother was a schoolteacher up until a few months after I was born. She taught second grade. At the time, we lived in a very little city in southeastern Ohio, in the foothills of Appalachia, actually. Her students could be anywhere from seven to fourteen years old, depending upon how much time they'd been afforded to be in school. She stopped teaching for many, many years to be a mother, which consumed all her time. Later she started her own preschool in New Jersey, a sort of Montessori progressive school.

She would probably say that she really didn't enjoy cooking. She didn't come from a family that enjoyed food. And I think that with eight kids, it was work versus joyful. But simultaneously, she loved food. When she was a young woman, like a lot of girls straight out of college, she went off to New York City as an employee of Procter & Gamble, which is a big company in Cincinnati. She was sent to New York to be a salesperson. Her first stop was always Chinatown. She loved Chinese food. She loved anything that was different. And there was a place called Dave's Luncheonette that was famous—you stopped by and had an egg cream after your Chinese food.

And she grew up reading the *New Yorker*. The librarians, from the time she was a little girl, would save the weekly issue for her. So she would read about food. She would read about Chinatown and about places in the outer boroughs. So for her, food was this thing that was part of another life that she hoped to give all of us. Even though she didn't like cooking, she cooked three meals a day.

It was our job to be helpful. We came home from school, did homework, and we had ballet classes. After ballet, we'd all jump in and help in the kitchen. We all had jobs before and after dinner that weren't necessarily connected to cooking: cleaning, putting things away, sweeping, loading the dishwasher, unloading the dishwasher, helping with laundry.

It was a big deal for us to eat out, growing up. We didn't get to go on vacations until much later, and then it was sharing a house with another family and still cooking all of our meals. We would go to the Outer Banks of North Carolina, this very pristine, not very popular destination. The big deal for us was that we would get crabs and throw down newspaper. That was eating out.

We moved to New York City from Cincinnati on January 1, 1977—my mother, my stepfather, and my siblings. So I've lived there most of my life. And my real father is from Brooklyn, born and raised, so we spent some time before then in

Brooklyn, visiting my grandparents on my father's side. For me and my siblings, we all love to share our feelings, thoughts, and experiences with food. I would say that in some way, it dominates our relationship.

Matthew cooks. We probably eat dinner as a family every night. If I'm shooting or he's doing a play, obviously that shifts around. But if we're home, one of us cooks every single day. We both love to cook and maybe it's boring to keep saying to each other, "What are we going to eat? Are you going to go to the grocery store?" But it's just what we do. We never understood how to order in, and now we're too old. I don't know how to use an app. If I want delivery, I'll still call the restaurant directly and order.

Yesterday, I made lamb. We actually went to a restaurant in Chinatown quickly after the show, but during the day, I'd made lamb stew and Matthew had made a white bean soup, so I knew we had all that. I like to have things in the fridge for matinee days.

I probably make lamb chops two or three times a week. We use Kerrygold butter and just a touch of olive oil so the butter doesn't burn. I salt and pepper the baby lamb chops, I throw them in, and that's it. You can smell the fat when it's cooking. We eat a lot of lamb in Ireland. We have a house way up in County Donegal. My husband's been going there since he was a little boy. We finally bought our own little house, because he shares his family home with his siblings. Ireland has the best potatoes. It's a cliché, but it's true. If you're there for the new potato season, oh, it's heaven. Kerrygold butter, York cabbage — I don't know what it is about a York cabbage that blows my mind. Lamb, lamb, lamb, lamb, lamb, lamb, lamb, the eggs, the rashers . . . any root stuff there is really good.

I never was very disciplined about eating. I'm not really good at denying myself something. And I was a dancer for so long, running around, so I was able to be that way. When I had girls, I didn't want them to have a relationship with food that was antagonistic or where they felt like this was their enemy and they were going to have to stake out a position with food. When I was growing up, we weren't allowed sugar, cookies, or chocolate in the house. And of course, all we did the minute we moved out was buy Entenmann's cakes and cookies.

I didn't want that with my kids. So in our house, we have cookies, we have cake, we have everything. And as a result, I think, you have a healthier relationship. My daughters will have the figures they have and hopefully they'll be healthy. And they're athletes and they enjoy food and they have different palates. You can't make someone like something they don't like or want. I hope that they can maintain their affection for the experience and find their own ways that are healthy for them.

I always loved shooting the food scenes in *Sex and the City*. They were in place from the beginning, probably from either Candace Bushnell's original source material or when Darren Star wrote that first coffee-shop scene. That was a great meeting place for the women to talk about the themes of each episode, to get the headline out. The characters would share their points of view, so we knew where everybody stood and it allowed for controversial conversation or titillating conversation.

Cynthia Nixon is a dear friend of mine and we've been working together since we were little girls. We would always audition together. We played siblings when were very young on records of *Little House on the Prairie* stories. We played Laura and Mary Ingalls. We played the children of Vanessa Redgrave in a movie. In those coffee-shop scenes, Cynthia and I always really eat. They always need to re-prop our plates. And when we finally wrap, they always say to us, "Do you guys want to take it to go again today?" And we're like, "Yes, we do."

We really like those scenes. And we'll very much go back and forth about, "What do you think?" They'll send the menu in advance now because they want you to order for the props department to have everything ready and multiples of it. So we'll go back and forth: "What did you order? I'll order that, you order that, and we can share." The lines between reality and TV are blurred.

When we go out as a family, we eat local. Especially after the pandemic, we were really concerned—there were a lot of small businesses and restaurants that were not part of larger consortiums that were really, really struggling. It was so easy to be supportive, because they're our neighbors and we know their family stories and we saw the collateral damage. If something closes, it's not just the restaurant, it's everything around it that lives and breathes off of it.

They're wonderful restaurants. Some are old and not inventive at all. They're not rethinking or deconstructing Italian food, but they've been in business forever. And then there are newer chefs doing really exciting things. And then you've got your local little delis and bodegas. It's a real privilege to live among them and to say that we are patrons and that we mean it.

Gene's is a wonderful restaurant on 11th Street in the West Village. It's this beautiful room, low ceiling, one of the prettiest bars you'll ever see in New York City. It's got marble steps you walk down and this gorgeous bar greets you that's been around forever. Famously good bartender, the locals sit there and eat. And the food is like veal scallopini, tomato sauce.

You get to your table and it's got cold vegetables on ice cubes, big radishes and carrot sticks and hearts of celery. Everybody in there is an older group and they're so lovely. They all say to us, "We're gonna go see your show." They're very community oriented. We go there a lot on Sunday nights, like if we're meeting other people. If we're not going to invite people to our house for dinner, we'll go to Gene's.

When I'm doing a play, I eat a huge meal after the performance. I'll eat a little bit before—yogurt, bananas. There's these eggs in London that I go mad for, the ones I want to put in my suitcase, but I'm not allowed. They're called

Burford. They have those orange yolks that are just, *Oh my god*. So we go through a lot of those. I'll have some lamb stew. I love your rashers here, your streaky bacon, and the kofta from our local butcher.

Sometimes when I take a job, I think, "Well, I'm really taking this just so I can go eat." And if I'm planning a holiday, I do endless months of research trying to find restaurants. *Where? Where? Where?*

Then you get to your destination, and they'll try to send you to the place that everybody else in the hotel is going to. And I'll say, "No, no, no, no. Please, where do *you* eat, Mr. Concierge, Ms. Concierge?" And they won't tell me because they think we want this fancy food. So I'll just follow the employees home. I literally follow them home and see where they live in their communities, their restaurants. That's where I go.

I think that wherever you travel, for whatever reason, you should try to embed yourself a little bit in the local flavor of a community. Sometimes for work I have to travel to do press junkets. Especially in the old days, you'd do these grand world tours and be given a guide, which was all wonderful and I was super grateful. But I would say to the guide, "Stop the van now, stop the van now. I want to get out here." And they were like, "There's just houses here." And I'd say, "Yes, exactly. I just want to see the houses." You feel like you're seeing *something* versus the same old boulevard with the fancy shops and the fancy restaurants.

*Sarah Jessica, what is your comfort food?*
I would say pork chops and I would just describe them more specifically as thin-cut pork chops on the bone. Put 'em in the pan with olive oil and salt and pepper and—*oh!* Heaven.

# WES ANDERSON

I have a few philosophies in life, one of which is always to say yes to Wes Anderson. "Ruthie, should we get a sheet from the upstairs cupboard and screen *Fantastic Mr. Fox* outside in the garden tonight in Tuscany?" "Yes, Wes." "Ruthie, shall we try again for the fourth time to make a perfect Bellini?" "Yes, Wes." "Ruthie, how about if we invite all the kids and friends and watch *Grand Budapest Hotel* before it opens in your living room in London?" "Yes, Wes."

Wes, who comes to The River Cafe with his wife, the writer Juman Malouf, and their daughter, chose to read one of our more involved recipes, for Roast Pigeon Stuffed with Cotechino, "for no other reason that any time I see this pigeon on The River Cafe menu, it is what I order."

I've always loved A. J. Liebling's writing. I think he's the funniest writer about food. We used some of his influence in *The French Dispatch*, where we show a tray of drinks that has everything from the apéritifs that you would have at three in the afternoon to the strongest digestifs that you might have at the very end of the night. We made our own versions of each. We also had a cook in the movie who makes some peculiar dishes. In fact, one is pigeon. We call it City Park Pigeon Hash. His food is meant to be specialized for police working on stakeouts, that sort of thing.

When my parents were together, dinner was more of a communal family meal. After my parents split, my mother decided she would like to be an archaeologist. So for ten years, she was studying for her master's and then her PhD while taking care of three boys. She was juggling a lot of things, so meals were a little more thrown together. There was nothing typical—every night was a different venue and a different situation. I think this is possibly why I've

always liked to eat in restaurants. In fact, if I'm not working on a film, and I'm working at home, dinner is the one time of day that I get to go out.

I went to two high schools in Houston, the second of which was where we made *Rushmore*. The food was not memorable, although I don't even think I'd heard of bagels before going to this school. Bagels did not become a huge part of my life, but I guess I started to see that there was a lot out there I didn't know about in terms of things to eat.

I live partly in Paris and partly in England. When we're in England, we cook at home every night. When we're in Paris, we go out to dinner every night. When we were first living in Paris, Juman and I tried new restaurants continuously. Then, over the years, I realized that my favorite kind of restaurant is a restaurant where I've already been, where I know where I would like to sit and what I want to order. I think that if you're a foreigner in Paris, it helps if you're a familiar face—if you've been there thirty times, that's a good way to establish yourself. I will say that in France, I have a tendency not to eat the healthiest dishes: the confit of duck, quite a few lamb chops, and more pigeon.

In Rome, we like to go to Tullio and Pierluigi. Maybe our other favorite place to eat in the world is Tokyo. The food there is so interesting and inventive and perfectionist. An interesting thing: the last time we were in Japan, we were there for a couple of weeks, and our friend had been trying to convince us to go to this Italian restaurant. I was like, "I don't want to go to an Italian restaurant in Tokyo!" It's called Cignale Enoteca and the chef is named Toshiji Tomori. Well, finally, the last night we were there, we went, and it turned out to be one of the better Italian restaurants outside of Italy and The River Cafe.

A group of us once went on the *Queen Mary 2* from New York to England: Jason Schwartzman; Roman Coppola and his wife, Jenny; Tilda Swinton and Sandro Kopp; and me and Juman. We showed our movies and did a few little talks during the journey. One of the great things was that we had a room on the opposite end of the boat from the kitchen. We often arranged to have a curry dinner, and we liked to watch them roll the cart down a corridor that was probably about a kilometer long.

I don't like to stop working during a filming day. On movies, often you stop and there's a very long break and then it takes even longer to get back from the break. So we have these little tables that are made to be folded up into suitcases. We set them up on the side of the set. We have a lunch brought out to us. For years, I tried to make it just soup, and to convince everyone that we would just eat soup and then get right back to work. And we did have some very good soups in Germany, where we made *The Grand Budapest Hotel*. But eventually, there was a mutiny. In particular, our key grip, Sanjay Sami, said you can't push a dolly all day and only eat a thin soup. So we started bringing Sanjay his own steaks and things. When we finish shooting for the day, we have a dinner with the whole cast and the department heads. We all live together in a small hotel, usually, and we have our own little dinner room. Our costume designer usually shows up very late, sometimes close to midnight, but we keep a plate for her, and usually a plate for the extremely large team of helpers who roll in.

When Owen Wilson and I first went to Los Angeles to work, our producers, James L. Brooks and Polly Platt, had their offices in the Sidney Poitier Building on the Columbia lot in Culver City. The studio commissary was still a busy place. I like the idea of having a canteen right there in the workplace. I've done a lot of work in restaurants over the years with Noah Baumbach. We wrote a movie in Bar Pitti in New York. We were there for probably six hours a day. And we still go there when I'm in New York. That's our canteen.

*Wes, what is your comfort food?*
I've always liked the Italian hamburger, *hachè di manzo*, with butter and sage. I would recommend it if somebody crosses paths with it.

# CAREY MULLIGAN

Ask Ralph Fiennes about Carey Mulligan, and he will tell you she was a brilliant acting partner in the movie *The Dig*. Ask Lorne Michaels about Carey hosting *Saturday Night Live*, and he will say she was one of the best in the show's fifty years. Ask Sir David Hare, who wrote the play *Skylight*, and Robert Fox, who produced it, and they will talk about Carey's authenticity, excellence, and her kindness to everyone involved in the production. Not to mention the fact that during the run she flawlessly cooked, from scratch, a Bolognese pasta in front of a thousand people every night.

Not many people know Carey spent her childhood in hotels as her father was the manager for Intercontinental. Carey now has a family of her own with the musician Marcus Mumford. She told stories about her nomadic childhood, hotel-made alcoholic birthday cakes, and eating her way through *Skylight*. She read our recipe for Scallops with Lemons, Sage, and Capers.

My dad was running the Britannia Hotel in London when I was born. Then he ran the Mayfair in Grosvenor Square. Then we moved to Germany, to Hanover and Düsseldorf, and he ran hotels there. Then he was at the Churchill in Portman Square. He also ran hotels in Vienna and Frankfurt.

We lived in hotels until I was eight. It was kind of all we knew, but when I look back on it, I think, "Oh, wow, that was kind of an extraordinary way to grow up." My brother and I would roll around with the maids, going into people's rooms after they checked out. I remember sitting in the basket with all the sheets in my hands, holding on, rolling around the corridor. And sitting with my whole body wrapped around a Hoover, going up and down the hallways.

In the hotels that we lived in, there was an apartment on the top floor for

It was very basic, but there was a musicality to it. The character is cooking during what turns into an enormous row. And so much of the physicality of the cooking was in the smashing of garlic and the chopping. I had to be cooking but also furious—but also controlled, so that I didn't cut my finger off.

There was a lot of comedy to the way that Bill Nighy would come over and glance and sort of judge the way the sauce was being cooked. Putting the oil in first or not putting the oil in, that was one of the little gags. And the theater would fill with the smell of cooking. I used to say to anyone who was coming to see the play, particularly my dad, "You have to eat before you come, because if you watch a play that's three hours long and you're hungry, you're going to hate it."

The food was totally edible. It probably wasn't great, but I ate it every night and it tasted fine to me. When we transferred to Broadway in New York, I was pregnant. I went through a phase of feeling incredibly unwell and nothing tasted good to eat. So for a while, I was just taking very small nibbles. But generally, I kind of loved it.

*Carey, what is your comfort food?*
We have a friend who lives near us who's a baby guru, Rachel Waddilove. She's amazing. She basically taught us how to look after our babies. Well, me at least. My husband was quite good at it already. Rachel said when you are breastfeeding, you must have a slice of cake, you know, all the time! But she also had this recipe for a chicken casserole that was really simple. The crust on the top was Weetabix and cheddar cheese.

So Marcus makes this delicious chicken casserole. The Weetabix is mushed up with a bit of salt and cheddar cheese and it melts, and it's heaven. Whenever I'm feeling a little bit depleted or done in, he'll make a big old thing of it. We'll start with fairly conservative portions and then just finish the whole thing.

with a bunch of other actors of a similar age. I'd never acted with boys before, because I'd been at an all-girls school. I loved it and made really good friends. We did one or two little productions there. Then I auditioned for a new film version of *Pride and Prejudice*, and that was my first job.

I moved out of my parents' house for *Pride and Prejudice*. It was a lovely production. It actually set me up for disappointment in future productions, because we stayed in such nice hotels and the catering was so lovely. The first month or so, we had really delicious snacks, yummy cakes and biscuits and delicious granola-y things that we could nibble on. After a while, they had to take out our corsets because we'd all been having a lovely time.

Then I moved into a flat with two boys in Highgate. I think I literally ate Pot Noodles every day whilst I did theater. I also got into a habit of having a double espresso before I did a show. I didn't really eat before the play. I did the espressos for years after, through *Girls and Boys* at the Royal Court Theatre in 2018, and then I stopped.

The Royal Court was my first theater, so it was special. I did *The Seagull* there when I was twenty-one, directed by Christopher Hampton. What I also love about the Royal Court is the downstairs bar. We would all go down there after the show. I remember eating cornichons back then. A glass of red wine and loads of little cornichons. But I don't remember going out for food much. I'd just go home and eat Weetabix at the end of the night. I was spending money on living in Highgate, so, yeah, I ate quite a lot of cereal.

When I started having success, I ate a lot of sushi. I was living in New York doing theater and a bit of film. I remember sitting down with a financial advisor. He looked at my bank statements and said, "You seem to have spent lots of money on rent and sushi." I was like, "Oh, shit."

When I did the play *Skylight*, it was the only time I ever had to eat onstage. It was a spaghetti Bolognese. I would cook it in the first half and eat it in the second half.

weren't properly kiddie birthday cakes. And they had very beautiful writing in icing.

There was always such a sense of occasion in the hotels, like a big display for Christmas or a big event happening. But I never minded it. I like being nomadic. I like being in hotels.

Dad worked in kitchens on his way up. He was the cook in our family. Whenever he cooks, I exit the building, because he likes things ordered and his way. For us to come in and start casually munching on something is not part of it.

My mum can turn her hand to anything, but she was never a passionate cook. My grandmother was a wonderful baker. My mother's Welsh, so my grandmother was in Carmarthenshire. Every time I went to her for any length of time, we would just bake and bake and bake. She made delicious Welsh cakes, which are little flat cakes with raisins. And a cherry-almond cake that just got better the longer you left it in the tin.

Acting was all I wanted to do from a young age. But I didn't think of it as a career until I was twelve. My mum and I went to see every musical, every time we went to London. We went to New York together, just the two of us, to see the Sam Mendes production of *Cabaret* at Studio 54.

I auditioned for a bunch of drama schools and didn't get into any of them. So I took a gap year, and it was in that year that I worked in some pubs. I worked in a restaurant on a barge in Marlow as a server and at the same time worked in two pubs, just picking up shifts. I liked the energy of it. I also quite liked being in charge of giving people drinks, being behind this bar at eighteen. I probably looked about fifteen, yet I was pulling pints for big, burly men and it felt like a powerful position to be in.

Luckily, I found another kind of way into acting. I went to Riverside Studios in London to do a young people's workshop, which was an incredible experience. I did it for months, once a week, where you would come together the manager, with our own mini kitchen. We didn't do room service, but we did have our linens changed every day. My mum always says that was a massive bonus.

My brother and I were bilingual, because we moved to Germany when I was three. I went to a German kindergarten, a Rudolf Steiner kindergarten. Then I went to school in Hanover, with a lot of military kids. Then we were in the Düsseldorf International School. And then we moved home.

It felt like being a diplomat's daughter or something. Someone would come and stay at the hotel, and you would greet them. It prepared me for acting in a way. I think moving around constantly did, too—always being the new kid. By the time I was eight, I'd been at three different schools in Germany. Then I went to a convent school in Buckinghamshire. And then when I was eleven, we moved again. And then when I was thirteen, we moved again. I was used to being new and having to introduce myself, adapt to people.

But we were amazingly lucky. We got to go skiing in Austria on our holidays. We ate lots of *käsespätzle* and Wiener schnitzel and delicious warm, brothy things to warm ourselves up. But because we lived an international hotel, the food I was regularly eating wasn't necessarily German cuisine.

I don't remember going to white-tablecloth restaurants at all. There was a pizza place in Düsseldorf that we would go to as a treat, a hole-in-the-wall kind of place. But at the turn of the millennium, my dad was running the Intercontinental in Vienna. There was a big millennium meal there. I was fourteen and my best friend came with me. We bought dresses and it was a proper white-tablecloth seven-course meal. That was a big, big deal.

One of my birthday parties when I was little was at the hotel in Düsseldorf. The pastry chef made a bunch of dough and we were all making little dollies out of it. They took them off and cooked them in the kitchen and brought them back. The birthday cakes, when we lived in hotels, were always very elaborate. I feel like they always had liquor in them. They

# JEFF GOLDBLUM

Jeff knows his way around a restaurant menu and has appeared in several food-centric movies, from Wes Anderson's *The Grand Budapest Hotel* to Lawrence Kasdan's *The Big Chill*, with its famous dinner and kitchen cleanup scenes.

It was during Covid when Jeff and I recorded our podcast episode. We were more than five thousand miles apart. I was in my bedroom in London; Jeff was in his home in Los Angeles. Specifically, for some reason, Jeff was in his closet. Partway through, he even took a Covid test. He held up one of our cookbooks and announced, "I've dog-eared the Slow-Cooked Fennel." This is a recipe I also love. It was taught to me by my mother-in-law, Dada Rogers. The fennel is fried in olive oil and garlic and then simmered gradually, adding water. The sliced bulbs melt and absorb their own juices, intensifying their flavor.

Hey, speaking of that fennel recipe, I came upon a poem by Longfellow from 1842, called "The Goblet of Life," that has a little snippet about fennel. It goes like this:

> *Above the lowly plants it towers*
> *The fennel, with its yellow flowers*
> *And in an earlier age than ours*
> *Was gifted with the wondrous powers,*
> *Lost vision to restore*

How about that?

Food is romantic. I love movies about food. Wes Anderson is a person of terrific sophistication. During the filming of *The Grand Budapest Hotel*, he had a chef come in and we took over this picturesque, spectacular little hotel.

We had these lovely meals that he'd invite us to every night, with a candelabra and so forth. Can you imagine? And the movie itself, of course, is about the provision of services, including food, to people.

Food has everything to do with who we are: how we situate ourselves in the community; how to coexist with every other creature without exercising brutal dominion; how to peacefully and more beautifully coexist with each other. It's only our political will and mismanagement that prevents us from figuring out how to feed everyone. And speaking of *The Grand Budapest Hotel*, that movie is not only about figuring out how to share food with everybody, it's about offering food and cooking in a way that's gracious, elegant, and artful. It's about fighting fascism. Sweetness and elegance are an act of politics.

I'm easy to please. I like all food. There isn't anything I haven't tried or wouldn't try and enjoy. It all looks great to me.

I grew up in Pittsburgh. My dad was a doctor. His parents were from Russia. My mom's dad was from Austria. My dad's dad, his last name was Povartzik, and he changed it to Goldblum. In our house, Dr. and Mrs. Goldblum had four kids. She used to cook. This is the '50s and '60s in America. So this is meatloaf time. This is canned vegetables. They even introduced us, on nights that they went out, to Swanson's TV dinners: Swiss steak and all that stuff.

But my mother made things, too. She used to do a potato salad, her own recipe. It was mayonnaise, potatoes, celery, and olives. She used the green olives that came with pimentos in them. My mouth is watering now and I'm getting a little nostalgic just thinking about it.

She also made spaghetti. She didn't call it Bolognese, she just called it meat sauce. She put it in a great big translucent dark-green bowl. Jeez, I loved that so much. And we had a barbecue outside, steaks on the grill.

The Dr. and Mrs. Goldblum used to go away on trips: to Las Vegas for some doctor getaway, or a cruise, things like that. They'd come back from Haiti with a couple of items. They painted a shuffleboard court on the cement in our backyard. Can you believe it? It was a blue-collar neighborhood. All the other kids were kids of steelworkers. I was a fish out of water already. A very strange boy in a strange family.

This was the beginning of the fast-food era. There was a place in Pittsburgh called Eat'n Park that we went to where you'd eat your food in the car. And we had chipped ham, something that people from Pittsburgh will know about. We used to make these kind-of Sloppy Joes but with chipped ham, covered in barbecue sauce. Delicious. On Saturdays we watched scary movies on TV, hosted by a guy named Chilly Billy Cardille. My older brothers were starting to drive. They went to this place called the Junction Pizza and brought back square-cut pizza. Man, I loved that.

We would all go out to Tambellini's, an Italian restaurant. That's the first place where I tasted this thing called a Caesar salad. It had hard-boiled eggs in it and I thought it was spectacular. There was a Chinese restaurant, Bill Ung's Tea Garden, that we went to once a month on a Sunday night. It was very standard Cantonese fare, but I thought that was great, too. Every eating adventure was great!

And then we went on vacations. We would get in our station wagon and drive to Atlantic City and get saltwater taffy on the boardwalk. When I was in fourth grade, we went to New York City. We went to Greenwich Village and had our portraits done by some beatnik artist on the street. We also went to this place called The Cattleman, a touristy steak restaurant. We got leftovers to take home and they wrapped them up in aluminum foil in the shape of a swan or something. I thought that was unusual.

I was so lucky. I have an unusual story. As soon as I decided to become an actor, I went to New York. I lived there for four years and studied with Sandy Meisner. And then, as soon as I finished school—even before—I started to get work. I've worked steadily for these last four decades or so without ever having to take a so-called straight job, except for one week when I sold pens and pencils on the phone. I was too sensitive for that. I wound up in the hospital.

I've had a lot of experiences with food on movie sets. In France, I've made movies where they have a bottle of wine on the table and they take a nice, leisurely lunch. But in Australia, where I did *Thor: Love and Thunder*, they had what is known as a walking lunch, meaning nobody takes a break. There's food that comes around and you just eat it as you go.

I have a digestive system like a hummingbird. So I need fuel. These days, I'm experimenting with whole grains. My wife, Emilie, she's from Canada and her mom is from Nantes, France. Her mom is a wonderful cook who prides herself on her cooking. They love their food in Emilie's family.

Emilie has taken to cooking and has been learning some of her mom's recipes. She's been baking bread and making crepes, croque monsieur, and croque madame. This morning, she cooked some scrambled eggs with cheese in them and she also made oatmeal. It was sweetened with maple syrup and she put in a little of this French butter that she likes, and some chia seeds. I can have that every day. See, I'm easy to please.

*Jeff, what is your comfort food?*
This is going to sound very primitive. I like cold cereal. If I wake up in the middle of the night, give me a bowl and give me some milk or a milk substitute. I experiment with different kinds of milks and different cereals. I'll take the first couple of bites when it's a little crisp. But when it gets not too soggy—just medium soggy—I'm very happy about that.

# FISHER STEVENS

Fisher Stevens and I were brought together by a love for the work of the artist Philip Guston. One night when Fisher came to The River Cafe with the producers of *Beckham*, the series he directed for Netflix, we agreed to have breakfast at my house the next morning.

Walking up the stairs, Fisher stopped at a Guston painting. It was hard to tear him away as he spoke about it and what it meant to him. A half hour turned into more than an hour as we talked about art, architecture, and food. We agreed we would continue the conversation on *Ruthie's Table 4* when I came to New York.

I was born in Chicago. I moved to New York with my mother so she could make it as a painter. We had our first loft in '71, '72, in the Meatpacking District. The artist Marilyn Minter and my mother shared a space. We lived in the loft and my mom was dating an actor—well, a maître d', but he was trying to be an actor. My mom ended up working as the coat-checker at his restaurant. It was called Charlie's, a famous theater restaurant.

We had trouble paying the rent. So the acting school that my mother's boyfriend had studied in rented the loft. They built a stage in our living room. I'd come home and there'd be an acting class going on in my house, which is how I got into show business, because there was a stage in our living room.

My sisters ended up moving back to Chicago with my dad, because the life was too crazy. But I stayed. When we moved to New York, what was so exciting to me was the food. My mom's boyfriend took us to Chinatown. Sometimes he'd show up with a bushel of blue crabs and we'd boil the crabs and eat them. And all these exotic foods: Vietnamese pho, I remember discovering that at thirteen years old.

I ate out a lot in my high school years. A lot of Chinese. I got to be so friendly with a Chinese restaurant on Sixth Avenue and 16th Street, Jin's Kitchen, that I actually ate with the family two nights a week, with the lazy Susan in the middle of the table. The food was much different than what was at the restaurant. The quantity and the selection. There were things that I couldn't recognize, but then there was some great stuff.

I became a snob, to be honest, because I had experienced these incredible delicacies. And by the way, you were able to eat brilliantly for nothing in New York in the '70s and '80s.

I dropped out of high school. I started auditioning at fifteen for plays. And I started working as a busboy in two restaurants in New York and as a bike messenger, making good money, more money than my mom. I got my first acting job at sixteen and had to change my name. My real name was Stephen Fisher, but there was already someone in the union called that. There used to be a sign for years in Brooklyn that said FISHER-STEVENS PAINTS. That's how I got the idea. But my dad always called me Fish. Everybody did.

The job was a movie, shot over the summer. It didn't pay that much, but I thought, "I'm going to make it." And then I didn't work again for two years. But I was auditioning and studying acting very seriously. There was a kid I knew through auditioning and high school friends, though he went to a different high school. It was Matthew Broderick. I bumped into him and he's like, "Hey man, I'm in this play. It's maybe moving to Broadway, but I just got a bigger play and I'm leaving. I'll get you an audition to replace me."

The play was *Torch Song Trilogy* by Harvey Fierstein, a revolutionary gay play. Matthew got me the audition and I got the job. And that was it—basically ever since then, I've been working. Then Matthew was in a Neil

Simon play called *Brighton Beach Memoirs* and he was going to leave that. He got me an audition to replace him in that, and I did.

When I was replacing Matthew in *Brighton Beach Memoirs*, he was making real money. He was about to go do *Ferris Bueller's Day Off*. He took me out to dinner at this amazing place on 52nd Street called Gallaghers Steakhouse. It was *the* place. The sports guys, everybody went there. Since Matthew was making bank, he bought me dinner a few times there. We would drink martinis. I was eighteen and it was illegal, but who cares now?

You don't want to go onstage with a full stomach. I've had to eat onstage, though. In *Brighton Beach Memoirs*, every night we had to pretend to have dinner and applesauce. But we'd just take a couple of bites.

The worst is in movies, because you have to re-create food scenes for coverage. The thing about *Succession* was that there were a lot of scenes where you're supposed to be eating but nobody's ever *really* eating because you can't re-create the position, and because they shot the show in big, giant chunks. There's a whole website devoted to "Why does nobody eat on *Succession*?" My character never sits still and is never invited to the table to eat. He's always just told what to do, sadly. But that was good for me as an actor, because I didn't have to worry about the food on my plate.

On *Succession* and Wes Anderson's movies, we did French hours. That means you don't break for lunch, but you only work for ten-hour days. In my early days of making movies, you'd shoot fourteen-hour days, but that would include an hour where you all sit and eat. On *Succession*, post-Covid, they found it more manageable if you didn't break, and they'd hand you a box lunch. The good news about being in a Wes movie is that you're usually in a smaller part, so you only work a four-hour day and then you can go and have a great lunch. If you're working a ten-hour day with Wes, as we did in Spain on *Asteroid City*, it will be a carton, but the food is good. Not to knock *Succession*'s catering, but it's much better on Wes's movies.

I was on my way to work on *Succession* one day and the phone rang. It was Leonardo DiCaprio's office, saying, "Listen, Leo and David Beckham had dinner last night, and Leo suggested you to direct David's life story. Are you interested?"

I wasn't, to be honest. I mean, I knew who he was. I knew he was beautiful. I knew he had a beautiful wife. I knew he was a brand. What really scared me was the idea of "He's a brand and he's going to try to brand me and make me do a branded-content film for him," which I wasn't interested in.

But I took the meeting on Zoom. Also, *Succession* was written by Jesse Armstrong and Tony Roche, two Brits. I told them about this opportunity, and they're like, "You *have* to do it. David Beckham is a genius." I said, like, "Really? He's that good?" They immediately went on YouTube and showed me clips of him, telling me, "You've got to dig. Do your research, man."

I didn't want to say yes until I met David. I was shooting *Succession* in Italy and told him I would come to London to meet him. He said, "Meet us at Harry's Bar for dinner. And wear a jacket." I went to a shop in Florence and bought a dress shirt and a jacket.

In London, I went into Harry's Bar and it was empty, about six o'clock. I walk in and there's this ass sticking out from under a table. I'm like, "Oh, I think that's David's ass." It was a comic moment—he almost bumped his head on the table as he stood up. He said, "So sorry, Victoria just dropped her earrings. I'm looking for them." And then we had this dinner at Harry's Bar, which is very fancy. I was nervous, dressed in this ill-fitting 40-Euro jacket from some store in Florence. David said, "Do you like red wine?" I said, "Yeah," because I love Bordeauxs. He ordered a 2004 Latour. And I thought, "This is going to be a fun movie to work on." We instantly got to know each other and that was what convinced me.

The other day, David was in New York. He called me and asked me to lunch. He said, "Meet me at Lucali's in Carroll Gardens." They're a place that has probably some of the best calzones and pizza in New York. They're legendary. I thought, "That's weird, they're not open for lunch."

I biked over there and it was just David, his friend Dave Gardner, and Nicola, who works with them. Mark Lucali himself was cooking, just for us. He made these pork chops with peppers and onions, unbelievable. Pasta fusilli with burrata and fresh tomato sauce. This was a Friday afternoon. We had two bottles of Barolo. David works out incessantly, six or seven days a week, so he can eat.

*Fisher, what is your comfort food?*
The thing that comes into my mind is pasta with pesto. Pesto—the basil, the cheese, the olive oil, the pine nuts—as I make it. That's the other thing: making it gives me comfort.

# OLIVIA COLMAN

While the films of Olivia Colman make us cry and laugh—they can also make us hungry. In *The Favourite*, Olivia conveys her authority by insisting on a cup of overrich hot chocolate. And there are tables laden with roasted venison, lamb, cakes, desserts, the Queen's symbols of wealth and privilege.

I met Olivia one night in The River Cafe. She was with her friend Maggie Gyllenhaal, and they had just wrapped filming for their movie *The Lost Daughter*. It is not an exaggeration to say they pretty much ordered everything on the menu. We immediately started talking about family and the joy of cooking.

A few months later, Olivia came back to The River Cafe for *Ruthie's Table 4* and went straight to the kitchen to cook, with the chefs, the very pasta she had ordered on her previous visit: Tagliatelle with Lemon, Cream, and Parsley.

We were not really a family of foodies. Food was always loved, but my mum was a nurse. She sometimes worked on Christmas Day and took shifts that other people didn't want. So, often she'd come home and it would be quick. We might sit on the sofa and watch *Doctor Who* with our food on our laps. My mum never really loved cooking. And her mum, my granny, sort of dreaded people coming 'round. Every time I went to her house, we'd always have the same thing: slightly overcooked salmon, new potatoes, and green beans. My mum, whenever anyone came for a dinner party, made Cod Mornay in a cheese sauce, with spinach and new potatoes. As simple as possible.

If Mum and Dad were very busy, I went to stay with my granny. She always had Orange Club biscuits and, hilariously, she left a bottle of Ribena [a blackcurrant soft drink] by my bed. So, sugar all night. My father's mother was an amazing baker. She kept a little larder, and she'd say, "Have a look in the cupboard there." There was always shortbread or fruitcake, or, sometimes especially for me, a little chocolate cake. We were allowed to go in and help ourselves.

During our holidays, we went camping on the coast, just a few miles from where we lived in Norfolk. We'd pick samphire, a salty green that grows in the marshes. We'd simply shake off the mud and blanch it. That's how we ate it. We also used to go cockling, gathering cockles to eat with mussels.

Overall, we weren't really travelers. But when I was twelve, my dad's best friend moved to Naples, having married an Italian woman. We went to Italy to stay with them, a summer trip to Ischia in the Bay of Naples. We had incredible food. We went to amazing restaurants, some of them in people's houses in the hills, and we didn't know what we were doing. So my dad's friend said, "Trust me," and ordered for us.

After that trip, my dad, who worked as a chartered surveyor, decided he wanted to get involved in the cooking and started making pastas and things. Really, it was an excuse to open a bottle of wine.

When I first left home, my mum gave me a Delia Smith cookbook, which was amazing. I so loved cooking for my two flatmates, Debbie and Olivia. I started to really enjoy going to the shop. Because we were on such a tight budget, I'd just get stuff for the recipes, nothing else off the shelf. Sometimes dinner was just jacket potatoes with loads of butter and cheese. Butter plays a big part in my life. Toast is basically just a vehicle for butter.

I went to Homerton, a teacher-training college in Cambridge, but I left after a term or so. I ended up working in Cambridge as a cleaner for a couple of years. I was the same age as everyone else, so I went to lectures in different subjects. No one ever questioned me. There's about thirty drama societies in Cambridge and I would cycle around all day, auditioning for things and learning lines, and then I'd go back and clean loos. Cambridge is where I met Ed. He's proper clever and was doing law then. He's a writer now. We discovered

Thai food together in Cambridge. The lemongrass and the coconut milk, it was so delicious.

When I started working in the theater, I ate quite late after the show. You're sort of on a high when you finish, and first you want to have a drink. But I remember doing *Hay Fever* at the Noël Coward Theatre in London, right next to Sheekey's, the seafood restaurant. We'd go afterwards, three of us—Amy Morgan, Phoebe Waller-Bridge, and me. We all smoked then, so we'd sit outside and order the little croquettes and the scallop-shrimp burgers. Oh, that was a treat. Phoebe and I first met on *The Iron Lady*, with Meryl Streep as Margaret Thatcher. Phoebe loves food and loves to eat, which is really annoying, because she is so tall and lean.

When I was playing Queen Anne in *The Favourite*, I was asked to put on weight. Queen Anne had lost seventeen babies and apparently was clinically obese. I put on about two stone. It was *easy*. Rachel Weisz and Emma Stone, they love food, but they ate sort of clean food. So while they had their healthy options, I would say, "I'll have one of everything and all of the puddings—oh, and if you don't want that, I'll have it."

But eventually, it started to get a bit gloomy: "I don't really want another pizza. I know I'm going to have to take it all off at the end." And I did. Just by the old-fashioned, boring means of eating a lot less and trying to move more.

Queen Elizabeth was very different. She was tiny, with a tiny waist. I don't have a tiny waist. So they got me a trainer before I started. In the scenes where the Queen entertained heads of state and that sort of thing, there was beautiful, lovely food. But she had lived through rations and austerity, and she was never irresponsible about that. Also, she was very healthy and outdoorsy and maintained a neat little figure, which doesn't come from copious amounts of food.

Thankfully, by my second season, Elizabeth was a bit older and her waist was not as tiny.

In our house, we always sit together and eat. We do a Sunday roast every Sunday. Just before lockdown, we took the kids on a holiday of a lifetime, to Sri Lanka. We ate the most incredible food three times a day, different curries. The two oldest, the boys, are the most adventurous. Our girl, the little one, wasn't so thrilled and ate plain pasta and rice. To be fair, she was only four at the time. But we all loved the dals and the coconut sambal.

Our middle boy became obsessed with Japan when he was very little. We enrolled him in a sushi course, and now he makes beautiful sushi and his own ramen, which takes three days to prepare. Ed is taking the two boys for a cookery course before our eldest goes to university.

And I love anything with truffles. We keep a little jar with a truffle in it, and every now and then we'll shave some over scrambled eggs, or on a mushroom pasta. Oh!

*Olivia, what is your comfort food?*
*Tarka dal*. It's soft lentils, and the *tarka* is the seasoning, or tempering, on top: ghee or oil infused with spices. I've never made it, but when I order it, I always get much more than we need so I can have it cold for breakfast. I could eat *tarka dal* all day, every day.

# BOB IGER

> Bob Iger is the CEO of the Walt Disney Company who built upon the Disney legacy while acquiring Pixar, Lucasfilm, and Marvel. When he came to dinner at The River Cafe recently, I proudly told Bob that I employ 120 people. He told me he employs 200,000.
>
> Bob is someone who cares passionately about the vegetable garden outside his kitchen, the meals he prepares for his family.
>
> In our conversation on *Ruthie's Table 4*, Bob described how he and Willow Bay, his wife and the dean of the USC Annenberg School for Communication and Journalism, fell in love over a first date at his favorite downtown New York restaurant—and the first dinner he cooked for her.

I lived with my parents and my maternal grandmother. She was from the old country: Poland. A nice Jewish grandmother. Her go-to meals were pot roast and stuffed cabbage. She liked to make matzo ball soup as well, and also made a mean apple pie.

My mother picked up some of her mother's cooking abilities but was not very adventuresome. In the 1950s in the United States, what was available was actually quite limited, at least in New York. The supermarkets, even the big chains, didn't have great produce sections. You'd never get fresh basil, for instance. So a lot of what we ate were canned foods: canned peas, canned carrots, canned green beans. Adventurous cooking was not my mother's middle name. She made some good desserts, but that was about it.

My grandmother died when I was sixteen, but until then, she was always part of our family meals. She shared the cooking duties with my mother.

My father wasn't much of a cook, although I remember him making scrambled eggs for me on occasion in the morning. He liked to make a good Jewish deli sandwich. Nathan's was the famous Coney Island hot dog emporium, and he loved that. He was a trumpet player. He had played some professional trumpet in his day.

He'd lost his lip by the time I was born. But he took me to jazz concerts. I saw Louis Armstrong play. I saw Duke Ellington, and that was a great influence on my life. Music is a true love of my life, thanks to him. His trumpet still sits in my office at home.

My father collected a lot of books, and for some reason we had a *Life* magazine book about the great restaurants of the world, and it included some recipes. I decided to impress a college girlfriend by cooking some Italian food for her, and I actually loved the experience. It was pasta with a light tomato sauce, very basic. I impressed myself. I began to use cooking as a means of presenting myself as an attractive date. When I met Willow and told her that I cooked, she said, "You *cook?*" Her eyes lit up. Suddenly I was far more attractive.

When I went into New York to begin work after college, I started cooking for myself quite avidly. I ended up taking a Mediterranean cooking class with a Frenchwoman of, I think, Egyptian descent. Then I ended up in jobs, working for ABC Sports, that took me around the world, and that's when I first got truly introduced to the world's food.

I started working for ABC Sports when I was twenty-four years old. I stayed there for thirteen years. I worked on a program called *Wide World of Sports*, which covered sporting events all over the world. I visited Beijing in the late '70s and went to South Africa and all over Europe, the Soviet-bloc countries, and Latin America. There was almost no place that I didn't visit. We lived and ate well when we traveled. I remember going to Taillevent in Paris, which I had no business going to, and the Hôtel de Paris Monte-Carlo. And having a steak at the Grill at the Connaught in London.

I cooked regularly until I became CEO of Disney, which was in 2005. After that, time management became a little bit more challenging, much to my wife's chagrin. But it's one of the things that I look forward to, having the time to cook more.

I love shopping for food, too. I like going to farmers' markets and discovering new things and tasting. The market in Nice, Cours Saleya? It goes on for blocks and blocks. I remember seeing more olives than I'd ever seen in my lifetime. There are a few in Paris that I like, too.

We have property in L.A. that has allowed us to plant quite a nice-sized garden. We grow a lot of citrus. We have great lemons, including Meyer lemons, and oranges of all sorts. We also have a thriving vegetable garden.

I find cooking relaxing, incredibly therapeutic. I must have a glass of red wine to sip from, and I like to listen to music. And I don't like intrusions. I like to take over the kitchen.

I taught myself about wine when I worked at ABC and was living in a building on the Upper West Side of New York. On the corner that my building was on, there was a wine shop called 67th Street Wines and Liquors. I had time on my hands as a single man in New York, and one of the salesmen took a liking to me and taught me a tremendous amount and got me interested in wine at an early age, well before I could afford a good bottle.

I'm very involved in the food programs at our parks. Not only have we hired a lot of great chefs, but we also have quite a wine program. We believe we're the largest buyer and seller of wine in the world, which you wouldn't expect to hear about Disney.

I very rarely have wine at lunch. It's got to be a very special occasion. A good glass of rosé sitting outdoors at a cafe on the Place des Vosges in Paris: that's license to have a glass of wine. But at dinner, yes. Pre-pandemic, I probably had wine maybe three or four times a week. It's probably six times a week since. I like one glass of wine right before dinner and one with the meal.

I fell in love with my wife over dinner. We had run into one another at an event in New York, and through a variety of complicated circumstances, it took us eighteen months to schedule the first dinner. We went to a restaurant called Alison on Dominick that isn't there anymore: not only really good food, but quite romantic. Dominick is a street in downtown New York. And that was our first official date, June 13th, 1994. We celebrate that anniversary more than we celebrate our wedding anniversary.

We've carried on a tradition of having dates since then. One of the nicest parts of my life is just being able to go out to dinner alone with my wife. If I know that I'm doing that, I look forward to it all week.

*Bob, what is your comfort food?*
A good margherita pizza. It doesn't need to be fancy. It can be very, very basic. I delivered a commencement speech at the University of Texas, which our older son graduated from. I talked about being bold and getting out there and changing the world. Certainly so much needs changing and fixing. But I also talked about embracing life. And my equivalent of stopping to smell the roses is savoring great pizza. So I put that into my speech.

# STEPHEN FRY

There is a well-known cartoon in *The New Yorker* magazine depicting President Franklin Delano Roosevelt in his pajamas, on his knees next to his bed, saying a prayer for his wife, the most active first lady in history. "Dear Lord, please make Eleanor tired tomorrow." It's easy to imagine the friends and family of Stephen Fry saying the same, as there's very little Stephen doesn't do.

He is an actor, comedian, television host, and director, and a prolific writer—he has written books on Greek mythology, three autobiographies, and countless columns in national papers.

But should you ask the people who know him well what Stephen is best at, they will answer, "Being a friend."

I would change the FDR prayer. I would say, "Dear Lord, we all need Stephen Fry. Please do *not* make him tired tomorrow."

Stephen read the recipe for our Lemon, Almond, and Polenta Cake.

I grew up in the Norfolk countryside. I had a strange childhood. It's going to sound like it was *Downton Abbey* or something, but it really wasn't. But my parents did have a cook and we had gardeners and an old-fashioned Victorian kitchen garden. We had a game larder and hung birds and things like that. So I was used to the fact that every day, the gardeners would come to the back door and Mrs. Riseborough, the cook, would select some of the vegetables. And I would hang around, age five or something, watching her.

Mrs. Riseborough was what used to be called a good English plain cook. She didn't do anything terribly fancy, but everything she did do was just right: pies and tarts and things. She would take her thumb, put little squares of pastry on it, and pull them back to make a rose that would go in the center of a pie.

Because of the kitchen garden, everything we ate was in season. My mother drove the gardeners mad because she'd go out when the peas were ready and eat the entire crop of peas. There were fruit trees trained against the outbuildings. And there were gooseberry bushes and raspberries and black currants, and four fantastic raised asparagus beds. Belgian asparagus, quite small and delicate. My mother had a constant war with the gardeners because she had this theory that you shouldn't eat asparagus after Ascot, which is in mid-June.

When I was young, up until I was about twelve, there would be dinner parties at our house, the men in dinner jackets and black tie. After dinner, the men would be left alone in the dining room while the women withdrew. I asked my mother, "Why do the men stay behind?" I'd heard that it was so that they could tell dirty jokes that the women didn't want to hear.

My mother, who had studied and taught history, said, "No, do you know what it is really? In the Victorian era, the women did not like drawing attention to the fact that they had to use lavatories." If they all left in one go, they could go up to use the lavatories together and then go down to the drawing room. But if the men *and* the women went into the drawing room after the meal, and a woman said, "I'm going to go now," everyone would think, "Oh, she's off for a piss, is she?"

My father just ate everything that was put in front of him. He was a scientist and his mind was on his work. But my mother was from a Jewish family. And Jews, compared to the British in those days, less so now, were obsessed with food. Partly because in some cases they knew poverty between the wars, when things were really short in Vienna and in Hungary, which is where my grandparents came from. My grandfather, my mother's father, was a good cook. He made the most beautiful dill and cucumber salads. I really got a taste for that kind of Central European flavor from him.

At age seven, I went off to a prep school in Gloucestershire, two hundred miles away. This was in 1964. There were things like hot-milk puddings made with semolina and tapioca. Something about milk that's been boiled makes me dry-heave. I said, "No, no, I can't." But they forced me, literally holding my nose. It was cruel, but of course, it happened to other boys and you just think, "This is life." I forced myself to throw up at the table so that they stopped doing that. It was written down: "Fry, S., allergic to hot milk."

It was, I wouldn't say Dickensian, but it was a world of chilblains and constipation and cold. What it does is make you start to obsess about sweets. There was a tuck shop in the school—*tuck* was the slang for goodies, for confectionery. You'd get obsessed with when the tuck shop was going to be open and how much pocket money you'd got.

This was the golden age of confectionery. Cadbury was producing new things like Curly Wurly and Aztec bars, and there were these amazing Barratt Foam Shrimps, and Flying Saucers made of rice paper, and Fruit Salads, four for a penny, and Blackjacks, four for a penny. I became so obsessed that I would start breaking out of school bounds and going to the village shop. It was in a little village called Uley, and I would spend whatever money I had on getting those sweets. By the time I was twelve, I was having huge amounts of fillings and even having teeth out.

I think a lot of it was preparation for smoking. There were these shredded-coconut fake brown tobaccos that came in a little wax paper with a Spanish galleon on it, which was like rolling tobacco. There were candy cigarettes that came in a sort of fake Chesterfield soft pack. And licorice pipes. And even more weirdly, the glamour of sherbet powder, which was a sweet white powder that fizzed on the tongue. You'd suck it up through a licorice straw. When you were fourteen or fifteen, you'd go for the real cigarettes. And then, when you were a little older than that, the real white powder. It's a terrible thought. I'm not excusing it or saying that it was the school's fault, but I, in later life, did become something of an addict.

At Cambridge, you had your rooms and what was called a gyp room, which was like a little kitchen. But it didn't have a proper oven or anything, so you couldn't do much there.

But because of my acting, I would stay on during the summer to rehearse with friends, for all the plays we were taking up to Edinburgh. You'd stay at totally different places than in your college, because your college would be given over to conferences and things like that.

One of these friends, Ben, was really good at cooking. He taught me the mirepoix: the carrots, the celery, and chopping them up. It's the basis of everything, from Bolognese and upwards, as it were. I really enjoyed learning that, seeing how it all worked. He also showed me what I now know is called deglazing. I'd say, "Oh, everything's stuck to the pan." And he'd take a glass of wine and just throw it in, scraping the bottom of the pan, and then it would all come to life. He had that confidence.

My theory about food is that certain ingredients know when you're scared. I love making mayonnaise, but it's a mood thing. If you're not quite confident enough, it knows and it will split. If you're *too* confident, it will split. You have to come up to it and show that you are master, but that you respect it.

When I left Cambridge, I was so fortunate, because the comedy stuff I was doing with Hugh Laurie and Emma Thompson won a new prize at the Edinburgh Festival Fringe called the Perrier Award. An Australian entrepreneur called Michael Edgley saw our show and said, "You guys want to come over to Australia?" And that's where I learned to eat.

This was 1981. Starting in Sydney. Doyles on the Beach was this amazing seafood place. You walk along the dunes and come to this beautiful shack where the food is things you've never heard of, like barramundi, a kind of fish, and the Moreton Bay bug, a kind of lobster—all these extraordinary seafood things. Also oysters. Oysters that were so plentiful and not, "Oh my goodness, I'm having oysters, I must be in Bentley's or in some other posh London restaurant that does oysters." It was, "Oh, yeah, have some oysters, mate."

And they were cheap as chips, as people say. That was the point. I'd have half a dozen plump Pacific oysters, not cooked. And then half a dozen cooked Mornay, Rockefeller, or Kilpatrick, these different ways of preparing them. Kilpatrick was a favorite of mine, because it involved Worcestershire sauce.

Wine was the other thing. I finally moved off the Lambrusco. They had things like Penfolds Grange Hermitage, which was nothing as expensive as it is now, £300 or £400 a bottle at least. And they had a way of categorizing wines which is so ridiculously obvious but unheard of in Britain: by grape—i.e., varietal. They would say, "This is a Shiraz. This is a Cabernet Sauvignon." And they'd tell you about the grape. Then you go back to England and every restaurant is Châteauneuf this, Châteauneuf that. What does that mean?

When I got back to London, I was wandering around Soho. We were doing a TV show and I was feeling lucky and flush with cash, relatively, compared to being a student. I was going down this street called Greek Street and I saw an attractive-looking restaurant. It was called L'Escargot, "the snail."

I wandered in and this fabulous woman, about three feet tall, came up to me and said, "Hello, dear." I said, "Oh, um . . . " I was obviously very nervous. She said, "You come with me" and sat me down. Her name was Elena Salvoni, a legendary maître d', an amazing, phenomenal woman. She chose for me, brilliantly, things that were just cheap enough for me to be able to afford. From then on, the richer I got, the luckier I got, I would go there. And this was in the high days of L'Escargot, when Princess Diana would go. Once I was having dinner there with my friend Rowan Atkinson, the comic genius. Rowan is the most wonderful person in the world, but he's not a late-night figure at all. In those days, I quite was. So we'd had dinner and it was half past 9 o'clock. Rowan said, "Right, well, I'll get a cab home." I thought, "Oh, well, I'll do the same." So I ordered one.

Rowan's cab came first. I was just about to leave when Elena said, "Could you go and cheer up John Hurt? He just left his wife and he's very unhappy and needs a bit of cheering up." So I sat down with John Hurt. Every now and again, Elena would say, "Your cab's still here, Stephen." I said, "Tell him I'll be five minutes." When I got home, the cab bill was £220. I saw John about a week later and said, "I told everyone I got *Hurt* on Thursday night." And he said, "Well, I told everyone I got *Fryed*."

I am a bit obsessed about my weight. I know that if I was fitter and lost a stone, I would snore less and puff less at the top of the steps. I tried Ozempic years ago. My doctor in America said, "I think I can get you some." The first week or so I was thinking, "This is astonishing. Not only do I not want to eat, I don't want alcohol of any kind. This is going to be brilliant!" And then I started feeling sick. I was literally throwing up four or five times a day and I thought, "I can't do this." So that was it.

I've got a really good kitchen at my house in L.A., which is under the Hollywood sign, in Beachwood Canyon. The house, which was built in 1923, used to be an art gallery. So there's this very long upper room, which used to be where the pictures were. One end of it is the kitchen, and it's open to the dining room part of it. So when you're cooking, you're chatting with everybody who might be there and there's plenty of room. You know how somehow surfaces disappear when you cook? "Where can I put anything?" I cook there more than I do in England. I love it. And my husband's a good customer. He seems to enjoy it.

*Stephen, what is your comfort food?*
It's a small silvery fish in a tin called skippers. It's not a sardine, although I like sardines, and it's not skipjack tuna, which is a different thing. You see them in supermarkets. You have them whole and they're soft enough to spread on toast. On toast, they are absolutely glorious to me.

# AUSTIN BUTLER

Shortly after he completed filming Baz Luhrmann's *Elvis*, Austin arrived in London to shoot the World War II series *Masters of the Air*. This was in the period when the Covid-19 lockdown had only just been lifted and people were reacclimating to socializing. My friend Kadee Robbins decided to start a new tradition, hosting a small group of friends for a weekly Sunday dinner. We did so for twenty-nine weeks. Austin, a Californian far from home, became part of this group. He is family to me now.

It was challenging trying to decide which chapter of this book Austin Butler should be in. Tradition? This would be fitting and in honor of our ritual dinners and card games. Or Family? Because Austin truly is a part of mine. When he comes to visit, we don't go out much, mostly shopping, cooking, and eating together, as family does. But in the end we chose this chapter: Discovery. Because, quite simply, being with Austin is, for me, always a discovery.

When he returned to The River Cafe for the podcast, he read our recipe for Grilled White Peaches with Amaretto.

I was born in Anaheim, right near Disneyland. We had grapefruit trees and an orange tree in the backyard. So the smell of fresh fruit evokes memories of my mom picking lemons and grapefruit and bringing them into the kitchen.

When I was born, she wanted to be a stay-at-home mom; she was a dental hygienist at the time. But my parents divorced when I was seven. She ended up starting a day care out of the house—she'd watch the children of the mothers who taught at the elementary school around the corner that I eventually went to. We always had little children in the house and she had to make meals that were really quick and easy. Things you'd get in the freezer aisle, like fish sticks and corn dogs. Nothing really gourmet at all.

As the years went on, she became vegetarian and then vegan. She got really into making things like portobello mushrooms and bell peppers stuffed with couscous. But when I was growing up, it wasn't extremely healthy in the house. It was efficient meals. She was working so much. When I started going to elementary school, I would walk home every day for lunch and she'd have a peanut butter and jelly sandwich waiting for me. We'd watch this home-decorating show called *Surprise by Design* and come up with things that we were going to do around the house. We'd get inspired by the show and lay a brick path in the backyard or plant little flowers. I just remember how excited I was to walk home every day and eat the sandwich that she'd made for me.

My dad moved into the garage of a person he worked with. It had a little miniature fridge where we kept all our groceries. We slept on air mattresses at night and pulled them up during the day to make room for a table. There was a treadmill in the corner. We shared our landlord's kitchen, but otherwise, we had just this one room.

I started cooking as a kid because my dad had to work. He would say, "Hey, I'll pay you $2 if you cook dinner tonight." It became a way for me to stock up money as a kid. We'd go to Costco and buy food in bulk. I'd make burritos with Dennison's chili beans out of a can and some sour cream and cheese. A special occasion would be getting a $5 pizza from down the road. Years later, coming to a place like The River Cafe or the French Laundry, I felt out of my element, because $5 sounded like a lot for a meal when I was a kid.

I moved out when I was seventeen. I started wanting to learn how to make food and how flavors fit together. So when I started to make money, I started trying restaurants in L.A. and New York.

There hasn't been a lot of continuity in many areas of my life since I was young, because I travel a lot. Even the nature of doing a film or a TV show, you make a family of the entire cast and crew and then it splits up. Through therapy, I realized that I was almost reliving my childhood—you have a family and then it splits up. So I'd seek out ways of having stability and consistency. So when I'm on location, whether in Vancouver or New Zealand or Australia or London, I find a restaurant that becomes my second home and I get to the point where I go there every day, and the staff knows me and I know them.

Suddenly, it feels like there is this thing separate from my work that feels like home. Even if I've woken up with anxiety or I feel sad or overwhelmed, I go to a restaurant. I'll come with a book so I get to read, and I know the people who work there. This morning, I could hardly leave the house. I just felt anxious for some reason. Then I thought, "I've got to get to The River Cafe." Once you get here, suddenly there's life around you and it sort of buzzes. You feel humanity wash over you, things that are happening outside of your own experience. And you eat delicious food. That really helps.

For a time, I lived in a beautiful house in Los Angeles that had belonged to Gary Oldman. He had built a pizza oven and I became obsessed with learning how to make the perfect pizza, using a specific type of wood. I got one of those laser temperature gauges so I could make it a thousand degrees. Learned how to make the pizza sauce and the dough from scratch. The first couple of pizzas came out kind of rough. Then I started to get really into a zone. It's amazing to me how fast you can cook a pizza, in thirty or forty-five seconds.

Then I thought, "What else can I cook in this fire?" There's a restaurant in Laurel Canyon called Pace that makes this salmon on a cedar plank. I thought, "I want to learn how to make that." So I got these cedar planks. You soak them in water and put the salmon on top, seasoning it and sticking it in the wood fire. It came out incredibly.

One of the best trips I ever took was to Italy, probably four years before *Elvis*. Spent a month just road-tripping with my girlfriend at the time. We started in Milan, drove to Portofino, and went to Cinque Terre and hiked between the little villages and visited the vineyards.

Then we drove to Florence, and after that, to a little bed and breakfast in Tuscany. It was run by this beautiful Italian woman and her husband. They had two daughters. One of the daughters would play piano in the afternoon and you'd hear it reverberating through the vineyard. The woman would bring focaccia up and we'd eat it around the pool in the afternoon. One night, her husband had caught a wild boar, so she prepared it for us and it was just absolutely divine. One of their daughters was dating a young man who was eighteen years old, half Israeli and half Italian. He told me, "You know, I'm a pilot. I can fly you if you want me to."

I said, "Wow, that would be cool." But I was thinking, "I'm not putting our lives in this eighteen-year-old kid's hands." The next night, his mom came to dinner and she was in the Israeli Air Force. She said, "You know, he's actually a very good pilot." So I thought, "You only live once." He offered to fly us to Elba, where Napoleon was exiled. I said, "Let's do it. I'll pay for gas. I'll pay for the plane."

We ended up getting in the car. Turns out he couldn't drive a car, though he could fly a plane. So I drove us all: me and my girlfriend, him and his girlfriend. We drove up to the little private area of the Florence airport. He went to a garage and pulled out, by hand, a four-seater Cessna. We went through all the preflight checks and took off. It felt like riding in a go-kart. I couldn't hear him at all. It was static in the headphones and I saw panic over his face. I was thinking, "He's the only person who can land this plane."

But it was only that he couldn't figure out how to switch a certain switch so that we could hear each other. Once he figured that out, peace came upon the airplane. Then he told me, "It's a dangerous landing place in Elba because you have to fly in this zigzag pattern." So I went back to thinking, "Oh, God, we're trusting this eighteen-year-old."

We ended up zigzagging through the mountains of Elba and landing safely, thankfully. We ate pasta with him and his girlfriend that day for lunch.

They flew back. We stayed and rode around on Vespas and ate pasta at all these different beaches on Elba. Went to the vineyards that Napoleon used to go to. He came back three days later, picked us up on the plane, and we flew back to Florence. It was magic.

I did *Once Upon a Time in Hollywood* with Quentin Tarantino. On one night shoot, at about three in the morning, he had this amazing crepe-maker come and make crepes. As we were eating them, he said, "Austin, you know what my thing is? I want to give everybody such a good experience on this job that their next job sucks."

So every night, there would be some new food thing that he would organize, to give you something to look forward to. The other thing that he did was, after every hundred rolls of film, he'd throw a party and it would have a theme. So grappa would come out, or there would be margaritas and a mariachi band.

When we wrapped *Elvis*, Baz and I were at his house in Australia with a small group. It was the first time that he and I were both able to go, "Ah, we did it." We put on vinyl records, danced, ate oysters, and just lived life.

Then the sun started to come up and Baz looked out. He said, "Should we go swim in the ocean right now?" We ran across the street and jumped in the ocean, around five in the morning. I said, "Baz, I can't believe I was going to go to sleep tonight!" He started singing "Nessun dorma" to me and going, "No sleep tonight. No sleep tonight." I hadn't heard that opera so he told me its story. Then he said, "I'll play it for you when we get back to the shore."

I took a second for myself in the ocean. I watched the sun rise and processed all that we had done. Then, as I slowly walked back to shore, I saw Baz holding a speaker above his head like John Cusack in *Say Anything*. He was playing "Nessun dorma," the Pavarotti version, blaring at 5:30 in the morning on the beaches of the Gold Coast. It was so magical and cinematic.

Then we made breakfast. We looked in the refrigerator and thought,

"Okay, what can we make?" There's this thing about filming where you have so many responsibilities that other people end up almost treating you like you're a child. They walk you to the bathroom. They walk you to your trailer. You're very spoiled in many ways, but there's something relieving about that moment when you're finally able to do something for yourself.

So Baz and I at breakfast—that was our moment. We opened the refrigerator: "Okay, we got eggs, we got asparagus, we got some spinach, we got some tomatoes, we got some Parmesan cheese." We made this great breakfast and cut off bits of a loaf of bread. Just a delicious meal. Then we just sat there as the morning sun laid down on us. It's one of the most glorious memories of my life.

*Austin, what is your comfort food?*
My mother's no longer here. She passed away when I was twenty-three. After a big week, or if I'm feeling really overwhelmed, I'll make a peanut butter and jelly sandwich. It brings back that comforting sensation.

The River Cafe

Rossini –
Prosecco with fresh
strawberries £12

## Tuesday 24th May

### Antipasti
Prosciutto di Dan Daniele – with new seasons' Charentais Melon
Mozzarella di Bufala – with spring herbs, slow-cooked peas, swiss chard & Selvapiana olive oil
Seppia Nero – Cuttlefish cooked in it's ink with Soave Classico, fennel seeds, parsley, tomato & soft polenta

### Primi
Taglierini – with English asparagus, herbs & aged parmesan
Linguine – with prosciutto di San Daniele, spring peas, mint & butter

### Secondi
Capesante ai ferri – chargrilled Scottish scallops with salted anchovy, chilli and grilled English asparagus
Branzino al forno – wild Sea Bass roasted with wild oregano, olives & lemon, with Tuscan roast potatoes and trompette squash
Fegato di Vitello in padella – Calf's Liver seared with lemon zest, marjoram and capers, with braised Italian spinach
Coscia d'Agnello – chargrilled marinated leg of lamb with salsa rossa piccante, wood roasted Violetta aubergine & baked fresh borlotti

### Dolci
Affogato with Espresso    Chocolate Nemesis    Lemon Tart

12½% OPTIONAL SERVICE CHARGE WILL BE ADDED
IF YOU HAVE A FOOD ALLERGY, PLEASE SPEAK TO US BEFORE ORDERING

# Food Is Art

A painting by Caravaggio lasts over four hundred years, while a pear and almond tart, which I might consider a work of art, disappears in five minutes. I know many artists, and I have yet to meet one who doesn't like to cook.

Food is artist-friendly—from Caravaggio's luminously rendered figs and persimmons to Wayne Thiebaud's bright layer cakes—and artists are food-friendly. The River Cafe is proud to welcome many artists as regulars. It's always a revelation to have painters, sculptors, and architects on the podcast and see food through their eyes. Ed Ruscha, for example, describes an almost *Wizard of Oz*–like culinary and artistic journey, from the Omaha of his youth, which he calls a "cultural wasteland in many ways," to his adopted California, where he grows his own ghost peppers and harvests his own pine nuts. So I wasn't surprised when he brought his own recipe for a cactus omelet to *Ruthie's Table 4*.

Food is art and art is food.

# NORMAN FOSTER

Of all the people I've spoken with on the podcast, the architect Norman Foster is the friend I've known the longest. We met in 1970, when I was twenty-two. He and his late wife Wendy were close friends and former architectural partners of my husband, Richard. We have since been through so much together, bonded by our love of adventure, architecture, and each other's families. After we finished recording his episode at The River Cafe, Norman, his wife Elena, and his son Eduardo, joined us for dinner, two families with a long history together.

Norman read a recipe for a favorite of his, Trofie with Pesto.

I grew up in Levenshulme, near Manchester, during the time of war and rationing. I remember the ration book as if it were yesterday. It was coupons, a government document. It's a powerful image and really quite symbolic.

My mother discovered dried eggs, which came from America: this bright yellow powder in a brown greaseproof package. And fruit was scarce. If you got a tangerine, that was a real treat, very, very special. After the war, when the shops opened, there were queues for sweets. Sweets were a rare delicacy. But occasionally Hershey's bars somehow found their way to children from friends of GIs who were stationed nearby.

I don't remember ever being hungry. My mother cooked the classic baked beans on toast, or dinner might be fish and chips from a fish-and-chip shop. We would have a roast on Sundays. I'd go round to the corner shop to get mustard powder, and I would make the mustard to go with the beef. That was a special day.

When I was a student at the University of Manchester, the only food we could afford to go out for was side-street Indian food. Quite humble restaurants, but good food.

My first time out of Manchester was a bike trip with a friend. I must have been sixteen. We took a train to London and crossed the English Channel. Our first meal in France was in a very humble café. When we were served our dinner, my friend and I automatically asked for the salt and pepper, because that was a ritual where we came from. Whenever food was served, you sprayed it with salt and pepper. I remember the look of absolute horror on the proprietor's face. He told us, "We have already added the salt and pepper." That was a turning point for me.

We cycled onward and ended up in Milan, where I discovered pasta and risotto. I had always associated rice with rice pudding, which was sweet and for me, not very nice. So properly made rice and pasta was a great discovery.

On subsequent trips I developed a taste for more exotic food. I'd work part-time jobs to raise funds and travel to France, Italy, and also Scandinavia, where I was studying the work of Jørn Utzon before he won the competition for the Sydney Opera House. Wherever I was, I tried the food and drink of the area. So there were simultaneous revelations about design, architecture, food, and, really, a whole lifestyle.

There were wonderful places in Spain, where food is really a cult, and cooking is a very male occupation. I'm thinking of parts of northern Spain, where that gastronomic tradition permeates society, and everybody lives it as a way of life. In Madrid, there's a total change of tempo and work patterns. The working day is longer and later. Nine o'clock for dinner is early. You're lucky if you can find a restaurant open at that time.

Italy was always fantastic. I would take the measure of the public spaces, like the main square, or *campo*, in Siena, or the square in Verona, or the shortcut through the galleria in Milan that connects La Scala to the cathedral. There was always a good pavement café and a great synergy of food and public space, though I wouldn't have called it *public space* then. I was interested in the urbanity of the city, which was unusual because architecture school is much more about the design of individual buildings than the infrastructure of a city.

I first met Richard at a Fulbright reception, where he was heavily bandaged from a skiing accident. The next time was when we were beginning at the Yale School of Architecture in 1961.

The dean, Paul Rudolph, was quite a character and drove everybody hard. There were so-called charrettes, where you would burn the midnight oil working together to map out plans. The only place that was open all night was a bar in New Haven called My Brother's Place. We went there sometimes in the middle of the night and discovered American food, things like pastrami sandwiches. We thought they were fantastic.

Philip Johnson was a visiting critic. Sometimes he invited students to have lunch in New York at the Four Seasons, which he had designed. It was at the base of the Seagram Building, Mies van der Rohe's still enduring early bronze skyscraper. There was an extraordinary sculpture over the bar, Rothko paintings, and a pool in the center. A breathtaking interior and a very classic menu—an incredible marriage of a great space, amazing taste, and classic furniture.

Later on, I'd go there for a drink on excursions with Richard and another architect, Jim Stirling. Jim once surreptitiously slid one of their ashtrays into the pocket of his coat. At the end, when Jim was given the bill, the waiter said, "Oh, by the way, this figure here—that's the cost of the ashtray."

*Norman, what is your comfort food?*
I think it's back where we started: pasta and pesto. With good cheese.

# TRACEY EMIN

Tracey Emin is a great artist and a good friend. Her episode of the podcast touched me and all our listeners deeply. Her food stories are as vivid and powerful as her art, a reflection of a bold and complicated life.

Tracey and her twin brother, Paul, were born in 1963 to parents who were married to other people. Her father, Enver, was a Turkish Cypriot who lost a fortune in real estate; her mother, Pam, partly of Romani ancestry, struggled to make ends meet. In the early part of their childhoods, Tracey and Paul enjoyed rich, eventful holidays in Turkey. Later, they suffered abject poverty and racism.

My dad was a fantastic cook. Grew his own vegetables. Actually, me and my dad grew vegetables on the roof of my studio back in the 1990s: cucumbers, courgettes, aubergines, potatoes, heritage tomatoes, green beans, everything. Then he would cook for me.

My mum, I hate to say, was a terrible cook. Though I did like it when she made me egg and chips. She was completely against my cooking. It was pretty radical for the 1970s. When we were being taught cooking at school, she wrote a note saying, "My daughter will not learn to cook. She is not going to be a slave to any man." She had very strong ambitions for me. She put me on the pill when I was fourteen to make sure I didn't get pregnant. She considered the idea of me having children to be a complete failure, not a positive thing, so she did everything she could to stop me from being a young single mother. She wasn't home-based. It wasn't her strong point.

So the food I grew up with was a strange mixture of amazing food that my dad cooked and really terrible food that my mum cooked.

My dad came to England by boat in 1948 on a £10 ticket from Cyprus. One of his grandfathers, my great-grandfather, was from Sudan and had been a slave in the Ottoman Empire. Around 1900, he was given his freedom in Cyprus, with fifty sheep. So we're Turkish Cypriot, known as this thing called the Black Turks, descended from slaves. I was brought up on pomegranates and watermelon.

Up until we were about six, my brother and I went to Turkey regularly. We spent two separate periods of six months there. All that time, we were eating Mediterranean food, Mediterranean cooking. We used to drive to Turkey from England. This is really cool: Dad had a brand-new Ford Zodiac, and in the back were these tiny wooden chairs with raffia seats. He stuck a hole through the roof, put bungee-type elastic things around the chairs, and then just sat us in the back of the car, two twins bouncing up and down in these chairs.

We'd drive to Turkey and stop along the way. Dad would get the Calor gas stove out and fry eggs and cook and everything. And we'd go to fields and take watermelons. It was really exciting and adventurous, these drives. I'm romanticizing it, but it *was* romantic—so different from the upbringing of everyone else I knew.

My dad never properly lived with us. He was married. He'd spend three days with his wife, three days with my mum, and, we'd always say, "One day somewhere else." So when he was around, it felt like a big treat.

Dad left us when Paul and I were seven years old. We were wealthy until I was seven, and then he lost everything. We went from trips to Turkey to squatting in a cottage, with my mum working in a hotel as a waitress and chambermaid. From high to low really fast, a reversal of fortune.

My mum was out most of the time, working. And at weekends as well, she'd be out 'til three in the morning. So we were on our own. Often my mum would leave us sandwiches. There was no sitting around a table. It was sitting watching telly with a tray, eating egg and chips when she came home.

Christmas was not Christmas, because Mum was always working. We had the Salvation Army one year, coming 'round with food and presents.

If my mum didn't have work, we had nothing. This is one of the most shameful things I can tell you about, but in a way, I'm sort of proud of her: when the hotel went derelict, she climbed up on the roof, took some lead off of it, and sold it, so we could afford something to eat. That is on another level. You hear about women shoplifting to get their babies food and it seems unimaginable. But it's not when you've been that poor.

I was brought up with absolutely no rules. This might be the Gypsy side of things. If I didn't want to go to school, I didn't go to school. If I didn't want to brush my teeth, I didn't brush my teeth. If I wanted to have sex, I could have sex, as long as I didn't get pregnant.

I left home when I was fifteen, the first day I could leave school. I came straight to London with two David Bowie albums and some clothes. I stayed in all different places, including a squat in Warren Street. That was very educational. I lived with several people who are now quite successful and well-known. I stayed with different friends. I stayed in a cupboard in Clapham for a time. It's a real mystery how I never got in trouble. But I was kind of sassy and streetwise.

For a long time, I didn't eat. I used to be so thin. For years and years, I didn't care about food at all. I was not anti-food, it just wasn't on my list of priorities. I went to Maidstone College of Art and the Royal College of Art, for painting. When I was at the Royal College of Art, I'd get into the studio at about a quarter to eleven in the morning and I'd stay 'til ten o'clock every night. I'd work at the weekends as well. I had no social life at all.

But the thing about artists and restaurants is brilliant, because then, after I left art school, one of the first things I did, as soon as I started to have money, was eat oysters. All of my excess income was spent on oysters. I used to try all different restaurants, different oysters, figuring out what I liked and didn't like. For a moment, I was on about a hundred oysters a week. And I used to cycle everywhere, and I was so fit! Lean, like a ballerina.

I now have a house in the South of France. I'm on top of a hill, looking over maybe 260 degrees of the sea—it's only behind me that I can't see it. It's really beautiful and in the middle of a nature preserve. I don't have any neighbors. It's a twenty-five-minute drive to the nearest little town to buy food. So what I tend to do is one big shop a week, and that's it.

I have this thing in the house that I call my war cupboard. It's full of stuff where, literally, if there was a war, I'd have enough to keep me going: tins and tins of sardines, all sorts of stuff. I also love going shopping for really nice food, putting it in the fridge, and looking at it. It makes me feel so safe and cozy and secure. I've got a vegetable garden as well. My favorite cooking is when I get down to the nitty-gritty and I have to be really inventive with what I cook, using the war cupboard.

I underwent surgery for bladder cancer a few years ago. While it was a success, it has affected the way that I eat. My diet's completely changed since I was ill. I eat vast amounts of fish, vast amounts of apples, fruit, all day long. I eat cold food much more than hot food. I don't know why. But I eat quite healthily. I'm quite forward-thinking on good food. When I eat something bad, it's because I really want to.

*Tracey, what is your comfort food?*
Apples. I eat probably about six to eight apples a day. Couldn't live without apples. I like Pink Lady apples, kind of sweet. I wash them, put them on the bread board, and get the knife. I don't cut them evenly. I just slice all sorts of bits off until I get to the core. So it's all different shapes. I make a big pile of apple pieces on a very beautiful blue Delft plate. And then I sit, anywhere, and just slowly eat, three apples at a time, in different bits, shapes, and pieces. It makes me feel so good.

# FRANK GEHRY

For years, every time a new Frank Gehry building opened, Richard and I would go see it: the Walt Disney Concert Hall in Los Angeles, the Foundation Louis Vuitton cultural center in Paris, the Guggenheim Museum in Bilbao. But one summer, in 2008, a spectacular Gehry building came to London, opening in Hyde Park—the temporary Serpentine Gallery Pavilion, designed by Frank and his son, Sammy.

For the few months the pavilion stood, we met friends there almost daily, watching the sunset, listening to people play music, eating, and drinking. This brave and beautiful structure made Hyde Park a better park and London a better city.

For Frank's episode of the podcast, I made a pilgrimage to Los Angeles to see my friend. He read our recipe for Fagione in Josephine Dorè: pheasant braised in sweet wine.

I was born in Toronto. My mother was from Poland, my father from New York. His father was from Russia, Pinsk, I think. My mother's family came from Lodz. They came over in 1913, I think. There was a pogrom in Poland. I found out later that the Jews were being rounded up and beaten up.

My grandfather, who delivered coal, had a wagon. I went to Lodz and saw where the rail tracks were, where he would have been. I went there when I was invited to a film festival called the Camerimage Film Festival. I went with David Lynch. I loved the people. We went to the city hall and they asked David and me to sign our names on the wall. I wrote, "My grandfather left in 1913. If he hadn't left, I wouldn't be here." I was immediately called by the mayor's office and they became very solicitous. They found all my grandparents' families. All of a sudden

they wanted to show me they really loved the Jews, blah, blah, blah, which was a bunch of bullshit. I did get a pretty deep education on my family. I found out my grandmother ran a foundry. There was folklore about it when I was growing up, but it was actually true.

They came across the Atlantic on a Dutch ship that got stalled mid-ocean, which was the reason my mother would never cross a bridge in a car. She had a phobia, so she would get out of the car, walk across the bridge, and meet us on the other side. They landed in Toronto. My grandfather got a horse and buggy. He was delivering bread, I think. He went on to have a hardware store, which I worked in as a kid.

We had a small kitchen. My grandmother, on the cookstove, made gefilte fish. That's why everybody says I do fish sculptures, because I used to go pick up the live fish from the market and put it in the bathtub. At night, as a kid, I would play with the fish in the bathtub. And then the next day, it was gone.

We never went out much when I was a kid. My family couldn't afford to. I do remember going to restaurants with my father in Toronto that had signs that said NO JEWS ALLOWED. He knew the owner of one because he was a gregarious guy, so we got to go in anyway. He wasn't friendly with the owner, but he had a business relationship with him.

My father had a heart attack and lost everything. We had to leave Toronto. He was penniless. His brother brought him to California. My mother and my sister, Doreen, came, and we lived in two rooms in an old building downtown.

I got a job as a truck driver. My father got a job as a truck driver. I delivered breakfast nooks and furniture. He did soda-pop delivery. My mother got a job in the Broadway department store in Hollywood, in the candy department. She ended up in the decorating department, selling draperies to Hollywood people. My mother used to compare me to other people's kids, like, "Hilda's son does this? Why can't you be more like him?" So I had a bad time.

It was very stressful at our dinner table. My father had a temper. He couldn't control it and took it out on me because he saw me as not understanding business. I was a kind of artsy type and he didn't understand that. And my mother supported that. I was interested in going to the symphony and going to art galleries, but not in things that would make a living.

I started my own practice in 1964. I'd worked on shopping centers with Victor Gruen Associates and stuff like that. I got some houses to do. I did some small buildings, and I got to know Peter Eisenman, Richard Rogers, Norman Foster, Michael Graves, and Charlie Moore. I wasn't a big force in architecture, but they sort of paid attention. From the very beginning, I hung out with artists like Ed Ruscha, Ed Moses, Billy Al Bengston, John Altoon, and Peter Alexander. I always thought of architecture as an art, and I would go to their shows and they would come to mine.

When postmodernism became the siren song of architecture, Philip Johnson, Michael Graves, Robert A. M. Stern, I wasn't buying it. I thought there was more to life than copying the past. I was at a conference with a lot of those guys, and when my turn came to talk, I got up to say what was on my mind. I looked at them and said, "What the hell? Is there only one way, to go backward? Isn't there something new? Isn't there any hope for the future?"

Then I said, "Ah, damn it, if you've got to go back, go back three hundred million years before man, to fish. Fish are very architectural. Their movement is beautiful. They suggest movement and it goes with cars and trains and planes. So just copy *that*."

I had no idea why I said that. After that, I started to draw fish on all my little drawings. I was doing a project with Claes Oldenburg in Venezia. The sponsors were a fashion house in Florence. They asked me to do a fish sculpture for their show. So I went to Cinecittà and did a drawing, and they made it. I never saw it. In Torino, they were just getting ready to open the Castello di Rivoli as a museum, and they invited me to be in the first show.

They gave me two galleries. In one gallery, I put all my models. They said they had something for the other gallery, but they didn't tell me what.

I walked in, and in the other gallery was this wooden fish made for the fashion show. It was the biggest piece of kitsch I'd ever seen. It was so embarrassing. I was freaked out that they were making this part of my show. And standing beside me was a guy from the Stedelijk Museum in Amsterdam who had spoken ill of my work many times before. He said, "How'd you do that?" I said, "What do you mean?"

Then I realized what he was talking about. The thing looked like it was moving. This piece of egregious fish kitsch had the movement that a fish has. It was a pure accident. The guy said, "That's brilliant. How did you do that?" I said, "It's pure." I told him I was interested in fish because of their movement.

The next thing I did was the show at the Walker Art Center in Minneapolis. I cut the tail off the fish, the head off the fish, and I made it abstract. It still had the sense of movement. And that's when I got hooked on the fish shape, using it to express as an architect.

I think that experience made the Guggenheim Museum in Bilbao. I love the food in Bilbao, by the way. I love the codfish, the baccalà, and I love the wine. Bilbao awakened whatever foodie I was, because we went out all the time.

In Los Angeles, I used to go out to Italian restaurants with Benny Gazzara, the actor. We had a lot of pasta and wine. There was a steakhouse like a train carriage called the Pacific Dining Car. It was in my neighborhood. We used to go there because it was around the corner from where I lived and you didn't need a reservation. I used to see Spielberg. He would be there, and a lot of other Hollywood people, but they would come at six in the morning for early breakfast when nobody was there, or real late at night.

I did think about food when I designed the cafeteria for Si Newhouse, the owner of Condé Nast, at 4 Times Square. The best thing I did with Si was take him to Japan for a week. Greg Walsh, who was my partner, had spent a lot of his life in Japan. So Greg and Si and his wife, Victoria, and me and my wife, Berta, all went together.

Si wanted to go back to the same restaurant every day, a little café with typical Japanese dishes. He ordered pork noodles every day. A month before he died, I was with him in Paris for the opening of the Louis Vuitton building. He was sitting there, not totally with it, and called me over. And he said, "Frank, the trip you took me on to Japan, it was one of the best ever."

I like to cook salami and eggs, as well as matzo brei. On Sunday mornings, I have matzo brei bake-offs with people. Matzo is unleavened bread used mostly for Passover. I break it up under water and get it sort of moist. I salt it and stuff, and I take a bunch of eggs and I beat them up and put them all over the matzo. It absorbs the egg stuff and then I fry it. That's matzo brei.

*Frank, what is your comfort food?*

I guess pasta. You don't have to eat a lot of it. It's kind of filling and you can drink some wine with it. And when you go to a restaurant, an Italian restaurant, the varieties are incredible. That gets exciting.

# JONY IVE

One of the questions I'm often asked is, Where and when did you meet Jony Ive, the man whose designs changed the world?

The answer? Jony and I met at a White House state dinner in May 2012. Barack Obama was president. Hope was in the air.

Jony's memory is that we both found ourselves in the library, pretending to look at the books. We immediately discovered how much we share. Of course, Jony, then working as the chief design officer at Apple, was an astronaut flying to the moon, while I was only the pilot of a small plane. But we both love the color white, wake up thinking about food, and, though we love to party, consider ourselves shy. We had also both lost our best friends and work partners in the past ten months—for him, Steve Jobs, and for me, Rose Gray—and were trying to navigate stormy skies without them. Jony and I quickly realized we could make the journey as co-pilots.

Since that serendipitous meeting, the White House has changed occupants a few times, but Jony and I still orbit each other: creating books, sailing Southern Italy, and always sitting next to each other at dinner parties.

One recent day, I was delighted to find Jony in The River Cafe kitchen, making Taleggio Pizza with our co-chef Sian Wyn Owen. There followed a conversation about food and our love for each other. No navigating is needed when Jony and I talk. The skies are bright and clear. We are happy. We are together.

I was born in North London, up in a place called Chingford. It's right where London was halted in its growth by the Green Belt, which is Epping Forest. Literally the road ended and the forest began. Our kitchen was not memorable, but there were one or two appliances that were. We had a big bread mixer that was made by Braun. It was probably the most beautiful thing we owned.

I was brought up primarily vegetarian. Curiously, both of my parents grew up vegetarian. So breadmaking somehow seemed important. A lot of bread was made. Oh, God, it wasn't very nice. It was whole meal bread, snappy, more like a crisp.

Both of my parents worked. My mother taught philosophy at a local school. My father trained as a silversmith and a cabinetmaker and then became a teacher and a professor. Eventually he was one of Her Majesty's inspectors for schools, helping to improve the teaching and the practice. His specialty was art and design.

I'll tell you something that's absolutely dreadful. Because my parents worked, my mother made sandwiches ahead on Sunday for me to take to school. Then she would freeze them and take out a sandwich the night before. It would dethaw in time for the next day, *just*. So the sandwiches were always chilly and always wet. Because when you freeze lettuce, the moisture leaks out. It was the tomatoes and lettuce defrosting that caused havoc in the sandwich department.

There was a television program in the U.K. in the 1970s called *The Good Life*, with Richard Briers and Felicity Kendal. It was about a couple who had an existential crisis and decided to become as self-sufficient as they could. My grandparents, my father's mom and dad, were like that. Because my parents worked, I was essentially raised by them. They also lived in Chingford and were also vegetarian.

They had a lifestyle ahead of the language necessary to describe it. They grew or made almost everything that they ate. In a tiny garden, there was a greenhouse, and everything was fresh. One of my enduring memories is of digging up potatoes: digging through the soil and seeing a shape emerge and realizing there was a magical potato down there. My grandmother would simply scrub the potatoes and boil them gently. She served them with mint that I had picked after digging up the potatoes. And there was a shocking difference to me between something that ten minutes ago was growing and what was now on the plate.

My favorite part, without a doubt, was harvesting and shelling the peas. I've shelled thousands of peas. Probably about 10 percent of them got to the table.

They also grew tomatoes. And they served lentils, which I could not bear. In the early '70s, Neal's Yard was the only place in London where you could buy bulk vegetarian food. I still resent the place. What's worse than a small bag of lentils? A sack. We had this old Volvo Amazon, and I remember helping my father put this huge sack of lentils in the back.

My grandfather was a chain-smoker. He had that rare ability to talk while smoking, with his cigarette bobbing up and down. He'd give me a private lecture about the importance of the quality and the makeup of the soil. He spent hours making up his soil.

They had thoughts and ideas that were, then, particularly unusual. They were terribly concerned about coloring in food. Nobody was talking about that then. We now know that some of the artificial dyes are carcinogens. And they had concerns about all the fluoride. They worked hard to find fluoride-free toothpaste. Then it was put into the water, which they were terribly upset about.

I don't have clear memories of sitting down together for a family meal. In the evening, my sister and mother and I would have dinner, but my father was always home late from work. We didn't have very much money, and we didn't have very much time together as a family. Both things were rare. My Christmas present from my father was to go with him to the workshops during Christmas break, which I'm sure was illegal. He said, "We will make something together, whatever you want, with the one condition that you design it." He didn't actually say "design"; he said, "Think about it and explain it to me, with a drawing." What a wonderful definition of design.

It's part of the human condition that we assume everything that is made and everything that grows is inevitable. Now, maybe that's necessary, because if we were truly startled and full of joy and celebration about everything around us, we wouldn't get much done, perhaps. But I love the simple joy and curiosity about a chair. How did it get here? How was it made? The same thing with a pizza, seeing floppy dough change into something rigid and crispy. When you understand process and celebrate it, it can be a glorious thing. You end up connecting to your environment in a much deeper way. I think it also brings a humility. You become very aware of your small part as part of humanity, part of our species.

Heather and I married very young. We got married up in Newcastle but moved down to Greenwich. We both worked so hard that we didn't have much of a domestic life. I started going to restaurants for the first time in my life. As a child, I went to a restaurant maybe three times, ever.

My first design group was called Tangerine. The studio was over in Hoxton. Possibly the best thing about it was that it was close to Brick Lane. I love curry. The culture of Brick Lane was so interesting. Many of the restaurants didn't have the license to sell alcohol, so you were typically going to buy alcohol at the off-license next door and then go into the Indian restaurant. I had some extraordinary things there.

When I moved to San Francisco, there was an entire culture of eating out. I mean, Chez Panisse was incredible. We have dear friends near to where our new studio is, in Jackson Square, who have a restaurant called Quince. They have another restaurant next door called Cotogna and a farm near Bolinas, just over the Golden Gate Bridge. I feel so unspeakably grateful for the ability to have fresh peas again. I mean, it's not quite as much fun as shelling them yourself, but it's great to have such simple and fresh food.

I've been in San Francisco for well over thirty years. Having such a close relationship with Steve, I got to benefit from seeing the area through his eyes.

He grew up in Silicon Valley. He'd point and say, "Jony, that used to be an orchard of apricot trees." He understood the surrounding area in relationship to San Francisco. I got a sense of, even though it's fifty miles away, you have Napa Valley, where there are extraordinary wines and vineyards that are really, really beautiful. I think the adjacent areas can make such important contributions to people's sensibilities and to the culture that are often not appreciated because they can't be seen.

Steve and I ate lunch together nearly every day. Monday to Friday, we would either have lunch in the canteen at Apple or go out together. He was a vegetarian—really a pescatarian. We loved going for sashimi together. He had, I think, an extraordinary palate. We could eat just a tomato with great olive oil and we were never happier. He also had a wood-fired oven in his kitchen that he used primarily for pizzas. He had a productive garden. I could discern from tasting how recently something had been taken from the ground.

Working and eating together was all one thing—when we talked and wondered and interrogated the world around us, and there was that fluency of it all being one conversation. There's a danger in how people talk about things that are easy to measure with a number, speed or height or weight. People, particularly with products, will do that. Those are the easy conversations, and Steve and I understood that. The insidious danger is that, because they're easy conversations, you make the terrible mistake of thinking they're important. There are many, many really important things that are ignored because there aren't easy ways to measure them. How do you measure the taste of a tomato? That is divine.

The thing that is so extraordinary about food is that, of course, there is a functional imperative of nourishment, but how incredible that it doesn't stop there! I love looking forward to eating dinner. And I think eating with someone is an amazing way to explore ideas.

What I love about sitting at a table is that normally, it's very unusual to have a horizontal plane in front of you. But when it has food on it, it signals that it is a sacred space that's different from a picnic or eating on a park bench. It signals that the world can miss you and you're just with the people you're at the table with.

In our kitchen at home we have a very large dining table, a Nakashima. George Nakashima was a woodworker in New Hope, Pennsylvania. I've collected his furniture for years. One of the first pieces was a rocking chair that Heather used when she was nursing our boys.

When you're planning a house, you try and imagine how you're going to use it as one big machine. But there were things that surprised us. The kitchen I love because of that big table. It's a higgledy-piggledy mixture of books and typewriters and every menu that we've had for dinner parties—hundreds of them—on the walls.

But there's a more formal dining room, with a very long English dining table from 1780 and a beautiful crystal chandelier that wasn't modified to take electric lights. We use it almost every day. We light the candles in the chandelier. Even if it's just two of us, we tend to eat in the dining room. I never, ever thought that would be the case.

*Jony, what is your comfort food?*
It would be peas, just peas. And if I'm honest, a chocolate digestive, because they don't have those in America.

# FRIDA ESCOBEDO

When I'm asked why I love Mexico, and why Richard and I traveled there for nearly thirty years, the answer is the culture, the cities, the food, the seas, the mountains, and the history. But what I love most are the people.

The architect Frida Escobedo and I met in 2018. She had just won the international competition to design the Serpentine Gallery's annual summer pavilion in London. Her building brought the refined spirit of Mexico to Hyde Park.

Richard and I threw a fabulous party to celebrate this bright and beautiful young woman.

When she visited us at The River Cafe, Frida read our recipe for Deep-Fried Zucchini Flowers. The stunning colors remind me of Mexico—and, when she is not around, of Frida herself.

I grew up in Mexico City with two sisters. When I was five, the 1985 earthquake happened. Around the same time, my parents got divorced. Two earthquakes. They moved into separate houses but in neighborhoods close to each other, so that they could both still see their children all the time.

My father is a doctor and my mom is a sociologist. We grew up with a cook. But my dad is also very much into cooking. He makes simple but really delicious recipes. He cooked for us mostly on weekends, but also for breakfast and dinner sometimes. One of my favorite dishes from him is *torrijas*, which is the leftover bread that you have from the week that is a little bit hard. You put it in an egg batter with vanilla and cinnamon. It's like a Spanish version of French toast. Instead of using powdered sugar, he uses this raw sugar that comes in a cone shape, called *piloncillo*. You melt the piloncillo with a little bit of lemon zest and create a syrup.

My father loved to have me in the kitchen and he would share these recipes, most of them coming from my grandmother. He's great with soups and stews, like a mole de olla, which is a lighter version of a traditional mole, more like a soup, with vegetables and meat, slightly spicy.

A mole is a very intricate, elaborate paste made of chilies, spices, chocolate, banana . . . it really changes with every family and region in Mexico. So it can be a darker chocolate, or it can be made out of squash seeds, or it can be green or yellow, depending on the nuts or the spices that you use. It's like our version of curry. You can make it with chicken, with rice, with eggs, with quesadillas or *enfrijoladas*.

In every Mexican house, you have a mortar made of volcanic rock called a *molcajete*. You use it to make everything from salsas to moles. And it's passed on from generation to generation. My father made a special gift of the one he received when his grandmother passed away. It's very old and smooth on the inside. When I moved into my first apartment, I asked my dad to give it to me, and he said, "Not yet." But by the time I returned from getting my master's degree from the Harvard Graduate School of Design, he said I was ready to receive the molcajete.

With my mother, what I remember is having desserts outside. She's really good at making them, but one of my favorite things was that on a rainy day, she would say, "Would you like to get some cake and tea?" And we would drive to Polanco, which was actually very far away from where we lived. We'd go to this place in a little passage, on a pedestrian street inside one of the older buildings. And we would have a tart or cake or some chocolate and tea. It was such a treat to have this in the middle of the week. It seemed like a little celebration, an intimate time between her and me. No one else was in that bubble, so it felt really special.

It was a shock to go from Mexico to Cambridge, Massachusetts. There was a culture of spending very, very long hours working on your thesis. I had a very generous scholarship, so I had a small apartment that I didn't have to share. It was a blessing for me, because I could really manage my time. I had a small kitchen and a group of other Mexican students who liked to cook, so we started something called *Martes de Mescal*, or Mezcal Tuesday.

We would cook for each other, some of us bringing ingredients from our trips home to Mexico. We would either smuggle moles and tortillas or just cook small dishes and serve them with mezcal. We also invited friends who were not Mexican. It started a nice tradition, because when you're in architecture school, it's really heavy. There's a lot of pressure, and it's competitive. So it's a good reminder that you have a support system and people who will become your lifelong friends.

Sometimes we went out for Chinese food or for other inexpensive versions of eating out in Boston. I tried Mexican food there once and it was terrible. Real Mexican food is so different from region to region. You have the food from the coast, which is grilled fish and oysters and shrimp, very simply prepared. And then you have the more elaborate cuisine of Puebla and El Bajío, where the salsas are almost baroque in their making. And then Yucatán, where you have the pulled pork. I love the food there. It's so tasty and comforting. *Sopa de lima*, which is a chicken broth with *lima*, a kind of sweet lime, is food for the soul. If something bad has happened to you, go and have *sopa de lima*. It makes everything better.

I'm designing a restaurant in the U.S. for a dear friend named Gabriella Cámara, who has a famous restaurant in Mexico City called Contramar. The food is amazing, but it's also become a gathering space, a happy center for culture and people-watching. Everyone wants to go there to see and be seen. It's a democratic space.

The only other thing I've seen like that is the staff café at the Met. It was a big surprise. It's a canteen for all the employees. Max Hollein, the director, goes there for lunch, and the curators go there, but also the maintenance people and office people. It's a place where you can encounter everyone, having casual and spontaneous conversations. I like that it's diverse and you can have food from all over: Mexican, Indian, Chinese, Japanese.

I live in Chelsea when I'm in New York. I'm there every month. I cook at night. It's my way of relaxing when I come back from work, because lunch is so short in America. I just make something simple. I feel like I'm taking care of myself again.

*Frida, what is your comfort food?*
My father's *torrijas*. It's the thing that brings me back to my feet and reminds me that everything will be all right. The other thing is my mother's tarte Tatin. I associate that more with the celebratory aspect of life. We usually have it for birthdays and special occasions. She cooks a tarte Tatin, and everything is sweet and crisp again.

# ED RUSCHA

There's a small work of art by my bed. It's a River Cafe menu over which the artist Ed Ruscha has painted, in red block letters, the word *YUM*.

I have been an admirer of Ed's since the early 1970s. But I didn't get to know the man until he came to London for his exhibitions at the National Gallery and the Tate Modern. Over breakfasts at Claridge's and dinners at The River Cafe, we became friends.

In keeping with his iconoclastic nature, Ed was the first person ever to read one of his own recipes on our podcast. Fittingly for someone who makes his home in Los Angeles and the California desert, Ed's choice was a Cactus Omelet, made with nopalitos, the diced pads of the prickly pear cactus. I met up with Ed at his studio in L.A., where we were joined by his loyal dog, Dexter.

I was born in Omaha, Nebraska, in the very center of the United States. We moved to Oklahoma when I was about five years old. So that's where I grew up. I think back on it as a black-and-white movie, but as I go back there occasionally, I see that it's more progressive than I make it out to be. It's caught up to the rest of the world.

Back then, it was a cultural wasteland in a lot of ways—like, there was no such thing as an artichoke or an avocado. No sushi. I remember when pizza came into fashion in the 1950s. We didn't call it just pizza but pizza *pie*. I was in high school and it became a popular thing then. There were a half a dozen places in Oklahoma City, including one place that's still there called Sussy's.

My mom was the cook. It was all meat and potatoes. I particularly liked her pies, cherry and rhubarb. It was the Bible Belt, and since we were Catholic, people there called us "mackerel snappers," meaning people who eat fish on

Friday. One food that was a really big hit was okra, which my mom served fried. We had local okra from the farms and good corn almost every day. During World War II, we had a victory garden, our way of participating in the war effort by growing our own food: tomatoes, corn, celery, various other vegetables.

The only international food we had was Chinese. But every Chinese restaurant had a sign on the outside of the building that said CHINESE AND AMERICAN FOOD. You could get chop suey, but just in case, you could also get a hamburger. We'd go out for barbecue, too.

In 1961, I went to Europe for the first time with my mother and my brother. She got a little Citroën in Paris and drove it all over Europe: Yugoslavia, Spain, Portugal, Italy, Germany, France, and the British Isles. We even went to Ireland to try to trace my mother's heritage, but we struck out there. We traveled together for four or five months. Food-wise, we were on a budget, so we didn't eat anything particularly fancy. But just stumbling onto those tiny little wild strawberries in France was great. I'd never had anything like them before.

I have fruit growing behind my studio in Culver City. I was fortunate to get this building with a large backyard that I had no use for. I'd always wanted to grow citrus, so I thought, "Well, I'll just put an orchard in there." So I grow oranges and lemons, and also figs, pomegranates, and cherries. And then I've got some raised beds. I grow bhut jolokia, an Indian pepper also known as ghost pepper. It measures out to be the hottest pepper in the world.

The other thing I like to cook besides the cactus omelet is chili. I make it without onions, beans, or tomatoes. It takes a few hours, but it's worth it.

I barely eat when I'm painting. I will maybe have a banana or a piece of fruit, and that's my lunch. I don't eat three meals a day like I used to. In the '60s and '70s, it was the artistic tradition to stop working at 11:45 a.m. and have lunch with wine. Or to work in the studio all day, very solitary, and then go out.

I used to go to Mr. Chow in Beverly Hills. One time I was going there with a friend, and he said, "Can I bring a friend along?" His friend turned out to be Groucho Marx. He came in, sat down, and we all had a good time. But Groucho had his own food sent over from Nate'n Al's delicatessen up the street.

I loved all the loud Hollywood parties, but I don't miss them one iota. I go to the desert, east of Big Bear Lake. It's not the kind of desert like Palm Springs, with palm trees. We have Joshua trees, crazy, beautiful trees that look very spiky. They got called Joshua trees because the pioneers thought they looked like silhouettes of biblical figures.

We also have piñon pines, from which I harvest nuts if the squirrels don't get to them first. You pick the pinecones off the trees and very carefully take the little seeds out of them. It takes you about an hour, and you have to get the sap off your hands by washing them with gasoline. But they're extremely delicious—far more so than the pine nuts you buy at the supermarket.

*Ed, what is your comfort food?*
I would say some sort of soup. It's a traditionally healing sort of food. Preferably some kind of vegetable soup.

# Food Is Politics

The policies, opinions, and goals of our politicians and social leaders are well known. But talking about memories of food brings out other, often surprising dimensions. Who would have known Nancy Pelosi has chocolate ice cream for breakfast? Or guess that United States senator Adam Schiff is obsessed with his air fryer?

In his podcast episode, former vice president Al Gore not only explained how to peel a tomato but talked about his advocacy for countering climate change on a personal level—he has turned his family's farm in Tennessee into a progressive model of sustainable agriculture. Darren Walker, the president of the Ford Foundation, grew up in poverty in the American South and now prioritizes eliminating food deserts in urban areas.

Food activism is becoming politically charged, and what better way to tackle our biggest issues than to begin at our most communal space: the dinner table.

# NANCY PELOSI

U.S. congresswoman and former Speaker of the House Nancy Pelosi and I share the same political and personal concerns. The difference is, I wake up every morning worrying about the world, while Nancy goes to work every day to change the world.

I had the privilege of hosting a dinner for her at our London home. She loves Italian food as much as I do. She was born Nancy D'Alesandro in Baltimore and married a fellow Italian American, Paul Pelosi, in 1963. They have five children.

It was autumn when we met for *Ruthie's Table 4*. The River Cafe chefs were cooking Risotto Amarone, braising *cicoria*, and roasting pumpkin. But the ingredient we talked about most was not particularly seasonal: chocolate. For much of her life, Nancy's breakfast has included chocolate—usually in the form of ice cream. She chose to read our recipe for Chocolate Sorbet.

My earliest memories are about loving chocolate. I remember once, when I was a very little girl, my parents told my big brother, who was a teenager, "You can have the car if you bring home some ice cream for Nancy first." He brought vanilla ice cream home. I put it under the bed. I never ate it because it wasn't chocolate. Why would he bring me vanilla ice cream? I've always loved chocolate ice cream. We didn't have sodas or soft drinks in our home. But we had chocolate ice cream. And as time has gone by, I've loved it darker and darker and darker.

It is not an urban myth that I eat ice cream for breakfast. Ice cream is convenient. It's right there. It has a long shelf life. I don't have it every day, but it's a great way to start the day. When I was younger, I used to have a pint of it before I went to sleep. But as time has gone by, the later the chocolate, the less sleep I get.

I was the youngest of seven children, six boys and one girl. One of my brothers died when he was young, so I was really raised with five boys. My mother, may she rest in peace, bless her heart, had a cook. She wouldn't like me saying this, but she wasn't a big cook herself. Her family was from Campobasso, which is in the center of Italy. And her mother didn't cook, because her husband cooked. He was a chef. We would see him break the neck of an eel and cook these fabulous meals.

My understanding is that he sold pasta. He had one of those shops that sold products from Italy. So he was a foodie, and my grandmother was treated like a queen. She never did any housework and I never knew her to cook one thing. My grandfather was so beautiful and wonderful. I loved him so much. Every time I went to see him, he was going to teach me how to speak Italian. And every time I'd go, he'd start by getting out a map: "These are the different dialects of Italy." I could give you the map of Italy and the different dialects, but I don't know how to speak Italian because we'd start with that map every time.

My father's mother was born in Baltimore, but her parents, my great-grandparents, one was born in Venice and one was born in Genoa. So there was a lot of that Northern Italian influence in the food we ate.

From when I was in first grade, my father was the mayor of Baltimore. When I went away to college, he was still the mayor of Baltimore. So our routine my whole childhood was, he would come home for dinner and then he would go out to make all of his speeches in the evening in black tie. Everything was very formal in those days.

We ate dinner at around 5:30 because he'd have to go out on the campaign trail or to civic engagements. My husband, Paul, was born in San Francisco. To this day, he likes to dine at eight o'clock and I like to eat at 5:30, like a peasant.

Our family was devoutly Catholic and fiercely patriotic, proud of our Italian

American heritage. My parents related their Catholicism to taking care of other people. My brother Tommy used to tell me that when he was a little boy, people would come to our door and Mommy would always be giving them food. Even in her old age, she was giving ice cream to children, and they knew to come to her door. It was all about nourishment, one way or another.

I went away to the only college I was allowed to go to, a woman's Catholic school in Washington, D.C., called Trinity College. It was not exactly a culinary delight. Don't tell anybody I told you this, but we used to go down to the dining room in the middle of the night and break into the freezer to get ice cream. It was locked, so you could only lift up the lid a little bit and then put the scooper in and pull some ice cream out.

It was hard to tell a flavor in the dark. You couldn't tell if it was chocolate or peach or strawberry. Sometimes we would order pizza so that one of us could say to the guard, "I'm waiting here for the pizza I ordered," while the others would go down and steal the ice cream.

After my husband and I got married, we lived in New York. New York for me was heaven. When I was a young girl, our family went to New York regularly to eat dinner and see plays, all that. So here we were, young, married, and in Manhattan. We didn't have children yet, the first year. We had, shall we say, Champagne taste and beer-bottle purses. So we'd save up and go to the best restaurants. Or we would just go to the neighborhood Italian American restaurant. New York was great because, for example, if you wanted to have chopped chicken livers, oh my gosh—the best place in the world for chopped liver.

Then we had children. We had no help. When you have five children in six years, help doesn't come anywhere near your house. It was intense, but I would love to do it all over again.

We had a lovely apartment on Beekman Place. We didn't realize how small it was until we moved into a big home in San Francisco. San Francisco is a very Italian American city. The Bank of America, which used to be based in San Francisco, was originally the Bank of Italy. And the influence is very Italian in terms of food. So it was a comfortable move for me.

There were certain things that I carried over from my childhood to my own children. We always had to have a tablecloth. That wasn't so unusual back then, but now it's almost seen as a luxury. We never had a meal without linens and a tablecloth. When we go out to dinner, it's very, very important that there be a tablecloth. The tablecloth is not only a tablecloth, it absorbs sound. So it's a little calmer when you have that.

When the kids were growing up, I had different things I would try. When they came home from school, I'd say, "Let's have dessert now, at four o'clock, and then we'll have dinner later." Then I decided, because they came home hungry, to have dinner at four o'clock. We tried all kinds of things to satisfy their appetites.

My children will not say that I was a great cook. I mean, it was standard fare. Then, as they got older, I just got tired of washing pots and pans. So I developed a practice where I would go to someplace like MacArthur Park, which was a restaurant that had the greatest ribs. Or we'd go to LaRocca, which was a seafood place. Or we'd go to Chinatown for Peking duck and I would bring it home.

We sat down to these meals with linens and I'd make a salad. When I went to Congress, my youngest daughter, Alexandra, said, "Mother, I'm so proud of you because you're a pioneer." I said, "Because I'm a woman member of Congress?" She said, "No. Remember when you used to cook? And then you stopped? Well, now a lot of people have stopped cooking. But you were the first to stop."

We had many events at our home, all the time. We always had food, so the kids would help prepare. When we had dinners—I hope none of our guests hear this—here's how we would do it. We bought one of those little inflatable pools for children, filled it with water, and washed the lettuce in there. Then you put it in a pillowcase, tie a knot in it, and put it in the washing machine on the spin cycle. You have to be careful, because sometimes I'll tell people about this and they'll get mixed up and put their lettuce in the dryer. It has to be the spin cycle of the washing machine. And then the lettuce comes out crispy.

I always say to other members of Congress, "Know your 'why.'" Why do you think you should be in Congress? What motivates you?

My "why"—why I went from the kitchen to Congress, from housewife to House Speaker—was that one in five children in America goes to sleep hungry at night. I couldn't handle it. I mean, we had five children. You think, "In America, one of these children will not have food and will go to sleep hungry." Now take that idea globally. It's sinful. It's immoral. That was my motivation. And if they were hungry, they weren't learning to their capacity. They were not feeling that their needs were being met.

It is a kitchen-table issue for some families. Are they going to be able to put food on the table, pay the rent, pay the utility bill, pay for their children to go to school if that requires some payment? So the food issue—that one in five children goes to sleep hungry at night—was my why. Every step of the way, I have worked for policies to alleviate that, not only food programs and lunch programs, but also improving the standard of living so that people don't have to choose between paying the rent and feeding their children.

*Nancy, what is your comfort food?*
Ice cream!

# AL GORE

Al Gore was one of the very first guests on *Ruthie's Table 4*, in November 2021.

Listening to the former vice president of the United States tell me how best to chop a tomato to make a Pappa al Pomodoro—a Tuscan tomato and bread soup—was more than special. Hearing that deep voice of his reminded me of the many times I had heard him speak: on climate change, inequality, and sustainability, both in public and in private.

The inconvenient truth about global warming that he warned us of in his film, *An Inconvenient Truth*, twenty years ago could not be more resonant in the world today. But even in the face of the alarming truths unfolding around us, Al remains a positive and strong political force.

Al spoke from his home in Tennessee, where he oversees his family's farm, Caney Fork Farms, regenerating the health of its soil, animals, waterways, air, and more. When he is in London and visits The River Cafe, he brings warmth and inspiration to everyone—especially me.

Every single year of my life, I went back and forth between Washington, D.C., and Tennessee. My father had been in the U.S. House of Representatives for about ten years when I was born and went to the Senate when I was four years old. As soon as there was a spring vacation or a Christmas vacation off, we drove back to Tennessee. It was quite a contrast to enjoy the food on the farm and fresh from the garden, and then go back to the old Fairfax Hotel in Washington, which was owned by a distant cousin. The food in Washington, D.C., was quite different from that in Tennessee. But in my mother's kitchen, it was pretty much the same in both locations.

It was a small apartment at the Fairfax, two bedrooms. My sister and I shared a bedroom. There was one bathroom in the entire apartment and a small kitchen. It did have a dining area and a living room, but that was it, it was a small apartment. Believe it or not, I really don't ever remember getting room service. My mother was a good cook. She was a lawyer, one of the first women to graduate from Vanderbilt Law School back in the 1930s. My sister, when she got older, was a good cook as well. I remember one time when my mother and my sister both went on a tear competitively, making soufflés. They just became entranced with the whole notion, and for several weeks, I would come home from school and there would be one or two different small soufflés there.

In Tennessee, we had fried chicken and barbecue, fresh vegetables. We would pay attention to when the new corn was ready and when the vegetables were coming in. We had a big garden on the farm. My grandmother also had a garden, which she worked in pretty much constantly, and she canned food. She was of the generation that really prepared for what might come by canning lots of food in her cellar, and I would help her occasionally.

Southern food has changed over time. It's very influenced by Black American recipes. I don't know that the full credit for Southern cuisine that should go to Black Americans has been widely understood, but it certainly is the case. Nowadays Nashville Hot Chicken is a distinctive brand that has gone far and wide. Barbecue is still identified with the South, and Tennessee takes a lot of pride in its barbecue. I had a barbecue team when I was in the U.S. Senate. Every year, they have a huge barbecue contest in Memphis, Tennessee. The judges primarily graded on taste, but the presentation was a factor, too. I was in the Senate, and the point of it for us was not necessarily to win the contest, but to meet all the people who came by.

I don't consider myself a great cook by any stretch of the imagination. But during the pandemic, like a lot of people, I picked up a few new skills because the chance to go out to restaurants was foreclosed. And I'm surrounded by a lot of fresh food at the farm.

I've been pretty much a vegan for over ten years now. I occasionally supplement my diet with some sustainable seafood. My kids are all good cooks, including my son, the youngest, who learned cooking from his grandmother, my mother. I remember when he was quite young, she taught him how to make bread. She had her own recipe that was absolutely delicious coming hot straight out of the oven. He loved it so much that he got her to teach him how to make it.

The family farm is now my farm. Starting a little over ten years ago, I converted it to a regenerative agriculture farm. We also have livestock. I am a vegan cattle farmer—there are not many of us! Rotational grazing, where you manage the livestock in cooperation with the vegetables and fruits, really is an effective way to make the soil healthier and make the farm successful. Regenerative agriculture is a farmer-led movement and it has also led to some new food chains. We sell at farmers' markets and to local chefs in Nashville. And we have several hundred boxes of produce and proteins each week that go through a program called Community Supported Agriculture. We deliver the boxes. We give 25 percent of them to a food bank in Nashville, and did so particularly during the hard times of the Covid-19 pandemic.

It's a connection that I established when I was a boy. Every summer of my life, I worked on this farm and developed quite an attachment to it. Then I moved back to Nashville and to the farm, which is outside of Nashville, when I made a transition out of politics and into the business world . . . involuntarily. But I've enjoyed it a great deal.

I have become close friends with quite a few of the chefs in Nashville, which is becoming quite a foodie city. Every year at the farm, I have a conference in the fall, after the harvest, called The Climate Underground conference, which looks at the health of the soil and the economic health of the farmers and the chefs. During the pandemic, a lot of restaurants struggled, but the chefs that have become friends over the years really stepped up to provide food for populations in the community that fell on hard times in the year 2020. In many communities, it's a remarkable development, that chefs have become a new variety of superhero.

There are so many so-called food deserts in Black and brown and Indigenous communities, where you might have just a gas station with an attached mart that sells Slim Jims, some kind of jerky, and snacks—food that's not very healthy for you. There has been a growing recognition in those communities and others that we would all benefit by developing a healthier connection to the sources of our food and paying more attention to the way it's harvested and prepared.

Where schools are concerned, I have partnered with Alice Waters from Chez Panisse in Berkeley. One of her programs is called the Edible Schoolyard, which has gone beyond the pilot phase and is now being expanded into the University of California system and in school districts around the country to educate children in school about gardening and growing and preparing food. They're trying to move past the era where people thought that food came from the grocery store and didn't give it any further thought beyond that. Of course, it's so much better and healthier in every way when people take responsibility for eating enough fresh vegetables and fruits, cutting back on meat consumption, and paying attention to the health of the meals they consume.

Agriculture can be one of the biggest solutions to the climate crisis. It cannot solve the crisis by itself, for sure. The main task is to stop burning all these fossil fuels. We are putting more than 175 million tons of manmade global-warming pollution into the atmosphere every day. But it was not until 1950 that the majority of the greenhouse gases came from something other than farming. And it was not until the 1970s that the majority of the accumulated global warming pollution was no longer from agriculture.

What happened was, in part, the use of heavy plowing and a reductionist model for growing food that says just get rid of everything except what you want to grow, and then use heavy chemical inputs and insecticides and herbicides and synthetic nitrogen fertilizer, which was only invented in Germany 115 years ago. In that stretch of time, we have seen a massive outgassing of carbon dioxide from the topsoils. People talk about planting trees to pull carbon dioxide back out of the atmosphere, and it's something we certainly need to do. But we also need to remember that if you look at all the carbon in every tree in the world, plus every plant in the world, there's three times that much carbon in the first ten centimeters of topsoils around the world.

By sharply reducing the amount of plowing and using natural fertilizing and pest-control techniques; using cover crops, always keeping roots in the soil, not letting it lie loose; using perennials where we can; using rotational grazing—these techniques can reverse the flow of global-warming pollution out of the soil and put a large amount of carbon dioxide back in the soil. So regenerative agriculture not only produces healthier foods and healthier communities, it also contributes to a healthier planet by becoming a key part of our arsenal in combating the climate crisis.

*Al, what is your comfort food?*
I would prefer one of The River Cafe's thin vegan pizzas. Accompanied by fried zucchini flowers.

# MALA GAONKAR

In the early days of our friendship, I was so taken by Mala Gaonkar, a founding partner of the investment firm Lone Pine Capital, as well as a writer and public health philanthropist.

Some time later, I went to dinner at her family home full of contemporary art. Mala was in the kitchen when I arrived, apron on, finishing the subtle curries, delicate rice, vegetables cooked from family recipes, and regional Indian desserts she'd prepared for us all.

Mala's focus is on multidisciplinary thinking, including using the tools of data science, AI, and behavioral science to solve public health problems.

There is also her short fiction; her new investment firm, SurgoCap Partners, founded in 2022, the largest hedge fund launch by a woman; and the immersive theater piece she cowrote with David Byrne, *Theater of the Mind*.

Mala read our recipe for Pistachio Cake, of which she is a devotee, having made it for every one of her sons' birthdays.

---

I'm from South India. My story is pretty straightforward in some ways for that period of Indian immigration to America. I was born in 1969. Many people don't know this, but as soon as the Civil Rights Act was passed, there was also a change in the immigration law. There had been veiled restrictions on people from certain places of origin. As soon as they were lifted, my parents were among the first Indians to come over to the U.S., to become graduate students and then academics.

If you or I were to go to Mars, it would be less of a leap than it was for them. They both came on scholarships from rural India. They came from the Malabar Coast, just south of Goa, which is a haven for spice growing.

They were both in the sciences, my father in the mathematical area and my mother in molecular biology.

I'm consistently astonished by their bravery and the gallantry with which they went out with open curiosity into the world. I would love to see us all tap into that a bit more. It was something they did with great gusto and they were happy. But they were also very happy to go back to India. Shortly after my sister was born, when I was about seven, we moved to Bangalore.

Neither one of my parents was really affiliated with the stove in any particularly distinguished way, but my maternal grandmother was a great cook. She always had something pickling and believed that anything could be pickled. At one point she even pickled banana skins. That wasn't successful, but she pickled hibiscus flowers and gooseberries.

In India, there's a lunch box everyone has called a tiffin carrier, with these stacked little stainless-steel boxes. There's a whole bento-box ritual to it, all these Ayurvedic traditions around how many sours and how many sweets, everything architected. My little tiffin was a bit less polished. But I'd take it to school, and I remember the tastes of yogurt and rice and pickles.

Breakfast was very simple, maybe a *dosa* or some lentils or a *rasam*, which is a spicy seasoned broth. And then I'd come home to a very simple supper. But it was all delicious because the food was very fresh. I'd go to the markets with my grandmother or the lady who helped out with the house. The markets were overwhelming, big piles of endless varieties of chilies and greens. I remember when the season for Kashmiri apple juice arrived. I have very strong, Proustian memories of these little flavors and smells, and of Indian street food, which is really just a spectacular celebration of humanity.

I went to Harvard and there wasn't much opportunity for cooking there. It was more just taking whatever was offered to you in the dining hall and adding hot sauce to it. But at that time of life, you're so overwhelmed with intellectual curiosity that you don't think about food as much. You're absorbing so much that's new in terms of relationships, friendships, ideas, and people.

I wandered from food into philosophy. The arc of that was very much around failing. I think it's important to make mistakes and fail a bit in life. I differentiate between failures of hubris and failures of curiosity; the latter is more where you're open-mindedly trying something and you mess up. That's how you learn and move on. My first class at Harvard was one where I did very poorly, but it was also the class that was most impactful. It was taught by the great philosopher John Rawls and it was about developing the ideal society. What we all had to do as a class was get together and decide what the ideal society would be. If you were behind an invisible veil and didn't know anything about your status in that world—your race, your gender—what kind of society would you create?

Ultimately we decided that we would want a society where the worst-off person would be not just okay but actually flourishing—because we could well be that person. That really transformed me. I'd had a very utilitarian view of the world—it was my way of coping, I think, with having grown up in a very poor country. Though the Rawls class, in terms of my transcript, was a failure, it was transformative in terms of my mind-set and what I did later, in trying to do a bit of good in the world.

My first big philanthropic project was around sanitation and subsidized toilets for poor populations across South Asia. Work was going well and I wanted to give back right away—I didn't want to wait until I was an elderly person. I thought, "Oh, this is going to be great. We've got all the answers. This is going to be about better sanitation for all." And it didn't really work. When we visited some of the toilets that we'd subsidized, most of them were being used as chicken coops.

The bottom line is that it was another failure—but one of curiosity and hope, I'd argue, but also a bit of hubris. I realized, okay, it's important to really listen, and that led me to Paul Farmer, a really dear friend and a great innovator in terms of how public health could be delivered. [Farmer, who died in 2022, was a Harvard professor and doctor who cofounded the nonprofit organization Partners In Health, which provides health care to the poorest populations of developing countries.] He was a real mentor to me, teaching me about listening to what's happening on the ground, rather than assuming.

My passion for cooking came with the birth of my children, Lucas and Rohan. We had just set up Lone Pine, so I was a young working woman and a mother. Their father, Oliver, and I came to England for his work. We thought we'd stay briefly but ended up staying twenty years.

I firmly believe that, when done well, business is a creative activity. I define "creative activity" as connecting different areas in fresh and new ways. To be good at pretty much anything, you have to think creatively, so I don't see the dichotomy between cooking and all the other aspects of my life as much as someone might from the outside. If you're a philanthropist and you want to do well—particularly in the public health area—the business of food, the public health aspects of food, and the creative aspects of food are intertwined in some really interesting ways.

I was introduced to David Byrne by our good mutual friend Brian Eno. One thing that David and I learned a lot about for our show, *Theater of the Mind*, is how the brain processes food. The brain creates illusions around taste. David told me about this West African berry called the miracle fruit, or Synsepalum dulcificum. It's a little olive-shaped red berry that grows on a bush. When you chew on it, it tastes quite normal. But it binds to the sweet receptors in your tongue, so temporarily, for a couple of minutes, if you eat anything sour, it activates the sweet receptor and you get this burst of sugar in your mouth. You could literally be chewing on a lemon and it will taste like an ice cream sundae—a crazy experience. So we put that into our immersive theater piece. Some people who went through it started yelling out in delight, like children, because it's such an intimate part of your sensory system, taste.

*Mala, what is your comfort food?*
I think of a very specific *rasam* that my grandmother used to make for me when I was ill. It was something I never could make and I never quite figured out the exact flavors.

But here's an interesting story. Someone told me about a woman who lives in Chennai. Her mission in life was to compile all of the pickle recipes and *rasam* recipes in South India into books. She systematically did this job. But the *rasam* book had gone out of print. So I wrote to her and got this PDF in the mail. Her name is Usha R. Prabakaran. Now she has her books on Amazon, *Usha's Pickle Digest* and *Usha's Rasam Digest*. I could not recommend them more.

The rasam I was looking for is very simple. You make it with a little bit of *toor dal*, which is yellow lentils, and you grind them up with coriander. Essentially, it's a lentil stock that you add chilies to. You do this by making a *tadka*, oil infused with some mustard seeds and a bit of chili or any other whole spices, which you sprinkle on top. It's delicious, and any cold you have will be cured.

# SIMON SEBAG MONTEFIORE

I would like to think that Simon Sebag Montefiore and I have much in common. We were both lucky enough to have what he calls loving and indulgent parents. In addition, our great-grandparents fled the pogroms of Romanov Russia, and we both see food as one of the focuses of our lives.

Simon and I also like to tell and listen to stories, about food and history, food and fiction, food and exploring. Simon has lived these stories—and documents them in his television programs and his books: *Catherine the Great and Potemkin*, *Young Stalin*, *Stalin: The Court of the Red Tsar*, *The Romanovs: 1613–1918*, and most recently, *The World: A Family History of Humanity*.

Simon specifically asked to read our recipe for Cannellini Bean Soup. Whenever he comes to The River Cafe, we give him a jar of beans to take home.

I chose Cannellini Bean Soup because bean soup has played a big part in my life. My career as a writer (and a lover of bean soup) started off in the early 1990s with the fall of the Soviet Union, when I was often in the wonderful country of Georgia. It became my favorite home away from home. I was there for all its wars, its coups, and its tragedies, and I came to love its food. *Lobio*, a kind of bean stew, is a Georgian national dish, along with *satsivi*, a chicken in walnut sauce, and *khachapuri*, their cheese bread.

The Caucasus, of which Georgia is a part geographically, is fascinating because it's the borderland of empires, Russian, Turkish, and Iranian. There's a huge Persian influence, a huge Ottoman-Turkish influence, and then the Russians. Georgian food is unique and special, but if I had to describe it, there is a touch of Persian and also of Lebanese and Turkish. But it's not like any other cuisine, because it's filled with coriander and tarragon and walnuts and *ajika*, which is a sort of chili sauce. It's very original.

Joseph Stalin was a Georgian. He was also a great trencherman. He loved *lobio*, *khachapuri*, and *chakapuli*, a lamb stew—one of his few winning features, I should say. His real name was Joseph Dzhugashvili. Many Georgian names end in "-adzi" or "-shvili," which means "son of." He came from Gori, which is a small town in Georgia, and until he was about thirty or forty, he was completely Georgian. He spoke Georgian. But his mother was very ambitious for him. She wanted him to be a bishop or archbishop and got him into the seminary in Tbilisi, where he trained to be a priest. There, he was taught Russian. If he hadn't been taught Russian, he never could have ruled the Soviet Union.

The interesting thing about Stalin is that he reinvented himself several times. He became Stalin, which means "man of steel," in about 1912. Stalin is a Russian-style name. But he was a Georgian in terms of eating and drinking. And the thing he really loved was Georgian singing. Surprisingly, he was the star choirboy of the seminary. His falsetto was supposed to be the most beautiful falsetto. And he remained a good tenor and often sang with his henchmen even when he was the dictator. So he was this rather sinister choirboy.

In Georgia, they have something called the *supra*, which is a feast, and a *tamada*, the person who is elected the toastmaster. Stalin was always the *tamada* at his feasts. Even though he was a Marxist, a Soviet leader, and became a Russian imperialist, too, he was always Georgian. His Georgian accent was very strong.

The *tamada* tells stories, makes toasts, and quite often goes around the table and clinks glasses with different people. But what's unique about Stalin is that he was a storyteller. Which brings us back to my food stories.

I'd been an investment banker, believe it or not. But when the Soviet Union was falling apart, I left investment banking and went out there. Some of my favorite moments were in Georgia, eating *lobio* beans.

I covered the Ossetian War in 1990 and accompanied Georgian forces into the war zone. Ossetia, north of Tbilisi, is a region that broke away from Georgia and is backed by Putin. Once, I was invited to a funeral supper at the top of a beautiful mountain with these amazing Georgian churches. The fighters leaned their guns against a tree. There was a huge table laid out for a *supra*. The food was piled high. Three boys had been killed in the village and this was their funeral supper.

We all sat down and the *tamada* took control. We made toasts; I made a speech, several speeches in fact; and everyone got drunker and drunker, and everyone wept, and more and more food kept arriving. Then, after a bit, I said to the soldiers, "I guess the funeral happened earlier and the boys were buried earlier?" They said, "No. They're with us." They lifted up the tablecloth and the bodies were under the table. So you can see why I have a visceral feeling for Georgian feasts.

I understood the Georgian way of telling stories through food because we Jews do that, too. My family was a very Jewish family. My father's family, the Sebag-Montefiores, were Jewish gentry, if such a thing exists—sort of fox-hunting Jews, though I don't believe Jews fit into any British class. My mother's family—she would kill me for saying this—were shtetl Jews from Lithuania, Poland, and Odessa. They got out when the pogroms began in 1903 to '04.

But they were tricked. They bought tickets for New York, but after about two days at sea, they were told, "I'm afraid that you're getting off here." In Ireland. So my family said, "Hang on a sec, we bought tickets for New York and we haven't seen the Statue of Liberty." They were told, "Sorry, look at your tickets." They looked at the tickets and they didn't say "New York" but "New Cork." So they got off there and settled in Limerick until they were driven out in a pogrom and came to Newcastle.

My father's family has a longer story. The Sebags came from Morocco.

Sebag, that's an Arabic name, and I am so proud to be descended from Arab Jews. The Montefiores were originally called, we think, Carvajal, which is Spanish. They were expelled from Spain in 1492. They went to Portugal, but they were expelled from there in 1498. So they went back to Spain and converted to Catholicism. But they were only pretending. They were crypto-Jews. When Philip II was trying to recruit governors to govern New Spain, which was Mexico, he gave Luis de Carvajal the job of governing a huge province, the New Kingdom of León, which covered today's Texas.

But there was a feud with the viceroy. Their servants spied on them. The Carvajals were denounced for secretly being Jews, and most of the family were burnt alive in Mexico City. This was around 1600. One son got away and went to Italy. He adopted the name Montefiore, which is the name of a Tuscan village. The Montefiores came to London in the 1790s, and one of them, Moses Montefiore, made a fortune, was knighted by Queen Victoria, was given a baronetcy, and became a British and Jewish philanthropist. He traveled the world to intervene for British interests and to save Jews from persecution from Morocco to Syria, meeting Tsar Nicholas I, the Egyptian ruler Muhammed Ali, and the Ottoman sultan. Quite a character. I am descended from his Moroccan nephew Sir Joseph Sebag-Montefiore.

My father was a doctor who was also a psychiatrist. We grew up in a very strange household, because the surgery was under our house in Kensington. He had all sorts of patients. He saw lots of people for free, but also he had well-known patients such as Peter Sellers, Dudley Moore, and Peter Cook. They actually did a sketch about him. Because whatever you said to my father, whatever terrible thing you'd done as a child, he would always say, "Don't worry, that's perfectly normal." So there's a sketch where they go to a psychiatrist, and to everything they say, he responds, "Don't worry, that's perfectly normal."

I've got three brothers. I'm the youngest of the whole family. We were always told, "Never repeat anything that you see in this house, because it would ruin your father." But my parents were very open, so we knew all the stuff that was happening. People would arrive in the middle of the night having had a row with their wife, or somebody was giving birth. It was like growing up in a theater. It was very exciting and fascinating—perfect training for a writer.

My mother did the cooking and there'd always be delicious food, but not really Jewish food. Actually very English. Roast chickens, roast lamb.

She was born in England. Her grandfather was the first Jewish lord mayor elected in Newcastle. When he was campaigning, they used to say, "We hear you lie in bed all day." He'd reply, "So would you, if you were married to Mrs. Woolf." It worked very well; it won him the election. I've got a picture of her in my room, and she does look quite beguiling.

Food was all-important in our house. We were absolute epicureans who lived for food—food and books. I still live for eating—and reading. Boarding school was a shock. The food was appalling, for a start. And because I was Jewish, I had to have special food. I remember once going to the kitchen and there was a very old lady plucking a chicken. They said, "That's your food."

After boarding school, I went to Cambridge and studied history. I ate in the dining room sometimes, but what I really loved doing was eating at a great Turkish kebab house called Omar and Ozzy. We used to go there every night, and we lived on that delicious food.

Whenever I travel anywhere, I want to experience the food. One of the reasons why I've often written about family history, such as in *The Romanovs*, or my global history in *The World: a Family History*, is that it's a way of conveying not only continuity but also depth, the juice and the grit of life. I've always wanted readers to know what people were wearing, what music they listened to, and what food they were eating. Food is what families do together. Even families that barely hang together still eat together, don't they? And of course, there are sometimes chefs who became part of history: one of the most famous was Antonin Carême, the famous French chef of Prince Talleyrand who also cooked for Napoleon, Tsar Alexander I, and George IV of Britain.

Food is a hugely important part of world history and my specialty, Russian history. Until about one hundred fifty years ago, there were still massive famines all the time around the world. But in the late nineteenth century and early twentieth, scientific improvements in fertilizer and medical advances enabled the explosion of the world population. Most of the famines in the twentieth century were actually man-made famines, failures of supply, or the consequence of war and political policies. In the 1880s and 1890s, there was a huge famine in Russia, which the Tsar Alexander III denied existed. After the 1917 Revolution, there was a series of appalling Russian and Ukraine famines.

There were two Russian revolutions, one in February '17 and one in October '17. For a while, it looked like the Bolsheviks would keep power but lose most of the Russian Empire. But they faced a spasm of wars, which they conducted from the center, basing themselves in Moscow, and they reconquered much of Russia. Then they started to retake all the imperial provinces and the ethnic groups that had been part of the Tsarist Empire. That included Georgia and Ukraine, which was very decisive, because Ukraine was the breadbasket of the Russian Empire.

Traditionally, Ukrainian grain was exported out of Odessa and Nikolayev to the world. But when Stalin started to collectivize the farms in the late 1920s, he especially victimized the Ukrainians and other minority peoples. The famine struck not just Ukraine but also North Caucasus and Kazakhstan. A million and a half Kazakhs also died during collectivization. There was a huge famine while Stalin sold food abroad. So the creation of the

Soviet Union really was based around shortage of food. That was how Stalin broke the peasantry and broke the Ukrainians—by starving them.

Putin has a special connection to food because his grandfather was a chef. Not quite Carême, but he was a chef at the Hotel Astoria in St. Petersburg. While he was there, he cooked for everyone, including Rasputin and all the grand dukes. When the revolution happened, he joined the Soviet secret police, the Cheka, later the NKVD, as a chef. He cooked for Lenin and Stalin. Stalin's chefs had to be secret police. They were called the "service staff" and worked within the NKVD.

I don't think Putin is an epicurean at all. He seems to be a very unsympathetic, harsh, somewhat joyless man. Not very interested in culture, though he does read history books.

When I wrote my first book, *Catherine the Great and Potemkin*, I was approached by the Russian minister of culture and also people in the president's office. They asked me, "Could you write a little essay about this subject?" because the book hadn't been translated into Russian.

I wrote the essay. Then they said to me, "A certain important person is very interested in reading your book and finding out about the Crimea and how Catherine and Prince Potemkin took it and Ukraine." This was in 1999, 2000. We were all filled with hope about Vladimir Putin, that he was possibly a liberal. George W. Bush raved about him.

You may wonder why Russians don't have their own books on this subject. The reason is because under Stalin, Catherine the Great and Potemkin were very out of fashion because their love lives were so decadent, so they weren't studied very much. After my book was translated into Russian, I was approached again by the minister of culture, who said, "A certain personage loved your book and he would like to give you a present."

Of course, with Vladimir Putin, I worried about what the present was going to be. But it was: "We are opening Stalin's archives. Would you like to be the first to have access to them?" So that became the book *Stalin: The Court of the Red Tsar*.

But jump ahead twenty-two years, to when Putin wrote his essay saying Ukraine doesn't exist as a state and as a people, quoting stuff from history books like mine. That's when I realized that he was going to invade Ukraine.

My wife, Santa Montefiore, is also a writer. We're very pescatarian. We love tuna and we grill a lot of swordfish. My favorite dish is an amazing pasta filled with fresh tomatoes, fresh onions, fresh chili, garlic, and fish. I often put sardines in it, or sea bass, and it's quite spicy. I put a lot of chili in it.

When I'm not writing, I don't do anything. I spend the whole time sitting in cafés, phoning people, texting people, and reading the paper. Which is the best thing. But when I am writing, I live like a cenobite, like a monk. I live in a very disciplined way and get up really early in the morning.

Writing *The World: A Family History of Humanity* was definitely the hardest thing I've ever done. Obviously it's an insanely ambitious project. It tells the whole of world history, from the Stone Age to the Drone Age, through families. Some of the families you've heard of: the Romanovs, Habsburgs, Rothschilds, Kennedys, Trumps. The Herod family of Judea. The Ptolemies of Egypt. Many of them are quite unpleasant families, like the Kim family of North Korea. We follow those families over five generations. But other families you won't have heard of. Some of them are enslaved families, some are families of doctors. The great thing about following family lines is that in terms of diversity, it's a great way to cover every place the same. And now I've just finished updating and revising my book *Jerusalem—The Biography: A History of the Middle East*—three thousand years of history. That's hard to do. But a balanced history of the Middle East is essential.

*Simon, what is your comfort food?*
Tarte Tatin, with the sugar burnt on top. It is the most delicious thing on earth.

# DARREN WALKER

Some years ago, a friend led me across a crowded room with the words, "Talk to this man *about food*, Ruthie. He's as passionate about it as you are." This was Darren Walker.

So I held back all my questions about the social, philanthropic work Darren was doing as president of the Ford Foundation, at the Council of Foreign Relations, the Institute for Urban Design, and the New York City Ballet.

Darren was born in Louisiana and raised mainly in Texas. Listening to him talk about the poverty in which he grew up gave me an understanding of where his deep values and ethical concerns originate. He read our recipe for Prosciutto and Figs, saying, "Figs are plentiful in the American South. I had them in just about everything."

I was born on August 28, 1959. Place of birth: Charity Hospital, Lafayette, Louisiana.

It was a really challenging place. I was born to a single mother. I never knew my father, but in many ways it made me resilient. I remember one person saying to my mother, "What ails your boy? Something ails your boy." Of course, what ailed me was that I was a little queer boy, and that was, for some, an anathema. That my mother seemed to be so comfortable and supportive of me was also an oddity.

My mother worked a lot and she always did her very best to cook. When she wanted to really treat us, she cooked my favorite jambalaya: shrimp, andouille sausage, and chicken in a deep-black roux made in an old skillet with bell peppers and onions. It was just divine.

We weren't far from the Gulf Coast. You could find shrimp and crawfish

and catfish, all the things that I used to love. Then you put McIlhenny hot sauce on it—on everything—and it was beyond delicious. My mother, to this day, intuitively knows how to make a great gumbo and great cornbread stuffing for the turkey at Thanksgiving. Gumbos, étouffées—these are the sorts of things that I grew up on. My mother, who is Creole, is a master chef when it comes to good old-fashioned Creole foods.

In the South, regular old working-class Southerners had in their backyards, before organic farming became chic, fig trees, pecan trees, mulberry trees, all sorts of trees I remember picking things from. It was a magical place in spite of the fact that we were poor.

There were certain occasions, though, when there were foods that absolutely repulsed me. Foods that members of my family, especially my elders, ate. I detest what I call slave food. For example, the remnants of the cow that the owners discarded. This would include the intestines, which are called chitlins. Pig's feet, chicken necks, the things that the enslaved people had to eat because they were not allowed to experience the bounty of the produce and poultry and meats that they themselves cultivated.

The contradictions of our culture play out in food. For me, part of it is just the trauma of having been poor and Black in America and saying, "Whatever is associated with that, I'll reject it." I'm not sure it's really fair, because there are lots of people who love chitlins and pig's feet. I mean, my French friends love pig's feet.

There would be no great American food without the food of African Americans, including the foods that we brought with us on the passage to America, such as the rice that is now so deeply embedded in American food, especially Southern food. When I think about the South and regional cuisine, it's important to understand the role of class and race and the status of African Americans.

Then we talk about the food of the Creole community. This is the complexity of the American South. Creole people are the people of the southern part of Louisiana. Creole is primarily a result of African enslaved women who were impregnated by their owners. Places like Martinique and Haiti were in some ways the origins of Creole culture, but New Orleans became the center of the Creole world. And it's important to understand the Louisiana Purchase. Thomas Jefferson facilitated the purchase of that massive part of America that France owned, where French culture and French foods were already established. The arrivals of large numbers of enslaved people really changed the texture of the food. It became more spicy, richer than in other parts of the United States, where the spices were really not a part of the food tradition. Food is a part of the racial history of the country.

My first restaurant experience was at the age of thirteen, when I worked as a busboy. It was a very nice seafood restaurant in Texas. When you're a busboy, you sit at the bottom of the organization, along with the dishwasher. Your job is to be as discreet and invisible as you can as you proceed around the room, taking away the things that people no longer want. That experience was profound because it was the first time that I truly understood what it felt like to be invisible, because people simply did not acknowledge my very existence.

The professionals who worked in the oil refineries dined there: an all-white clientele. The back of the house was primarily Black and Latino. What it did for me was instantiate a sense of what it feels like to be marginalized. And I think about that today: how many people feel invisible.

I went to the University of Texas in Austin, which, for me, coming from my background and community, was like going to Paris. The reality of race and class really plays out in college. I lived in a dorm with people from all over Texas—almost exclusively white, because University of Texas at that time had over forty thousand students, but fewer than a thousand were African Americans, and half of them were athletes. So it was, from that perspective, a very lonely place. But I'm an extrovert by nature and I found my way.

I was very engaged. I was the leader of the student union. In the process, I made friends with some interesting people. I recall a debutante party where Frank Sinatra was the talent and another with the Temptations and Earth, Wind & Fire. There's nothing like Texas debutantes. They give the best parties and their parents spend extravagantly.

I was introduced to caviar at one of these parties. In retrospect, I realize it wasn't great caviar, but I knew that I was tasting something that was really good because it was with Champagne. To me, there's literally nothing better.

Then I went to New York because, like so many people who feel alien in their own community, I was enamored of the idea of New York. I also wanted to make money. I'm unapologetic about that, because when you grow up poor in America, the thing you don't want to be ever again is poor in America. I was lucky. I went to, first, a big law firm, and then to a large bank. I had a great run on Wall Street. I enjoyed it. I didn't love it, but it provided me with a level of financial security that was necessary.

What we at the Ford Foundation have worked on is helping to address the issue of food deserts—to finance supermarkets, food shops, and cooperatives that bring fresh foods from farms and other places.

I was never hungry as a child, but I was limited. As I look back and reflect on some of the things we ate, it's not a surprise to remember the levels of diabetes. For example, I recall visiting my family back in Rayne, Louisiana, after we moved to Texas. We'd spend weeks in the summer there, and I recall walking on this dirt road past various little shotgun shacks and seeing people without their limbs sitting on the porches—often overweight men and women without a leg, or with their leg missing from the knee. Someone would whisper, "Oh, that's diabetes."

Then I think about what we would have for lunch sometimes: a slice of bread, a slice of bologna, and what my great-aunt would call sweetened water. She'd take an old mason jar, put water in from the faucet, and then just saturate it with sugar, shake it, and pour it into our little plastic cups.

When I moved to Harlem in the mid-1980s, no one really wanted to live there. The Apollo was the only thing left. The Renaissance Ballroom, Smalls Paradise, the Cotton Club—they were all gone. What had replaced them was massive disinvestment. I met the most brilliant man, Reverend Calvin Butts, who is the pastor of the historic Abyssinian Baptist Church in Harlem. He and another member of the church, Karen Phillips, had a dream: a vision to redevelop Harlem, to create an NGO, a nonprofit that would take many of the thousands of vacant properties in Harlem and redevelop them. So that's what I did. For eight years, I worked for him developing over a thousand units of affordable housing. We helped develop the main commercial street in Harlem, 125th Street.

Harlem was a food desert. There was no supermarket. There were no fresh foods to be found other than at the local bodegas, which were stocked primarily with brown things: brown lettuce, brown vegetables, things close to their expiration date. This is why we fought so hard for a supermarket that would bring fresh produce. That supermarket came, but along with it came higher-income people. The risk is always that gentrification means that the winners are the new residents and the losers are the people who have been there and get pushed out.

Today when I visit Harlem, you come off the subway onto 125th Street, and on the one side, you see Whole Foods, Starbucks, H&M—I mean, there used to be nothing there but literally abandoned buildings. It has been transformed, and there's both good and bad associated with that transformation.

I live the New Yorker life that I always wanted to live, which means I eat out every night. When you live in New York City, the combination of dinner parties, galas, and great restaurants means you can choose simply not to cook.

I lived in a lovely apartment with a ten-burner Wolf range. My mother came to visit after I'd been living there eight months. She said, "Son, I think something's wrong with your stove." So I called down to the porter. He went into the kitchen and said, "You never turned the pilot light on when you moved in." And of course I said, "What's a pilot light?"

*Darren, what is your comfort food?*
Fried chicken, old-fashioned potato salad, collard greens cooked with ham hocks, and my mother's cornbread.

# MARK CARNEY

> Mark Carney has done a lot in his career: he's been the U.N.'s special envoy for climate action, the governor of both the Bank of England and the Bank of Canada, and, as of this book's publication, the prime minister of Canada. Our families have spent holidays in Tuscany together. Mark is a serious political force and a really good cook.
>
> On the podcast, we talked about his belief in the possibility of truly sustainable agriculture, the comfort foods of his childhood, and his mother's passion for baking cakes.
>
> Mark read our recipe for one of his favorite desserts, Torta di Capri.

When I was young, I was an enthusiastic baker, inspired by my mother. She grew up in an abandoned mining town in British Columbia called Britannia Beach, which is in a spectacular location on a body of water called Howe Sound. There's a road that goes through the town now, but at the time she was growing up, it was isolated. A boat came by once a week with all the supplies she would need to bake.

Then she moved to the Northwest Territories with my father. That's where I was born, effectively in the Arctic of Canada. She baked a huge variety of things, from cakes to pies to cookies—or biscuits, as we called them.

My baking muscles have atrophied a bit, but when I was growing up in Edmonton, baking was a tremendously comforting and enjoyable thing to do. All of my mother's cooking was comfort food. The exception was oatmeal. My room was in the basement. If I came upstairs and my mother was making oatmeal, that was a bad sign. It meant that it was at least minus thirty degrees outside. I had a negative Pavlovian response to oatmeal. I have since overcome my aversion to it, but it took decades.

Our household food was pretty traditional, variations on meat and two veg. There was a period of time in the mid-'70s, during the inflation years, when there were a lot of casseroles, things made to stretch the ground beef a little further. Maybe that's one of the reasons I became a central banker.

The Bank of England has a formal dining room, absolutely spectacular, that was designed by the architect Sir John Soane. It brings to bear the full majesty of the bank and the United Kingdom. If there's a G7 meeting or something like that, you have it there. But there is also a very good cafeteria on Threadneedle Street, which is where most of the bank staff eat. I wanted to keep up some of the bank's traditions, but I wasn't going for lunch every day in the state rooms and finishing it off with some port—though there were many days when I wish I had.

In 2014, I went to a lunch in Rome attended by Pope Francis. There was a World Cup final between Argentina and Germany going on. Pope Francis is Argentinean, and the previous pope, Benedict, was still alive and German. It was an elaborate lunch, with a pasta course, a fish course as the main, and then cheese and dessert.

The pope told this parable at the start of the lunch. He stood up and said, "Look, we're going to have a nice meal together. We're going to start the meal with wine. Wine is many things. It has a bouquet, a color, a taste that complements the food, and alcohol, which enlivens our senses. But we will finish the meal with grappa. And grappa is wine distilled."

Then he made an interesting analogy. He said, "People are many things. They're rational. They're passionate. They're curious. They're altruistic. They're self-interested." Then, referring to the market economy, he said, "The market is self-interested. Your job"—and here, he pointed to everyone at our conference, sixty-odd people from business and finance—"is to turn the grappa back into wine. To turn the market back into humanity." And he sat down.

The big issue with food and climate change is that around 20 percent of greenhouse gas emissions come from agriculture and land use. A substantial proportion of that could be reduced through regenerative agriculture, reforestation, and growing different foods.

The reality with climate change is there is no one simple solution, no silver bullet. There are many things we need to change. One is to ensure that we have sustainable agriculture. As the world becomes more equal, we can not only feed everybody but also feed everybody in a sustainable way, to a high standard. That requires knowing where food comes from and sourcing it as locally as possible. We have a long way to go on that, but I find that my children and their friends have an acute awareness of these issues. They have a passion about them that gives me hope for change.

When I was writing my book *Value(s): Building a Better World for All*, I realized that I was most productive, as I suspect many writers are, in the morning. I would meditate for fifteen or twenty minutes, drink a liter of water, and write for a couple of hours before eating. My friend Nikolai Ahrens, who is a very accomplished chemist, told me that the most important thing for cognitive function is to drink a liter of water first thing in the morning, because your brain dehydrates overnight. So I began doing this.

I'm not super close to Jeff Bezos, but I mentioned this to him when I was on a hike with him in Switzerland. I next saw him about ten years later. He said, quite remarkably, "Mark, I think of you every morning when I drink my water." Which is fair, because I think of Nikolai every morning.

*Mark, what is your comfort food?*
Can I say one thing before I answer? I mentioned my Pavlovian response to oatmeal. My Pavlovian response to the food we've eaten together in

Tuscany—*fiori di zucca*, fried zucchini flowers, and *bistecca alla Fiorentina*, the amazing sliced steak—is the exact opposite. It's a feeling of warmth, of absolute heaven. The ritual around both of those things is extraordinary, with a great sense of human connection.

But I'd say my comfort food is pasta pomodoro. It is a simple recipe, very few ingredients. It probably takes two hours to prepare the sauce. You have to cook the onions for a long time, until they dissolve in the olive oil. Then you add the tomatoes and a bit of garlic and reduce it all down. Totally comforting.

# ADAM SCHIFF

A visit to London by Adam Schiff—a U.S. congressman at the time we recorded his episode, now one of California's two senators—is an important occasion. I had the honor of hosting a dinner for Adam in our home. He had just returned from Ukraine and a meeting with Volodymyr Zelenskyy. Over dinner, he spoke to those of us present about what he had learned. We continued the conversation on *Ruthie's Table 4*, where Adam also talked about the meals he grew up eating and the food he cooks his family today.

He read our recipe for Spaghetti with Tomato and Arugula.

I wish I was not a big eater, but I do love food. I meet people from time to time who can take or leave eating. I don't understand them. I think they're from another planet.

My strongest food memories of childhood were of the High Holidays, when we'd get together with my grandparents and they would make a great big meal. My father was an immigrant from London. His parents emigrated from Eastern Europe. My other grandparents were born in the United States, but their parents, my great-grandparents, all came from Eastern Europe. When we got together for the holidays, it would be a lot of matzo ball soup and challah bread and brisket. It was quite a feast, including a lot of things that I didn't want to go near, like chopped liver.

There is an eternal debate in Jewish households about whether a matzo ball should be light and fluffy or the kind that, when you drop them, they go through the floor. I just want to state unequivocally, without hesitation, that they need to be the kind that fall through the floor. I'm firmly in the camp

of the very substantial, very heavy matzo ball that doesn't get lost in the broth. Politicians—sometimes we have to make difficult decisions.

My mother was a good cook but didn't like to cook. Nonetheless, we ate at home all the time. My father was a traveling salesman in the *schmatta* [garment] business and building business. A lot of our meals were very standard fare. A lot of canned food. But my favorite meal that my mother used to make were these little boneless chicken pieces that she breaded and then put cheese on. She made them with a side of spaghetti, so it was kind of like a mini chicken Parmesan.

It was a big deal when we could go out to one of our favorite restaurants. I think this is why I love to go out to eat, because when I was a kid, it was such a rarity. I like to claim to my wife—because only a husband can make this claim—that I'm the ideal husband because I don't want a home-cooked meal. I really love going out. You're not distracted by the phone ringing. You're not distracted by the TV, or this kid wants to run off to do homework instead of finishing the meal. You're at a table, focused on each other and the food.

I was part of the first U.S. delegation to Ukraine since the war started. One of the things that became apparent is that when the Russians blockaded Odessa, not only were they trying to cripple Ukraine's economy but, since Ukraine has been the breadbasket of Europe and provides a lot of the grain to Africa and other places, the Russians were also blockading food that a lot of people need to survive.

It caused not only a great increase in food prices but also risks of starvation in many places. So part of the appeal that Zelenskyy was making, asking for the weapons to sink the Black Sea fleet and the equipment he needs for de-mining, was, "This is important to Ukraine and it's important to our economy, but it's also important to the rest of the world because of the food-shortage issue."

We have experienced a revolution in the global economy as a function of automation. But one result of this is that millions of people in the middle class are at risk of falling out of it. A lot of families have to work harder than ever to try to get into the middle class. At the same time, these structural changes in the economy have produced great concentrated wealth. So while we have students in our colleges who can't get enough to eat, we have captains of industry literally flying into space on tourist trips.

I had a meeting some years ago with a group of community-college students from my district. It came up, in kind of an offhand way, that they had food banks on the campus for students. I was astonished. These were students from three different community colleges, and they all said they had food banks on campus.

This was still before the pandemic, so the economy was strong. Yet the hunger was greater than ever. It really pointed out to me some strong structural problems. Even when the economy was doing well, it wasn't doing well for millions and millions of people, including college kids. So I introduced a bill to try to expand the free and reduced-lunch program that we have in K–12 to go up through community college. That was the genesis of the Food for Thought Act, which we've been working to get passed, to address food insecurity for community colleges and minority-serving institutions.

My cooking, pre-pandemic, was pretty basic. But then we were not going out to eat, and it was a huge lifestyle change. So I got myself a few gadgets. I think this is, like barbecuing, a male thing: you like to cook with gadgets.

I got an air fryer and a pressure cooker. I started making curry tofu in the pressure cooker with vegetables and potatoes. It seemed to be a pretty fail-safe device in terms of coming out well.

Likewise, the air fryer. An air fryer circulates hot air around the basket or the pot, so it is like deep-frying, but you're using air, so there's no oil. It's kind of a healthy version of frying. I have to tell you a funny story. I was at a political event in Los Angeles. I gave my speech. Then a brand-new assembly member went up to the microphone, a real sharp up-and-comer. He was saying some nice things about me, and then he said, "And I got some of the most important advice from Congressman Schiff when I was getting started: the most important advice I've ever gotten."

I was waiting to hear what sage political advice I'd given him. He said, "He told me to get an air fryer."

My cholesterol has been high. I tried medications like statins, but they didn't sit well with me. So my wife, who is a very healthy eater, suggested that I try being vegan.

I'd been vegan for about three days when I was at an event in my district. At any event in Los Angeles, you talk about food, and I was talking about a great restaurant I'd been to called Crossroads Kitchen. The person I was talking to recognized that it was a vegan restaurant. She said to me, "Can I tell people here you're vegan?" I thought that was kind of a strange question. Why would people be interested in that? Then I realized where I was: in West Hollywood, at an animal welfare event.

I said, "Well, to be honest, I've only been vegan for three days. If you tell people, I'm going to be pretty locked in. But I need the incentive. So go ahead, tell people."

That was several years ago. I do allow myself to cheat from time to time, truth be told. I usually cheat when I'm traveling because it's hard for me to always find vegan food. I also cheat during Thanksgiving, because my first Thanksgiving as a vegan was just an awful experience.

We were at a nice little place in Pennsylvania for the weekend. Our kids were with us, and we had ordered in advance two vegan meals and two traditional turkey dinners. They brought these two beautiful plates for our kids, and then they put out our plates. It looked like someone had opened a Gerber's baby food jar and poured it on the plate. It was not at all satisfying. So I thought, "Okay, on Thanksgiving, I'm going to make an exception."

I have a challenge for your listeners. On behalf of vegans the world over, someone figure out how to make a good vegan pizza. I have yet to find one that I really like. Most of the places you go to use something like Daiya cheese, which is made of coconut oil. It doesn't taste anything like the real thing. So I put this up there with the heart-lung machine: somebody invent a good vegan pizza.

*Adam, what is your comfort food?*
Pasta is hard to beat. I have so many fond memories of it, as a kid through adulthood. There's nothing more comfortable than a great Italian meal with some wine and some bread, and worrying about the carbs tomorrow.

# MICHAEL BLOOMBERG

A few years ago, the Serpentine, a small museum in London's Kensington Gardens, gave a party for three hundred people to celebrate its new chairman, Michael Bloomberg, the businessman and three-term mayor of New York City. We listened to the inspiring words: "Government cannot do everything. Private philanthropy has to step in and we at Bloomberg consider ourselves just lucky to be able to do so."

A true and generous dictum, but what I remember most from the mayor's moving speech was the last line: "Come to New York City, and if you want to have coffee or lunch, just call me. This is my number . . ."

I did go to New York City soon after, number in hand. I never made that call, something I will always regret, but here I am, almost ten years later, having that coffee with Mayor Bloomberg, ready to talk.

Michael read our recipe for Linguine with Fresh and Dried Oregano.

My mother always cooked everything in a pressure cooker or straight out of the can. It was Del Monte peas, cooked in the water that comes with the peas. It was brisket or chicken.

One time, I came home from Boy Scout camp, and I said the food was better there. She said, "Why don't you go back?" But the recipes that she used were good enough to get her to 102 years in perfect health.

Food was relatively plain in our house. Most things that I see on a menu today, my mother wouldn't have known what they were and certainly didn't serve them. My family was Eastern European in background. In those days, coming from overseas, you tried to strip out and throw away your culture, whether it was food, clothing, religion, or even names. We anglicized our

names. Today, it's the reverse: "I'm a Dominican American." "I'm an Italian American." But in the great migration waves in the 1920s, the goal was to become as American as you could possibly be.

But food brought us together. There was me; my sister, two years younger; my mother; and my father. He worked as a bookkeeper and made $6,000 in the best year of his life. We always waited for him to come home, around sixish. My sister and I set the table. My mother did the cooking. My father helped in clearing the table and doing the dishes.

When we sat at the table, my father would pick somebody, any one of the four of us, including himself, and that person had to spend two minutes saying what they did that day. Then the conversation was everybody else chiming in about what they had done. We did this virtually every night. I later tried to do it with my daughters, but everybody traveled, including me, and it just didn't work out.

Here's a good rule for everybody, and if we all followed it, the world would be a better place: don't do anything that you'd be ashamed to tell your kids about when you got home at night.

I went to Johns Hopkins University in Baltimore. Then I went to Harvard Business School and lived in Cambridge, fifteen minutes away from where my mother was living. My father had died. If my mother hadn't lived close, I never would have gotten through, because she had to type my papers. I still can't type and I can't spell, much to her embarrassment.

They had a luncheon hall at Harvard where we ate. I certainly didn't have the money to go out to restaurants. I don't think we ever went to a fancy restaurant as a family. We only ever went to Carroll's Diner in Medford, Massachusetts. I love dive-y places where everything comes in five minutes no matter what. They've got fifty things on the menu. How they do it, I don't know, but it all tastes good. I'm not fancy.

For the first two or three years that I lived in New York, I cooked all my own meals. Baked beans and hot dogs, that sort of stuff. On Sundays I'd make French toast and read the newspapers, eating an enormous amount of French toast covered with maple syrup and salt.

Now I go out to dinner virtually all the time. My attitude is, there are twenty-five thousand restaurants in New York City, and each one probably has twenty different things on the menu. So that's five hundred thousand possibilities if I go out, versus one if I had stayed home.

I like to cook, and my girlfriend, Diana Taylor, likes to cook. It's just that, in our lives, there isn't time. Shake 'n Bake chicken is the last thing I made—you get this stuff in a bag, you put the chicken in it, you shake it, and then you broil the chicken in a baking pan. It's so good. Not for your waistline or cholesterol, but it tastes good.

For the fifteen years that I worked at Salomon Brothers, we did not have food in the office. There might have been coffee, but I don't even remember that. But when I started my company, Bloomberg L.P., I went and I bought a small refrigerator and a coffeepot.

My job is to get people together. It's the synergy of working together that increases the odds of being successful. It's hard for people to be their best if they can't run ideas by other people and learn from them.

How do you get people together? Well, you have a building where they have to come to, first rule. Second rule is, to the extent it's possible, don't have walls. Have open spaces. Part of the design that Norman Foster did for us was to not put the elevators in the middle—to instead have a big open space, with the elevators and all of the infrastructure on the outside. If the CEO walls himself off, what kind of a CEO is he? I don't want that person in my company. I have a desk right in the middle of the bullpen, like everybody else.

Food is another thing that gets people together. It gets you to sit together—not so much the food itself but the fact that you're sharing it, doing the same thing that the other person is. Now, if the food is good, that's also a benefit.

I think government has some responsibilities regarding food. One is if people don't have enough food, we've got to find a way to get it to them, particularly children. I think government has a responsibility to make sure that the food sold in stores is not dangerous. I think we should warn against certain things and point out the calories.

Another public health challenge in America is smoking. I don't think the government should force you to not smoke, but I think it should certainly tell you about the dangers. In New York, we established a rule that you can't smoke in a place where people work, so that nobody has to choose between their job and their health. You can go outside and smoke, and you can buy cigarettes. I'll defend your right to do that. But waiters and waitresses should not have to choose between their health and their career. We were the first big city to have a no-smoking law for restaurants, to protect the workers.

*Michael, what is your comfort food?*
I'm addicted to popcorn with probably too much salt, although the doctor says I have low blood pressure, so I don't have to stop. And Cheez-Its—I could eat bags of Cheez-Its.

# Food Is Food

Rose Gray and I founded The River Cafe wanting to share our love of Italy and its food. We wanted to cook meals of the quality we enjoyed there and have a restaurant that felt like home.

On *Ruthie's Table 4*, we have welcomed chefs, restaurateurs, and cookbook authors. For Danny Meyer, Martha Stewart, and Jamie Oliver, their careers are an extension of childhoods where food was at the center of family life.

Wolfgang Puck's path from Austria to Beverly Hills was long and sometimes lonely and wracked with self-doubt. Yotam Ottolenghi bridged Israeli and Middle Eastern food, bringing flavor, color, and joy to London.

There is no single way to be a success in the world of food, as the guests in this section show.

# MARTHA STEWART

When Martha Stewart made a twenty-five-minute pilgrimage from her London hotel to have lunch at The River Cafe back in 1992, so began a friendship that has lasted more than thirty years.

In her *Table 4* episode, Martha looked back on her first visit to the restaurant with warmth and humor. But the best part for me was her memories of being a young girl from New Jersey whose grandparents, all four of them, had immigrated to America from Poland.

Martha didn't start out living a Martha Stewart life. But she has been one of the most influential people on how we eat and entertain today.

I grew up in Nutley, New Jersey. My mother taught sixth grade at the Washington School there. She took off, I think, eighteen years to have six kids. She went back to teaching when her sixth child, Laura, was old enough to go to kindergarten. Dad was a pharmaceutical salesman. I was the oldest daughter. It was boy-girl, boy-girl all the way down.

I learned how to cook at my mother's side. The kitchen was the hub of our home. It was a really ugly kitchen. My father renovated it himself. He put down pink linoleum squares on the floor. And pink Formica countertops. Pink! Then he put in birch cabinets, which were okay, except that he put very ugly hardware on them. We had a nook where we all sat, with a big picture window looking out onto the garden. It was called the breakfast nook, but it was large enough for eight people.

That was all one side of the kitchen. And there was one little oven with a broiler in it. For eight people. We had no domestics. We went shopping every

Friday morning. Mr. Maus from next door, this German baker, had a big Buick. He and his wife would drive us because we only had one car and Dad took it to work. So they would take us to the co-op, and we'd load up the car with a week's supply of groceries.

We also had a large garden. That was only during the warm weather, though. My mother did a lot of canning and preserving. We had a great big freezer in the basement and a large refrigerator where overflow was kept.

We fished. We'd bring home a hundred bluefish. We froze and ate a lot of bluefish. We also had farmer relatives in southern New Jersey who had cows and grew corn, really good corn. Being from a Polish background, you learn a lot about agriculture and you learn a lot about cooking and preserving.

It was a fun house. There's an old Polish joke that asks, "What's a Polish vacation?" It's sitting on your neighbor's stoop. That's what we did. We sat next door on the Italian stoop, or we sat next door on the Irish stoop, and we ate everybody's food. It was a very nice neighborhood, and I learned a lot. I learned how to roast a potato the best way. I also learned from Mr. Maus how to make beautiful, beautiful yeast breads. He had a big bakery down in his basement. I still have his bread-making bowl, a big yellowware bowl in which I make all my dough. For the most recent Thanksgiving, I gave my whole staff panettone with a recipe I learned from Mr. Maus a long time ago.

Dinner was important and conversation at the dinner table was important. Everything from current events to what was on the radio program *The Shadow*. We had a radio but not a television. We would have to sneak out and visit our neighbors to watch TV.

After dinner, Mom would sit there with her one cigarette she smoked per day, a Chesterfield. She looked so sexy. I loved how she looked. She sat there after everybody was in bed except for her daughter Martha, who was cleaning up. I was also sewing a lot because I made my own clothes.

Dad made breakfasts. He would make eggs with smiley faces made out of maraschino cherries and green peppers, to lure us down to the kitchen. He had an intercom in the house. If you ever read *Cheaper by the Dozen*, it's a fabulous book about a couple who had twelve children. It was written in Montclair, New Jersey. Dad would make believe he was that father. On the intercom he'd say, "Rise and shine!" I'm not allowed to say that in my house at all.

We were brought up on fresh, good food. Grandma Helen, my father's mother, lived down the street, and she made the best gefilte fish. She would bring home a giant carp that would sit in the bathtub. And then she would make the most delicious mousse of carp, which turned out to be gefilte fish, with a wonderful sauce. She was great.

The other grandmother, Grandma Ruszkowski, lived in Buffalo, New York. She lived next door to a slaughterhouse, so I witnessed how animals were slaughtered, and early on I learned a lot about how to treat animals and how not to treat animals. Also, she would go to the farms up in New York State and bring home the most beautiful golden cherries. She would do canning because they didn't have freezers. I learned how to be a good canner from her.

We had no money to go to restaurants. Six kids, all preparing to go to college. There was no time. My big treat from my dad was, he went to restaurants to take out his doctors he was selling drugs to. So he got to experiment and visit restaurants in New York City. He would bring me home a pomegranate from Chinatown.

I started going to restaurants as soon as I could work. When I was around thirteen, I started to model in New York City. A girl across the street was a model and a ballerina. She said, "Martha, you should really come see my agent. She'd love you." So I went to see this lady, Eileen Ford, and she accepted me as a part-time model.

So I would work after school, and on Saturdays, I would work modeling live at Bonwit Teller. It was fun. And instead of fifty cents an hour, I was making more like $20 an hour in New York. That was a *lot* of money. Then I got some TV commercials, and that's what really paid. It paid for my entire college education. The residuals in those days were very lucrative. I did that until I went to Barnard College.

I started having boyfriends who took me out to dinner. One of my boyfriends, the guy I actually married, lived in the Ritz Tower on Park Avenue and 57th Street. The Ritz Tower had Le Pavillon downstairs. That was his lunchroom. And there were other lovely French restaurants to eat in. I ate at a Japanese restaurant uptown on 120th Street and Amsterdam called Aki. That was very good. So I started to experiment with all different cuisines early on.

I took some detours, like to Wall Street. I learned how to be a stockbroker. I traveled a lot, tasted foods all over the world, and fell in love with different cuisines and tried to learn how to make those things. That was all more hobby than profession. When I wrote my first book, I was already forty.

In my mid-thirties, I retired from Wall Street and I had to do something, so I started a catering company. Catering is the worst job on earth. It's sort of like being a stockbroker: it's all about money and getting stuff done on time. It was a pretty horrible business. You're building a restaurant every night and tearing it down at the end of the evening and loading it into the car.

I knew my marriage was over the night I drove back into the driveway on Turkey Hill Road and nobody came out to help. That's what happened because I was devoted to the work. That's when I started thinking, "What can I do to make something that my children and grandchildren might know their grandma for?" And that was to write a book.

My first, *Entertaining*, came out in 1982. I was maligned for not having gone to cooking school. I never worked in a restaurant. But I learned from watching. I'm a really good observer and I have had the opportunity in my career, with the TV shows, to have the finest chefs in the world cooking with me. Nobu Matsuhisa even gave me a sushi jacket because he thought I did very well with the sushi knife. He let me cut fish behind his bar on 57th Street. That's pretty high praise.

*Martha, what is your comfort food?*
I raise my own chickens. The eggs are so delicious. No matter how you cook them, they're good.

# DANNY MEYER

It's constantly said how cutthroat the restaurant business can be. Danny Meyer was one of the people who convinced us otherwise. Two years earlier, he had opened Union Square Cafe in New York City and shown how a restaurant could succeed and uphold strong values. Treat the staff with respect. Talk down to no one. See to it that customers leave feeling better than when they arrived.

In 1994, Danny opened a second restaurant, Gramercy Tavern. In 2001, he and his partners launched Shake Shack in Madison Square Park. What started as a single hamburger and milkshake stand is now an international success, operating at massive scale while maintaining Danny's personal professional credo of kindness.

When I have a question about fair policies for the people who work with us—or about anything else, really—who do I call? Danny Meyer.

Danny read his own recipe for Fried Chicken.

I grew up in St. Louis, Missouri. We had a lot of cooking going on at home. My dad was in the travel business and he was the first American agent for an organization called Relais de Campagne, which would later become Relais & Châteaux.

So we had French people living in our home; people would work in my dad's office by day, and then, at nighttime, they were around the table. French was spoken every night. We kids didn't understand what they were talking about, which encouraged us to learn French. There was always a bottle of Beaujolais on the table. So, without knowing it, I was getting a little bit of an education.

Both of my parents cooked. My dad taught me how. His favorite dish was ratatouille, and we had a dog by that name. So I grew up with the smells and sounds and fun of cooking. It was just part of my upbringing.

I got to go to France pretty early in my life, and then later Italy, where I was a tour guide, working for my dad. He started selling group tours, and when my sister, who's older than I am, turned twenty, she got to pick a city, and she picked Copenhagen. When I was twenty, I picked Rome. My brother picked Paris.

Interestingly, we all three had a kind of love affair with the place we picked. I returned to Rome to study political science, and that was supposed to lead me into being a lawyer, but I would have been the world's worst lawyer. Thank goodness I converted quickly and thought, "Why not embrace where my real passion is?"

I grew up appreciating French food, but in St. Louis, we didn't really have French restaurants. We had great smash burgers and frozen custard, both of which would one day lead to Shake Shack.

St. Louis had and has an amazing immigrant population. It began with lots and lots of Germans. That's how you get restaurants like one we used to go to called Schneithorst's, and Anheuser-Busch, the beer company. Lots and lots of sausage makers, lots of beer companies. There was also a neighborhood, and it still remains, called The Hill, which was Italians from the south, primarily. They had their own style of cooking. To this day, they all have almost the exact same menus. So their carbonara has cream in it, which you would never do. And toasted ravioli with marinara sauce.

There was one restaurant that is still around called Kreis'. It's a German place, and they gave me an idea that I used when I opened Union Square Cafe at the age of twenty-seven: have a nightly special you can depend on, every night of the week. So you knew if you went in there on a Monday night, that was chicken and dumplings. If you went in on Tuesday night, it was sauerbraten.

We did that when I opened Union Square Cafe, because I love the idea that you could create a habitual regular. And they also remembered my favorite table. Well, probably every kid liked to have the table underneath the cuckoo clock, but it meant the world to me that they remembered that I did.

You'll always go back to where you feel most loved. James Beard was constantly accosted in airports, restaurants, everywhere, because everyone recognized the bald head and the bow tie. The question everybody asked him was, "What's your favorite restaurant?" And he said, "My favorite restaurant is the same as yours. It's the one that loves me the most."

I couldn't stop discovering things everywhere. So when I was at Trinity College in Hartford, Connecticut, I would go to their Little Italy and find the best grinders. Every city has a different name for submarine sandwiches. In Hartford, they're called grinders. It was all inexpensive stuff. The best pizza. The best espresso.

Because of my dad's travel business, until I was twenty-one, I could fly anywhere that Pan Am flew for $44 round trip. So every time we had a three-day weekend, I got myself down to Kennedy Airport. I would almost always go to Rome. I went to Venice once in the middle of winter, which, at that time of year, is the loneliest place on earth. I did go to London and really enjoyed it.

I was in London by myself for two weeks. I had this book, I think American Express published it, of their reviews of a hundred restaurants. I didn't have much of a budget, so I saved up for the ones I could get into. There was one restaurant that I went to and they wouldn't take me as a solo diner. So I made a reservation for two. I walked in and I kept looking at my watch: "Where's my friend? Where's my friend?" I finally ordered a decent bottle of wine for myself so they wouldn't kick me out. No solo diner is going to order a whole bottle of wine. But I was also learning about hospitality from how *not* to treat people, because they weren't very nice at that point.

When I first broke the news to my parents that I was not going to become a lawyer as everyone had expected, but instead I was going to go into the restaurant business, I said, "I want to be a chef." Because I had seen people like Alice Waters, Joyce Goldstein, Jeremiah Tower, Wolfgang Puck, and Paul Prudhomme. A lot of these people had liberal arts educations, so I wasn't going to let my parents down. It got up to the point where my dad said, "You better get some cooking in," and he set up two *stages* for me in Bordeaux at places that had been part of Relais & Chateaux.

The first one was called La Reserve, in Pessac-Léognan. The day I got there, they had just lost their second star, so everyone in the restaurant was completely demoralized. As a matter of fact, on day two, four of their cooks left because, God forbid, they did not want to have a one-star Michelin restaurant on their résumé. What that meant was I got a big promotion, meaning I got to open the oysters and pull the feathers from birds and chop the shallots and all that kind of fun stuff.

I also got to cook family meal for them. That was a big deal. I'll never forget, I made my grandmother's spareribs with her barbecue sauce: *"Côtes de porc! Côtes de porc!"* They loved it. Then I made a pasta for them. I could not believe my eyes: all these Michelin-level cooks, you know what they dressed my pasta with? Ketchup. They started pouring ketchup all over the noodles. I've never seen that in my life, but I guess they consider that to be a good pasta sauce.

My first night in New York was the night John Lennon was assassinated, December 8, 1980. It was not necessarily a nice city back then.

I wanted to open a restaurant that, if only it existed, would be my favorite restaurant in the world. I had no interest in it being an exalted restaurant. I wanted it to be a place that you would feel equally comfortable wearing jeans or wearing a coat and tie if that's what you felt like.

You could eat at the bar from the day we opened. We had good wines by the glass. But I had the bejesus scared out of me, because early on, as I was planning this thing, my uncle introduced me to the guy who was the food and beverage director at the Harvard Club: "You need to talk to this guy, because he knows everything about restaurants."

The guy starts grilling me: "What kind of restaurant are you going to open?" I said, "I don't know. I'm going to have a little French stuff, a little Italian stuff, a little California stuff." He said, "I'm going to tell you right now: it's not going to work. When people decide where they want to eat in New York they say French, Italian, Chinese, German. No one says, 'Let's go out and eat eclectic.'"

I was taken aback, but fortunately, I did not let that stop me.

The common skill set in all of our restaurants is that you can actually really, really advance the workplace culture and the hospitality culture for all of your stakeholders. I care as deeply about the guest experience and the workplace experience at Shake Shack as I do at The Modern or Gramercy Tavern or Manhatta.

So for example, if you're going to get a job at The Modern, which has two Michelin stars, we're going to look deeply into your work résumé. Do you have the wine knowledge? Do you have the culinary knowledge? At Shake Shack, I don't think one person has ever been asked, "Can I please see your credentials for how well you make milkshakes or burgers?" We hire 100 percent for emotional skills and hospitality skills. And we believe that we can teach and train people. If I have one job, it's truly fueling the culture, how we do things.

*Danny, what is your comfort food?*
Really good fried chicken. I don't make it that often because it's a bloody mess and there's so much good fried chicken you can get out there. But when I do make it, it's very, very simple.

# NIGELLA LAWSON

Nigella is family. I can't remember the day I met Nigella, for that would be like remembering the day I met my sister or my cousin. We both came into cooking professionally—in Nigella's case, as a bestselling author and television host—through a love of Italy and its food. We have both known the heartbreak of losing people we love.

Nigella chose to read our recipe for Summer Minestrone, which dates back to the earliest days of The River Cafe. We serve this soup of fresh peas, asparagus, broad beans, and green beans at room temperature. "Room temperature, which is something the Italians really get, allows you to taste flavors so vibrantly," she said. "And although it's an Italian soup, the sweet starchiness of the peas reminds me of an English summer."

My mother was a good cook. She married very young, at nineteen, and had her first child, my older brother, at twenty. She felt things very deeply but didn't always express them. So she would erupt quite a bit. She was fantastically impatient.

One of the jobs that my sister Thomasina and I used to have was to make mayonnaise together. One of us would whisk and the other would pour the oil. Whoever was whisking, you weren't whisking fast enough. And whoever was pouring, you weren't pouring slowly enough. I remember being in the kitchen with fondness and gratitude, yet it would be so unfaithful to the truth if I didn't say it was also a source of great tension. It was frightening, but I did learn a lot. My mother was a very spontaneous cook.

I associate her with food, yet she had a very troubled relationship with it. She had eating disorders, which I didn't really take on board until I was in my teens. It was difficult, because it was a repudiation of something that gave her pleasure. The heartbreaking thing is, she died when she was forty-eight. I was told by the doctor that she was terminally ill just three weeks before she died. I didn't tell her until two weeks before, because I was waiting a bit, just to get more tests and things. When I told her, she said that it was the first time she could eat without anxiety or guilt.

My father didn't cook, except to make his own breakfast, which I think is quite an old-fashioned male thing to do. Somehow, they don't feel that cooking eggs is too much of a dent to their dignity.

We went out to dinner only on special occasions, like birthdays or the occasional treat. There was a Chinese restaurant on King's Road called Choys, I remember that. I found family meals difficult. It's an odd thing. I was clumsy and I'd always knock something over. I found myself slightly inhibited within a family group. I came into my own later. I didn't enjoy meals a lot until I had a bit more control and could decide what I wanted to eat. For that reason, a tasting menu is my idea of hell.

I went to Italy before university, and it made such an impression on me. In the olden days, you did an entrance exam to go to Oxford. I thought I would like to study Italian. So I pretended, at the interview, that I was going to go to school in Italy for the year before, the gap year. But I didn't. I just turned up in Italy with a friend. We had a one-room *pensione* in Florence and worked as chambermaids. All I can say is, if anyone ever stays in a hotel and wonders whether people try on your clothes and put your scent on—yes, we do.

Our pensione was run by a married couple who came from Arezzo. They had a son called Leonardo. And his grandmother, *la nonna*, lived there. Every now and then, they would go to their farm and she would be left there. We weren't normally allowed in the kitchen, but the minute they were gone, I was let in because the nonna wanted company. She wanted to chat. I watched her cook.

The thing I remember most is that wonderful Italian way of making *rosbif*, which is almost pot roast. I would watch her put the oil and garlic in and then remove the garlic when it was brown; in the north of Italy, the idea of leaving in lots of garlic is odd. Then she'd put in a very small amount of meat, which she browned, and rosemary and a teeny bit of wine. She'd cook it so it was not quite fried but not really poached, either. There was something so enormously different about it. And, again, served at room temperature.

She also made *purea*, mashed potatoes. Whenever people say, "Italians don't use butter," I feel like you should have seen her mashed potatoes.

We didn't have an awful lot of money to spend. There was a bar I went to where you could sit and have a Campari soda. You'd have a selection of crostini and choose different soft cheeses, whether it was mozzarella, burrata, or a creamier one that had a stripe of anchovy on the top.

I didn't really want to go back to Oxford. I'd been very shy at home, but when I had to speak Italian, because I was speaking a different language, I was a different person. I was more voluble. I was less shy. I found my voice.

To go into a place and not to have all these connections is freeing: being completely independent, earning your own living, fending for yourself. It was as if I had decided at a young age that I wanted to be Italian. And then I proceeded.

John, my husband, was absolutely gorgeous. Not a great eater. No—he was a great eater, but he just didn't like an awful lot. He was picky.

I remember the first time I cooked for him, at my flat on Chesterton Road. We were just friends at that stage, but I thought I would cook something. It was based on a Claudia Roden recipe: courgettes with saffron and some sort of sauce. You made the sauce and put the chopped zucchini around the chicken. John took one look at it and said, "No gravy for me, please."

He adored tinned potatoes: little new potatoes that come precooked. His idea of a real treat was tinned fruit salad with evaporated milk. He *did* have a sweet tooth. We had a big oval table overflowing with people. I don't do children's food and non-children's food, but there are certain things that I'd make that were easier and people liked. Sometimes it would just be an indoor picnic: bread, cheese, ham, salami, tomatoes.

*Nigella, what is your comfort food?*
I guess I'd say my mother's way of cooking chicken, which is a bit like a chicken soup. Anything chickeny and brothy is a comfort.

But in different moods, all food is a comfort. There is such a beauty just in the ingredients. Sometimes when you've peeled an onion, the way the skin looks on the chopping board, it's just wonderful. Or the smell as you grate lemon zest and it changes the air. It reminds you that you're alive and you're taking pleasure, and to be grateful.

# YOTAM OTTOLENGHI

Yotam Ottolenghi was born and grew up in Jerusalem. His cooking and outlook are informed by the Italian and German heritage of his parents, as well as the Palestinian culinary traditions he learned from his neighbors. Yotam is largely responsible for bringing to London the subtlety, flavors, and joy of Middle Eastern cuisine and, through his wildly popular cookbooks, introducing the rest of the world to the beauty of tahini, za'atar, and sumac. We talked about separation and connection, family and friends.

He read his own wonderful recipe: One Jar of Butter Beans with Preserved Lemon, Chili, and Herb Oil.

My parents were born in Europe just before the Second World War. They immigrated with their parents as little kids in 1939. My mother was from a German Jewish family. My father was from an Italian family in Florence. They met in Israel years later.

The food culture of the city, Jerusalem, was the food of Jewish immigrants, from wherever they came. But it was also the food of the Palestinian population, which had such a rich, wonderful culinary history.

I was born in 1968. I grew up in a world in which we ate very European food at home. My father was cooking traditional Italian dishes and my mom was kind of an international cook, but with a very Germanic approach to cooking. But when we went out, we used to eat Palestinian food, Arabic food. I always thought that I was quite lucky to have had been exposed to all those kinds of foods from quite a young age.

My paternal grandparents couldn't really separate themselves from their Italian background, so they used to have food sent to them. They'd get an-

chovy paste, olive oil, biscuits, cookies, packages of Italian produce, and Parmigiano. They lived about an hour from where we lived, in a suburb of Tel Aviv. I used to go to their house as a kid with my dad, and the smell was just completely different. It smelled of Italy. They used to travel in the summer to a house they had in the hills outside Florence that I went to when I was growing up.

In Israel at that time, there wasn't a cuisine as such. It was just so early on, and everything was new and young. A national cuisine had not evolved. The Palestinian food was extremely evolved, but what people now call Israeli food is something that evolved later. When I was growing up, there was the food that the Polish Jews would have cooked, or the Russian Jews or Libyan Jews or Moroccan Jews or Iraqi Jews. Each one had their own cuisine. I always like to say that in Jerusalem, it was survival of the fittest. The best food from every culture would surface.

You had Sephardic salads and mezzes. You'd have the babkas that came from the Ashkenazim. In some of the restaurants in Jerusalem these days, that's what's featured: the best of every culture that makes up the city.

Both of my parents cooked. My father, because of his Italian sensibilities, cooked in a way that was quite minimal: great ingredients cooked with care and attention. When he made polenta, he'd just stand there and stir it for forty-five minutes, until it was just right, and add the cheese. It was so different from the way I ended up cooking, which is quite a maximalist: a lot of ingredients, more akin to maybe how they cook in North Africa or Southeast Asia, in the sense that I use quite a lot of spices, cook them down, and create something that is a base for a sauce. He didn't cook like that. He was a professor of chemistry at the university. So he had a deep understanding of ingredients.

Like all Italians, he loved *his* food the most. There were certain combinations that he would just not have. Sweet and savory food, never, because he was from northern Italy. Maybe in Sicily or Puglia they'd have that, but not in the north. Something Moroccan like a tagine with prunes? He wouldn't touch that.

My mom was a teacher. She had these international cookbooks of the '50s and would try a Malaysian curry or a gazpacho. For her, the most important meal in the day in our house was breakfast. We had this spread of food—again, not very Italian. Before I went to school, there were freshly sliced vegetables; some cheese in brine, like feta; and fresh bread and eggs.

We didn't have great restaurants in Jerusalem in the way there are now. The Six-Day War had happened not long before I was born, the war in which Israel occupied East Jerusalem. In some ways, these were the pre-traumatic times. It was obviously complicated, but it was relatively peaceful. We used to travel a lot to the Palestinian restaurants in the West Bank.

In Jericho, we had these incredible meals. We would have these delicious spreads, from hummus to labneh, the strained yogurt. They had wonderful oranges, like Sevilles, so you'd have orange juice, freshly squeezed. Some of the oranges were used for cooking. The citrus was perfect for lamb on the grill. They'd cook a lamb and rice dish called *maqluba*, which is layered and flipped upside down. And they had amazing, wonderful olive oil and freshly baked breads: pita and other variations on the flatbread theme. The Palestinians cook their bread in a taboon, which is a kind of earthenware oven.

My dad called me *goloso*, which is the Italian word for glutton, because I loved eating so much. I made them take me to this one restaurant in the Arab part of East Jerusalem that served seafood, like shrimps and squid. They were Christian Arabs. We'd go there and have a plate of prawns with butter, garlic, and lemon, and I just thought it was the most delicious thing I'd ever had. And so exotic.

But I never thought I was going to become a chef. I studied at Tel Aviv University in the '90s and got a master's degree in comparative literature and philosophy. My first apartment that I had, with my boyfriend at the time, was by Carmel Market, the main food and vegetable market. This was when I started to cook, because I was at university and, like so many students, I found that food was not forthcoming anymore.

On Friday, I would go and buy fresh herbs and vegetables and cheese. They had incredible cheese stands: all these Balkan cheeses sitting in brine, different types of feta. I use the word *feta*, but there is a whole range of young cheeses that vary in saltiness and texture, from something more like a ricotta to something much firmer.

We'd have other student friends come over. I remember just starting to understand how to marinate a chicken and grill it and make a salad to go with it: very baby steps in the kitchen. I fell in love with cooking, but I still didn't think it was going to be a career for me.

But academic life turned out to be very insular. I was speaking to seven people who knew what I was talking about and the rest of the world wasn't remotely interested. The opposite happened when I started cooking, because all of a sudden, everybody's interested. That dichotomy, between somewhere where you really have no one to share your passions with and a world in which everybody is interested, was such an eye-opener for me. I realized, "*Yes*, I want to try and engage in *this* conversation and not in *that* conversation."

When I came to London in 1997, I hadn't yet made up my mind about who I wanted to be. But I thought, "I'm going to take a year off." And I went to the Cordon Bleu in Marylebone Lane. I took a course there and thought, "Okay, maybe there's something for me here."

A bit later, my good friend Noam Bar came back from traveling the world and said, "Let's do something together." He had studied business, and I was at the restaurant Baker & Spice at the time. He said, "Let's open a shop."

It took about a year to make it all happen. Sami Tamimi, who became our other partner, wasn't quite ready to join us. It was originally supposed to be just a bakery in which I would be baking. When Sami joined at the very last minute—this was in 2002, when we opened on Ledbury Road in Notting Hill—we decided we were going to have two sides to our offering: freshly made salads and savory food mirrored by a mountain of cakes.

I wouldn't call what we do Middle Eastern. It wasn't until 2012, when we published *Jerusalem: A Cookbook*, in which we talked about our heritage and background—Sami's Palestinian background and my Jewish background—that people started saying, "Oh, Ottolenghi is a Middle Eastern restaurant."

Because, yeah, we had tahini and sumac and all those things, but we also used miso and soy and pomegranates and chilies and cumin, which are not specific to the region. There's something about the little strip that goes from Tunisia and Morocco in North Africa through the Middle East and then through South Asia, all the way to Southeast Asia. There's a certain language that I think we all use—it's kind of a sunny temperament. Sometimes you find something in Mexico that speaks the same language. It's chilies, it's garlic, it's citrus, these intense flavors. The Middle East has them, but other places that have them, too. We love to borrow from all those parts of the world.

What I find interesting is that this thing called Israeli cuisine did not exist fifteen or twenty years ago. When I did a show for the BBC years ago called *Jerusalem on a Plate*, I was trying to formulate what was actually going on there. What occurred to me was that it was all so new and fresh, and nobody felt that they were committed to one way of cooking. There was something very liberating about the sense that everything is possible.

It's a very Israeli thing. There's a laissez-faire kind of "whatever" attitude. I think it has to do with the fact that it's not indebted to one part of the world, one terroir or one cuisine. It's a magpie of cuisines that comes together really nicely.

And there is a very, very strong underlying Palestinian tradition of cooking that underscores this. People don't talk about it enough, for political reasons. I don't think it's a bad thing that Palestinian cooking has become so much part of what is perceived as Israeli cooking. But it's really important to tell that story. Many of these dishes belong to Jewish diasporas of other cultures, but Palestinian cooking is a massive factor in the way the new Israeli chefs cook.

*Yotam, what is your comfort food?*
Things that my Italian grandmother used to cook. She used to make gnocchi alla Romana, thinly spread semolina gnocchi on a tray dotted with butter and cheese. It would go under the grill. They had great Parmigiano cheese they got from Italy, and she would grate it on. That semolina, soft and milky with the grated, melted cheese on top—it's just such a childhood flavor and definitely the one that brings the most comfort to me. I've never managed to do it even remotely as well as she did.

# WOLFGANG PUCK

I'm often asked who inspired us when we opened The River Cafe. One of the answers is Wolfgang Puck.

With Spago, his groundbreaking L.A. restaurant, Wolfgang turned the culinary world upside down, serving sophisticated pizzas made in wood ovens. Even in airports, he could elevate fast food. He took kitchens out of the basement so diners and chefs could see each other. He brought the drama of the kitchen to the table.

Wolfgang is legendary for being generous with his knowledge: teaching, inspiring, and mentoring young people who aspire to be like him. When he came to The River Cafe for dinner with his family, it felt like a visit from the gods to everyone working here.

I asked him to read one of his own recipes, for his exquisite grilled chicken with garlic and parsley, which we fondly call Chicken Spago.

My father was actually very wealthy. My mother worked for a doctor in a small town after the war, in 1948, '49, '50. But my father's mother told him he could not marry my mother, because she came from a poor background. She started working in restaurants when I was a little kid while my grandmother, my mother's mother, took care of me.

My grandmother used to work in the fields on a farm, in a village with fifty people. We didn't have refrigeration or plumbing. For water, we had the spring outside. You had to pump water from the spring and bring it in. If we wanted to wash ourselves, we had to turn on the stove to heat up the water. For milk, I'd go with a can to the dairy farmer and get it filled it up.

My mother became a professional chef, but she didn't own a restaurant.

She worked at a small hotel on a beautiful lake in Carinthia, which is the southern part of Austria, next to Italy and Slovenia. She was like an angel. Then my stepfather came along. He was a coal miner and totally crazy and alcoholic. I don't know the yin and the yang of how they got together, but it was impossible for me.

I went to school, and in the summer, I went to see my mother at the lake. I helped her in the kitchen sometimes, and I went swimming and picked up tennis. When I was fourteen, my school finished and I had to decide what to do. I actually wanted to become an architect, but we didn't have the money for me to go to Vienna. So my mother found me a job as an apprentice in Villach, a city in Carinthia, fifty miles away.

My stepfather said, "Cooking is not a profession for men. You should be a carpenter or a mason or a mechanic. Cooking is for women."

I left for my apprenticeship. I was fourteen years old and I went to the train station with my little suitcase. As I was walking out of the house, my stepfather said, "You're good for nothing. You're going to be back in a month, crying for money."

I said, "I'm never coming back."

I started the apprenticeship and the chef was as crazy as my stepfather: drunk all the time, throwing things. Sunday lunch was always the busiest day. Three or four weeks into my apprenticeship, on a Sunday, I was making the mashed potatoes. That was my job, along with peeling onions and carrots and washing the spinach. We ran out of potatoes. At the end of the service, the chef screamed at me like crazy: "You're good for nothing! Go back home! You're fired."

That was the worst day of my life. I walked onto a bridge and thought, "I'm going to jump into the river and kill myself." But as I was standing there, I began thinking. "What will happen if I die? Will I go to heaven or hell?" All of these thoughts were going through my head. After a while, I thought, "You know what? I'll just go back tomorrow and see what happens."

I couldn't sleep all night. I went really early to the restaurant. The apprentice who was above me was so happy to see me. He said, "Oh, you're back! I don't have to peel potatoes." He hid me down in the vegetable cellar and I peeled potatoes there. After a few weeks, the chef came down and saw me. He started screaming, "What are you doing here? Get out!"

I said, "I'm not leaving."

So he called the owner. The owner had a little more empathy. He also had another small hotel in town, so he sent me over there. The chef there was a lady. She said, "Just do your job, be quiet, and don't do anything stupid." Sure enough, I stayed there for three years. After that, I left for France.

I went to Dijon first and worked in a restaurant called Trois Faisans, the Three Pheasants. I started learning French. And after a year or so, we got a star in the *Guide Michelin*. The restaurant had never had one before, so there was a party. I looked through one of those red guidebooks and saw that there were one-star, two-star, three-star restaurants. I decided that I would not go back to Austria until I had worked in at least a two-star.

So I wrote to Paul Bocuse, to Maison Troisgrois, all these famous restaurants. The first one to say yes was Baumanière, in Provence. Raymond Thuilier, the chef, was the most amazing person. He only started cooking professionally when he was fifty years old, and he was so passionate about ingredients. He had a lot of land, too. He had the best Cavaillon melons, strawberries, peas, and green beans, really small.

When I was there, Monsieur Thuilier was already seventy years old, but so passionate, going back and forth into the dining room. He came into the kitchen once with Elizabeth Taylor. All of young guys were like, "Oh my God."

Working there was an amazing experience to have at that age. I worked at Baumanière for two and a half years. M. Thuilier was the first person who respected me and made me feel good.

Then I worked at L'Hôtel de Paris in Monaco, a grand hotel in the old style. I didn't like working there, so I asked M. Thuilier if he could help me find another job. He found me work at Maxim's in Paris, which was a three-star restaurant at the time. I went in as a chef de partie, and, after a year or so, I was appointed the night chef, responsible for the kitchen from 10:30 p.m. to one in the morning. When there was a show at the opera or the theater, people came in afterward, all dressed up, to have dinner at midnight.

A friend of mine said, "If you want to make money, you have to go to America." I was always fascinated by the movies, the big cars, John Wayne, the cowboys, and everything. It was also the time of the hippies in San Francisco. I thought, "I want to try marijuana." You couldn't find it in my village. So I went to America, first to New York.

I didn't like it. It was nothing like Paris. But Charles Masson, who owned La Grenouille, found me a job in Indianapolis. I'm a big fan of Formula One racing. So when I heard "Indianapolis," I thought of the Indy 500. I imagined the city being like Monaco, maybe on a river.

I had almost no money left. I took the Greyhound bus there, which felt like it took thirty hours. When I got there, I said, "Shit. *This* is Indianapolis?" It was flat with a few high-rise buildings in the center.

I was a chef at a French restaurant there. I stayed a year and got my green card. Because nobody immigrates to Indiana, I was the only one at the immigration office. From there, I moved to Los Angeles, where I had a job downtown in a restaurant run by the same company as the one that ran the restaurant in Indianapolis. About six months later, I met Patrick Terrail. I started to work at Ma Maison in the morning, and, at night, in a restaurant downtown called François, because I wanted to make money to open my own restaurant.

Orson Welles was one of my first guests at Ma Maison. He came early for lunch, around eleven or so, and would say, "What did you make today?" I would give him a little taste. He'd say, "Well, I want to see the how the whole thing is." So I gave him a whole plate at 11 o'clock and then he had lunch at 12:30 with his guests.

Little by little, all these people came, like the director Billy Wilder, who was also Austrian; Jack Lemmon; and one of my favorites, Sidney Poitier, who I'd already met at Baumanière.

It was hard at the beginning. I used to make an omelet the way I learned in France, soft on the inside and cooked on the outside. They'd send it back and say, "It's not cooked." And fish, too. We got beautiful king salmon from Alaska and I made it so it was still a little undercooked in the middle, how I like it. One customer came with the plate into the kitchen and said, "My salmon is not cooked. What is wrong with you?"

My then-girlfriend, now my ex-wife, Barbara, tried to talk me out of what I was going to do at Spago. She said, "How can you do that? Working at Baumanière and Maxim's and then opening a pizza and pasta place?" I said, "You know what? I want to use great ingredients but have fun." Especially in Los Angeles, where it's warm. You go to New York, and the bankers all have their suits on. In L.A., people are in the movie and record business and dress totally different.

David Hockney did the cover of my first cookbook. A friend of mine opened a fancy French restaurant where you had to wear a jacket. David went in wearing a sweater or something and they wouldn't let him in. He came back to me and told me. I said, "Should I call them?" He said, "No. I will never go back there again."

The seating at the original Spago was important. I didn't know that at first. We had these window seats and everybody wanted to sit at them. One time, Sammy Cahn, the famous songwriter, was seated in the center row, not at the window. At the next table over, by a window, were Alan and Marilyn Bergman, who wrote hit songs for Barbra Streisand. Sammy called me over and said,

"Wolfgang, I won two Oscars. They don't have *any*. How come I have to sit in the second row?" I said, "You get the same food wherever you sit."

Later, we had the head of MGM, Daniel Melnick, and I noticed he was seated in the back of the restaurant. I went up to him and said, "Dan, we have a better table up front if you want it." He said, "What do you mean, a better table?" "By the window." He said, "You know, wherever I sit is the best table. I don't care where it is."

We used to serve smoked salmon and brioche with dill cream, in a very traditional way. One day we ran out of brioche and I thought, "What am I going to do?" So I just cooked some pizza dough in the oven, cut it into slices, and put the dill cream on it. Then I put the smoked salmon on it, with a little caviar on top. It was perfect: the crispy crust, still warm, with the smoked salmon on it. All you need is glass of Champagne, and you're good. That's how we came up with smoked salmon pizza, which is a staple of Spago.

I think L.A. is one of the most exciting cities in the world. Why? Because we have so many neighborhoods, like Little Tokyo, Koreatown, Chinatown, Little India, and Little Ethiopia. Going to restaurants in Monterey Park, you feel like you're in Hong Kong. When you go to a restaurant there on a Sunday, it's all families at big tables with the dim sum carts coming around.

We used to get prawns from Santa Barbara Island. I always grilled them, but sometimes they got mushy. Then I went to a Chinese restaurant where they made drunken shrimp, dropping them into a broth with wine in it. I thought, "Wow, they're crunchy and firm." So I learned from that. And then one day, I said, "I'm going to open a restaurant with French techniques and Chinese ingredients." We opened Chinois on Main in 1983.

One big lesson I learned from my early years was that I never wanted to be like my stepfather or the first chef I worked for. If someone makes a mistake, I'm going to show them how to do it right. Sometimes it takes more than once, but you want to teach people. Later on, I opened a cooking school.

Byron, my second son, was always interested in cooking. When he went to high school at Harvard-Westlake and he was in chemistry class, he wanted to do molecular gastronomy: "We can learn chemistry, but with food." He was really into what Ferran Adrià did at El Bulli. Now he is a chef. I want him to take over one day, because it is a family business.

*Wolfgang, what is your comfort food?*
I reach for simple things. If it's in the morning, it might be some good oatmeal. And sometimes I feel like eating a goulash or Wiener schnitzel from my childhood.

# ERIC RIPERT

At The River Cafe, we spend our days cooking Italian food—ravioli stuffed with spinach and ricotta, veal shin cooked in Chianti and sage. But when we are off-duty, our talk often turns to French food: bouillabaisse, pommes dauphinoise, tartes Tatin.

Eric Ripert, co-owner of my favorite French restaurant in New York, Le Bernardin, is an extraordinary chef—and a thoughtful and generous man. He told me about the influences of his two grandmothers (one Italian and one French), his early days spent in Parisian kitchens, and the philosophy he employs in his own restaurants.

We thought there could be nothing better than having him read one of his recipes: a fish soup inspired by one of his grandmothers.

One of my grandmothers was Italian and the other was from Provence. They both made fish soup. But my favorite memory is of the one from the Italian grandmother, because on the weekend, the family would gather together—all the uncles and cousins and my grandfather and grandma—and they would go fishing and scuba-diving and catching whatever they would catch. My grandmother was in charge of the lunch. She would make the table for twenty to twenty-five people.

She would prepare a lot of things: salads, appetizers, and the fish soup. Whatever fish was coming back, it was cleaned very quickly, and then she made the soup there onsite. We would eat it an hour or two later under the trees where it was cooked, in an area between Antibes and Cannes.

My two grandmothers inspired me a lot. The Italian one was cooking Northern Italian soul food. My grandmother from Provence was doing the same with Provençal food, which is a little bit similar to Northern Italian but has some subtle differences.

My grandmother in Provence, she was from the region of Avignon. They were obviously inland, and she would do, like, a baby leg of lamb roasted. My Italian grandmother wouldn't do that, but she would do osso bucco. My grandmother in Provence would do a coq au vin. My grandmother in Italy didn't know what a coq au vin was. Subtle differences, but they were important.

My mother was obsessed with the Nouvelle Cuisine chefs: Michel Guérard, Paul Bocuse, that generation. At home she cooked lunch and dinner, those elaborate meals with an appetizer, a main course, cheese, and dessert. And different china and a different tablecloth from lunch to dinner. She was cooking for me, my stepfather, and my sister, when she was old enough to be at the table with us, because she's much younger than me.

It was amazing because my mother was a business lady, in the fashion industry. She was importing the brand Courrèges from Spain and Andorra, very busy. But she would wake up at 5 a.m. to prepare the meals and later on finish what needed to be finished, all the little details. If she was doing, I don't know, a baba au rhum for dessert, she would leave time for the baba dough to rise. She did it for the love of doing it. She wanted to feed her family.

At fifteen, I could not go to school any longer because my grades were so bad. I ended up in the principal's office with Mom, and he explained to her that I had to find what was called a vocational school.

I looked sad, but I was really happy, because I wanted to go to culinary school. The principal promised my mother that he would do everything possible to send me to one. He had a friend who was the principal of the culinary school in Perpignan, and I was accepted. I was a very good student there. I really loved everything about it. The first year, we were waiters and cooks. We were learning both. We had some classes of oenology. I was having a blast and my grades were excellent, except for math, where I was still a bit weak. I was good in Spanish because I'd lived part of my childhood in Andorra, so I could speak Spanish and French. I didn't know English yet.

In the kitchen, I was a little bit bored because we were learning old-fashioned recipes from Escoffier, basically. But I knew I was learning the basics, so I was very diligent. At my exam, which was after two years, I had to do a goulash and rice pilaf with langoustines in a sauce Nantua. I did a good job and graduated with honors.

I was like, "This is the beginning." I wanted to be the chef that I am today. I wanted to be in a restaurant that had a big kitchen with a lot of equipment, a lot of cooks, a lot of waiters, beautiful china, and a great wine cellar. That was my dream.

And so, at seventeen years old, I wrote a letter to each of the eighteen three-star Michelin restaurants in France. Nobody answered.

Then I wrote to the two-star places. Maxim's answered with a letter saying, "We don't have a spot for you." But three months later, I received a letter from La Tour d'Argent, which at the time was a three-star.

It was 1982 and they were celebrating their four-hundredth anniversary. I called them and I said, "I'm Eric Ripert. I received your letter. When do you need me?" They said, "Tomorrow." I was like, "Tomorrow is going to be tough." But three days later, I was there with my suitcase in Paris.

The kitchen there was very old-fashioned, a lot of abuse: verbal abuse, physical abuse. That was the culture at that time. I have to note that I was the youngest in the kitchen and I was not necessarily the best, and they were patient with me. But at the same time, very abusive. In France then, the philosophy, which made no sense to me, was to break you psychologically and rebuild you as a champion. I think it was more an excuse to let the chef be abusive and have those tantrums. I learned this the hard way.

I was obviously down sometimes, but my vision of becoming the chef that

I became never wavered. I stayed at La Tour d'Argent about a year and a half. The chef called me in his office and said, "I heard that you want to make a change. I will tell you when you're leaving." I said, "Yes, chef, of course." A month later he said, "Go to this place called Jamin. The chef, his name is Joël Robuchon and he's waiting for you." I was nineteen and had no idea where I was going. I met with Joël Robuchon, a very sweet man. He told me that I would start in a month.

Joël Robuchon was very different. He was not a screamer. But he was very, very difficult. It was a painful experience because he was so demanding of himself and the team. He was never happy. Every day he had some negative comments, but not necessarily articulating what was wrong. Just frustration. He was looking at every plate coming back in the kitchen. When something was left on a plate, even a tiny bite, it was a disaster.

I did a year and something there and then I went to do my military duties. I was, of course, sent to the kitchen. This was in Castelsarrasin, near Toulouse. On my first day, we were making calamari Américaine. I was like, "Hey, this is cool." But it was basically frozen calamari with a béchamel sauce, ketchup, and brandy. At night, they did spaghetti and they managed to burn the spaghetti in the water.

I went to see the general. I said to him, "I don't mind doing my military duties, but please get me out of this kitchen." He laughed at me and he said, "I'm going to send you to the commandos. You're going to learn."

I was a skinny little guy. I looked at him and said, "I can't do that." He laughed and said, "You want to be my waiter?" And I became, for the rest of my stay in the military, the waiter for the general. I didn't cook.

On my last day, I received a message that I thought was a joke. They said, "It was Joël Robuchon, calling for you." I called the number and it really was him. He said, "Thank you for calling me back. I heard that you're done with your military duties. I would like for you to come back and be the chef poissonnier at Jamin."

At the time, I had a girlfriend. Many things were happening in my life. I was not excited to go back to Paris. I said, "Can I think about it?" He said, "Yes, of course. You have thirty seconds." And I was like, "Yes, chef."

I did two years with him, in charge of the fish station. Then I went up to him and said, "I'd like to travel the world. Can you help me?" He sent me to the Watergate Hotel in Washington, D.C., and I worked with Jean-Louis Palladin, who was an extremely talented chef.

It was very relaxed there, a small team. Jean-Louis Palladin was very creative. I was happy because it was a different experience. I learned classic food at La Tour d'Argent. Then I learned rigor and technique with Joël Robuchon. And then with Jean-Louis Palladin, I had a lot of inspiration to be creative.

Then you have to learn to manage a team. That I learned from Gilbert Le Coze at Le Bernardin. When I joined, in 1991, I was twenty-four years old. He said to me, "Look, I want someone to take care of my kitchen. If you respect the philosophy of Bernardin, which is 'The fish is the star of the plate,' then you can do whatever you want here and I will support you."

I had his support until he passed away in 1994. Then I became partners with Maguy Le Coze, his sister, and the rest is history.

In America, I find the kitchens, in general, to be very civilized. I have zero tolerance for misbehavior. If you misbehave but it's not a big mistake, we give you one more chance. But after that, you're not working with us any longer. You have to be a team player. You have to work with others. And you have to be polite and kind and grateful and motivated and hardworking and passionate.

I stand in the pass and look at every plate that goes out. I also work a lot in the kitchen. And I taste a lot. We have tasting spoons made of cornstarch. They're inexpensive and biodegradable, not like plastic. I have only one meal a day. The rest is testing.

We test all the preparations, all the mise en place, all the sauces. We have about forty different sauces. We test and we comment. Before we test, we calibrate our palates. We use industrial Swiss cheese that is not really good but perfect in its seasoning, neither too salty nor too bland, very neutral. Some days you may find the cheese salty, which means your taste buds are very sensitive to salt. Some days you may find it very bland, so you know your taste buds are dull. You know more or less where you stand. We test the sauces, the vegetables, everything else, and we give immediate feedback to the sous-chefs.

I'm very direct. Whatever is right is right. Whatever is wrong is wrong. I'm very articulate in my criticism. Maybe the sauce was cooked too long and we lost the vibrancy that we were supposed to taste. Positive or negative, I'm very detail oriented in my criticism.

*Eric, what is your comfort food?*
If I really want comfort, I cook for myself and my family on the weekend. I like to share. I will never see myself having a glass of wine and eating while not surrounded by friends and family. For me, the weekends are sacred. Since I'm the only guy in the kitchen with white hair, I'm allowed to take my Saturdays and Sundays.

# ALICE WATERS

Rose and I are often credited for bringing open kitchens, farm-sourced ingredients, and female chefs to the world of restaurant dining. As happy as we were to receive this recognition, we were always quick to note that Alice Waters did it all first.

Alice, who originally trained to be a Montessori teacher, is not only the cocreator of Chez Panisse, the farm-to-table restaurant in Berkeley, California, that she has run for more than fifty years. She is also an activist who has taught the world how food can uplift children, make them healthier, and bring communities together. Her foundation, the Edible Schoolyard, has taught kids how to grow fruits and vegetables, whether in a disadvantaged urban area or on the grounds of the White House.

One further note: on our dessert menu the very first day we opened The River Cafe was Alice Waters's Lemon Tart. It's been on the menu ever since.

---

I just picked some lemons from my backyard this morning. They smell so good. They reminded me that the first really successful dessert at Chez Panisse was a Meyer lemon sherbet that we put inside a lemon cup. People were so surprised by the taste.

Meyer lemons have a sweet, floral flavor, sort of ethereal to me. Lindsey Shere was our original pastry chef and is still a partner in the restaurant's ownership. Her family lived up north on a farm and they grew Meyer lemons. That was the beginning of our connecting directly with farmers. I went ahead and planted a Meyer lemon tree in my backyard. Lemon desserts are still among my favorites. My mother made lemon meringue pie for my birthday every year. It was one of the only things she knew how to make.

I grew up in the late 1940s in New Jersey, where it was very cold in the winter and very hot in the summer. But I fell in love with the vegetables and fruits of my parents' victory garden. They planted it during the war as a way to help send food to the soldiers in Europe. Roosevelt had asked everybody to do that. But they also did it for financial reasons, because we were a family of six. My parents canned their tomatoes for the winter and always had squashes in the basement. They kept that garden their whole lives. The seasonality of food was deep inside me from the start. I loved corn and tomatoes in the summertime more than anything.

The idea of Chez Panisse really began with the Free Speech Movement at Berkeley, under the leadership of Mario Savio. He said to all of us, "You need to visit other cultures, to understand the way people think around the world. If you can, you should take off your junior year and go to some other country." So I did. I went to France in 1965, and it really did change my life, not just because the food was so extraordinary, but because of the beauty and culture of France. I fell in love with the cathedral of Notre-Dame sitting by the Seine, drinking a glass of wine. I walked everywhere. I loved the farmers' markets. I came home and told my friends, "I want to live like the French." They felt the same way. In our naïveté, we thought, "Well, maybe if we open a little French restaurant, the food will come." And it did.

We were never out to make money. My parents mortgaged their house so that I could buy the building we were in. In those days, it cost practically nothing. They subsidized the beginning of the restaurant, no question about it. But it really began with a group of us. Some of us knew how to do pastries; some of us knew how to make soup. It was very collaborative in that way. Later, we got some more experienced people in the kitchen and things changed. But it's always been kind of an extended family.

As I look back over these fifty-odd years, probably the most important decision I made was when I had a child, my daughter, Fanny. I realized that

I could not cook six days a week. So I decided that we would divide the job in two: I would work three days but I would be paid for six, and someone else would do likewise. It worked so beautifully that I did it for the café upstairs and for the pastry department. So instead of having one chef in each department, you had two. And it meant that there were many points of view. For the people who were leading the kitchen, it made life civilized. They could be with their families and go out to other restaurants. And the young people who came to learn in our kitchen experienced our collaborative approach. That decision really did change Chez Panisse.

The restaurant had only one set menu each day. I wanted it to be like the little restaurants in Paris where you eat things you may not have ever had before, curated according to the season—and to what we loved to cook. And because we made it very affordable, people liked it a lot. They came because it was in an old house and they felt like they were eating at home.

That is really, I think, a product of my Montessori training, which says that you need to appeal to all of the senses, because they are the pathways into our minds. I wanted the restaurant to smell good. I used to burn rosemary out in front of the restaurant so it would smell like the South of France. I knew that a fireplace in the kitchen would give off a good aroma in the dining room. I knew that candles on the table would be beautiful.

But it was primarily the sense of taste I was looking for when I got back from France. I wanted to eat and live like the French, and I didn't find true taste until I found the farmers and the idea that you only eat food in season, and only local food. I fell in love with those wild strawberries we got in the fall, and all of a sudden, they were gone. I was told, "Oh, you have to go up in the woods and pick them." At first, I didn't believe that people would spend the time doing that and bringing the strawberries down from the woods and sell them to the restaurateurs. But that's what we ended up doing. We bought the food directly. Once we started doing that, every farmer in the state wanted to sell to Chez Panisse, because we left out the middleman. That's what is so critical, because the farmers need to make back the real costs of farming. Our farmers also took our composted food back to their farms.

When Fanny was little, I had a garden out back of my house. I planted things that were very aromatic, like little wild strawberries she could pick. I was very intent on making school lunches that she loved. As it turned out, she shared them with her friends, because they all loved the lunches she brought in. She loved to eat and became a connoisseur. Now she is really engaged with food as part of her work as an artist, and she's doing a website for new mothers, to help them learn how to cook for their kids.

Thirty years ago, the principal of a school in Berkeley called me up and asked if I could help him beautify his school. It was a middle school with eight hundred students from various places—among them, they spoke twenty-two different languages. I was very intimidated when I saw this big, huge piece of land. Yet from the very first planting of that vacant lot, their parents wanted to help. And the kids wanted to pitch in after school.

It was amazing how quickly it changed the whole nature of the school. You could make a kitchen a classroom; you could make a garden a classroom—and not just for teaching cooking or gardening, but for teaching the academic subjects. The Edible Schoolyard Project was a model of shared human values and the Montessori way: learning by doing in a kitchen or garden classroom. It's amazing how much kids learn and how happy they are to be in those classrooms.

It's also about school lunches and discovering what kids like. They were already into things like hummus and pita bread, but who knew that they would like wilted greens and all kinds of fruits and vegetables? They just hadn't been exposed to them.

The success of that program has created an amazing network of Edible

Schoolyards in practically every country in the world—more than 6,500 schools in different climates and cultures. It's what has made me so sure that school-supported agriculture can change the world. There's something deep inside all of us that is connected to nature and to food. Coming back to gardening and cooking is almost like coming home. It's not something that's difficult for children to embrace.

When Michelle Obama was First Lady, I talked to her a lot about the Edible Schoolyard Project, and she loved the idea. She knew about FDR's interests and his wife's interest in victory gardens. Roosevelt even had a garden on the front lawn of the White House for a time. Michelle found a chef, Sam Kass, who planted a garden behind the White House. He had a beehive, too. It was amazing.

I am optimistic about the possibility of changing how we procure food for public schools around the world. Many other countries, like England, are able to do this because of long, ingrained histories of gardening. Unfortunately, we don't have that in the United States. While many people are involved with gardening and selling to schools, we need some leadership to show us that this is possible and absolutely essential for the climate.

We can't keep shipping food around the world. That's an idea that comes from fast-food indoctrination, that we should have whatever we want whenever we want it. But you can't bring an unripe avocado from Mexico and hope that it's going to ripen by the time you get it to Denmark in December.

It's really a beautiful thing to be seasonal. You're always eating something at that moment of perfect ripeness, when it has such a distinct flavor. Right now, we have passion fruit on all the trees around Berkeley, and people are bringing their fruit over to Chez Panisse. We're buying it and making passion fruit syrup. We've never done that before, and it is delicious.

*Alice, what is your comfort food?*

For me, the great thing about food is that it connects you to the beauty of nature. I go outside and just throw myself down on the ground, smelling the herbs. I love rosemary. I love to fry rosemary and sage. I love to sprinkle them on just about anything. It is aromatherapy and very powerful.

# JAMIE OLIVER

When I am arriving at The River Cafe in a taxi, I can't tell you how many times the driver has turned to me and asked, "Is this the restaurant where Jamie Oliver cooked?" One even informed me that The River Cafe was owned by Jamie. I thought, "Why correct him?" Jamie is our prodigal son—he knows that whenever he walks through our door, he is home.

Jamie came to work with us when he was just nineteen years old. A few years later, a documentary was made about our restaurant—*An Italian Christmas: Recipes from The River Cafe*. Jamie cooked mushrooms. The camera loved him and so, it turned out, did the public. By 1999, Jamie had his own television program, a cookbook, and a column in *The Times*.

Jamie is also an activist. In 2002, he opened Fifteen, a restaurant that employs and mentors disadvantaged young people. He has campaigned to have the government provide free and nutritious school lunches.

Jamie read our recipe for Pork Cooked in Milk. "I was lucky enough to be taught it by you and Rose, and the idea of cooking meat in milk was something that I had never known," he said.

I had been working at Antonio Carluccio's Neal Street Restaurant for a year and a half, and I knew it was time for me to move on. I had just read the first River Cafe Cookbook, the blue one, and it changed everything. It was like fresh air, and I knew I had to get there. So I phoned up and I came in for an interview. I was quite skint and was wearing a really cheap suit. Honestly, if it had gone near a candle, it would've quickly gone up in flames. But I turned up in a suit, with a terrible tie, because my dad always said, "Make an effort." I remember all the chefs looking at me, thinking, "What's he doing in a suit?" Because you don't wear suits at The River Cafe. Even the customers don't.

I started straight away. It was an amazing time in Britain: Cool Britannia, the music scene, the fashion scene, the photography scene, the art scene. And The River Cafe was on fire. I remember cooking for New Labour before they got in and when they got in. I remember seeing the Millennium Dome as a sketch on a tablecloth, just a few meters away from the pastry section while I was making Chocolate Nemesis.

It felt like a family straight away. And I'd grown up in a family restaurant. I'll share this bit of advice from my dad to me: "Whoever you work for, treat their business like it's yours. And you haven't got one job—you've got every job. If the phone rings, pick it up. If the floor needs mopping, mop it." Coming into The River Cafe, it actually felt like a family, which is not that common even now in restaurants. What Ruthie and Rose were doing was so untraditional from what the machine teaches. I felt like I was being liberated.

My dad was a trained chef. He'd started really young and grew up in a pub that did very good food, the Plough & Sail in Paglesham, which is in a dead end near the River Blackwater.

I was born in South Ockendon in Greys, Essex, right in the estuary of Essex. An area that got devastated in the war. Dad was the youngest license-holder in the country at the time. I believe he was seventeen. And then he had me at twenty. As soon as I was born, we got a tatty old pub in a little village called Clavering. It was built in the sixteenth century and I grew up there. The chalkboard menus were written daily, so that gave me some sort of connection with The River Cafe changing menus daily. The game was local. The fish was only on Tuesdays and Thursdays, lots of live crabs and lobsters and whole fish. Whole animals were brought in to be butchered. He had a brigade of at least six on every shift. And the pastry was a proper pastry, an Anglo-French or Swiss-style dessert.

I thought this was normal for a pub, but even now, it's not normal. More typical is freezers full of stuff you can reheat. I remember that the head chef was paid more than Dad paid himself. I said, "Well, that can't be right." And he said, "No, no, we've got to invest in the quality and get the brigade steady." The pub had a bar side and a restaurant side, so there was slightly two tones of cooking happening. They had the kind of things that you would get, I guess, at the Wolseley or Rules: classics, simply cooked game, beautiful Dover sole, everything homemade.

Mum was a classic landlady. Not like an *EastEnders* landlady, but quite glamorous. She'd get ready for two hours. I remember the smell of that hairspray from the gold canister, and her hair in rollers. And then all of a sudden, this outfit came on and the hair was out. She'd go down about 8:15 and start working the locals: "Oh, hi, Sally." It was a busy pub. I guess in a sort of cheesy sense, we went from a working-class family to a middle-class family in about thirteen years.

We lived upstairs, Mum, Dad, me, and my sister, Anna-Marie. There were two bedrooms and a front room. Because it was a sixteenth-century building, there were gaps all around the edges, and everyone smoked a lot. If, God forbid, I ever get anything unhealthy with my lungs, it was because I had passive smoke as a child.

In the front room, we had a little table. Mum cooked down in the commercial kitchen in between shifts. They both cooked well. My mum and dad still cook today, but they're retired now. They did that in lockdown.

I was in the wash-up by age ten, and the wash-up involved a lot of veg prep, not dissimilar to at The River Cafe when you are picking the herbs and so forth. I really wanted to get into the kitchen, so I was fully in the kitchen by about eleven.

Probably by the time I was sixteen, I'd done the rotation of the kitchen maybe three times. I remember I had to develop the skill of teaching cooking. If there was a twenty-year-old who'd come in from college to get a job as a commis chef, I was fourteen and I'd have to train him. And obviously when you're fourteen, you haven't got a hair on your chin, and these twenty-one-year-olds look like men. So I had to develop a way of teaching without getting a slap. And that was to make them feel like they were teaching themselves: "Are you left- or right-handed? Okay, work from left to right. Okay, so this is this dish, and we prep this and prep that, and we put that on ice. Just try and set it up so the service can flow."

But being young, I was cocky as well, so I often ended up in the freezer. They'd throw me in for about fifteen minutes for backchatting. I'm sure it was illegal. But I'm sure it was with love.

I always tell people there are two ways to run a kitchen. One is through fear and one is through family. Family's a bit slower, but you get much more back in return. Fear is very efficient, but you get so little back in the long run.

I wasn't supposed to be working the night I was filmed for *Christmas at The River Cafe*. My girlfriend, Jools, who is now my wife, was off as well—she worked at The River Cafe in the front of house. We hadn't had a night off together for ages. The phone rang about four o'clock; one of the team was sick. I had to come and put the shift in, and that's when the crew was there.

Actually, they were kind of in the way, because I was catching my tail. I was an hour and a half late to cover someone and I was running hots two, one of the busier sections. It was fritto misto, tagliatelle with girolles, and risotto. And the slow-cooked pork. I didn't think anything of it. The night it went out on TV, many months later, I didn't know I was in it because I was working. But the phones started to ring the next day, literally the next day.

A TV producer named Pat Llewellyn got ahold of me. The next thing I knew, I had a TV show, a newspaper column, and an advertising campaign with a supermarket chain as the Naked Chef.

When I did my first cookbook, I couldn't write or type, so I did it on a Dictaphone. The responsibility of delivering it was like a nightmare.

I remember writing down what I would and wouldn't do on TV, and I wrote,

"Stripping down restaurant food to its bare essentials." The words *stripping* and *bare* turned me into the Naked Chef. I didn't come up with the title. But before that, the working title was *Forking Gorgeous*, so thank God.

Probably more than anything, *The Naked Chef* hit a moment. Timing's an interesting master, isn't it? It was a bit of a whirlwind. It felt like being in a pop band. Because I was younger and I wasn't married at that point, it was very lairy. Thankfully I had Jools, who I'd been with since I was eighteen. She was my rock. And I had good friends in the business, and I had Ruthie and Rose, and I had Mum and Dad, so I felt safe enough.

When I set up Fifteen, it was such a beautiful premise. People asked, "Why did you do it?" I said, "I wanted to, I could, and I did." It was as simple as that. I was young enough, stupid enough, and able enough to do it. I was a twenty-four-year-old kid who'd gone from having no money to having money in the bank, and I spent all of it on Fifteen, which was a charity. My dad was so worried about me. He thought I'd lost the plot, because he'd never made an easy pound.

Being that kid who had struggled at school, I wondered, "Is there anything that we could do for kids who had gone off the rail or got lost or had problems with the law or were homeless?" We set it up as Fifteen because the restaurant would take fifteen kids every year and train them for sixteen months. Really, it was a beautiful blend of the values that I'd learned at The River Cafe, from Mum and Dad, and from Gennaro Contaldo at Neal Street Restaurant. I mean, it was a very different restaurant, but you could see the genetics in the recipes.

Some of these kids were drug dealers and fraudsters. We'd take them to catch wild salmon, and then we'd get a farm salmon and do an autopsy to show them the difference. Seeing is believing, and you start to get their wonder. Maybe you haven't won them over yet, but then you do that with pork, and then you do that with foraging, and then you do that with olive oil.

And slowly but surely, about nine months in, there's that consistency. That's one of the things I learned about lots of the people that I love: consistency of how a person is, how they dress, how they look after their yard, whatever it might be.

I think most of these young kids got in trouble with the law because they had no consistency. We graduated over 80 percent every year. For context, that's the complete opposite of the government; they rehabilitate young offenders with a success rate of about 25 percent. We did Fifteen for seventeen years until it, sadly, closed.

At the moment, neither of the two big parties have child health on the manifesto as something that can be voted for. There's been an amazing bit of work done independently, just recently. They said if you just gave every student a free school lunch over a twenty-year period, Britain would be over £40 billion better off. They look at it very surgically, around productivity. What's interesting is, all the math says, "Invest in the system, treat all the kids same." Free school lunches definitely would make the food better, more consistent, but, more importantly, it would give young people from poor postcodes much more hope and the ability to thrive.

People forget it's the biggest restaurant group: thirty thousand–odd schools, nearly five million meals a day, eighty-five thousand lunch cooks. It's an incredible workforce, bigger than the military, out there cooking for kids every day.

I had this genius idea of, "How about we do an annual School Food Awards with real prizes and real incentives? How about we celebrate the best up-and-coming lunch cook and the best primary school, secondary school, special school?" So we've got eight different awards that we are going to launch. We're trying to get as many people as possible behind it. Hopefully it'll give us an opportunity to share what good looks like.

*Jamie, what is your comfort food?*

A dish inspired by my time at The River Cafe. It's a spaghetti arrabbiata. One of the ways I was taught it, and I know there are many ways, was to gently heat oil and put whole fresh chilies in and let them gently cook. You put a little hole in the chili so it doesn't give aggressive heat. Then the beautiful tomatoes go in, and a little garlic. The little hijack on this was, I remember seeing Ruthie and Rose using vodka as a base for risotto. You cook it all away, and it leaves this clean taste that is amazing.

    I incorporated that hack. So: oil and chili, slowly, slowly, slowly. Don't rush it. Then lemon zest, garlic, vodka. Cook the vodka away. Then in with the tomatoes—and this magic sauce happens. Then simply add garlicky *pangritata*, which are crispy breadcrumbs, and spaghetti. I will curl up on a sofa with that.

# SIAN WYN OWEN
# JOSEPH TRIVELLI

Everyone is interested in process. How do actors memorize their lines? How does a car get designed? How does an airplane stay up in the sky?

In my case, the question I'm most often asked is: How does a restaurant work? How do you know how many portions of sea bass to order? What do you do when a chef gets stuck in traffic and is late for work?

The answers to these questions are simple. It's people. And two important people for me at The River Cafe are the brilliant executive chefs Sian Wyn Owen and Joseph Trivelli, each of whom has been at the restaurant for more than twenty-five years—and both of whom worked with Rose.

They, together with executive managers Vashti Armit and Charles Pullen, not only represent a connection to the past and the original vision of The River Cafe but represent the future, shaping the restaurant, teaching and inspiring young people, and cooking and serving the food of Italy we love.

**Joseph**

My first day at The River Cafe was terrifying. I had written a letter about why I wanted to be a chef at the restaurant and given it to Rose Gray after a lunch. Rose invited me to come the following week to work. Ruthie was away that week, and I was just terrified until she came back. Then Rose made me a cup of tea and I thought, "Okay, I think I can get on with this."

I remember leaving at the end of the day and thinking, "I got through the day." I had wanted to work here for a couple of years at that point, and it meant so much, I could barely cope with it.

**Sian**

I met Rose on my first day and she said something I still always quote. She said, "I'll teach you to slice a piece of prosciutto at the perfect thickness. I'll teach you to cook beans perfectly. I'll teach you the art of simple cooking." And I remember thinking, "That sounds easy." But actually, that is the essence of The River Cafe. Simplicity and the *understanding* of simplicity. I've never understood it more than watching Ruthie: how every time she prepares a dish, she takes away one more thing. But at the beginning I was scared. I had come through London kitchens that were very hierarchical and aggressive and male-dominated. My preconception was that The River Cafe would be more of that. So when I arrived and saw two women running a restaurant in an utterly different way, I was wowed.

I remember thinking, "This is the life goal." I'd wanted to be a chef since I was a teenager. I read cookbooks like they were novels. The Italian repertoire of course, but the ones that really got me into cooking when I was young were the French-inspired ones—the Roux Brothers, Sophie Grigson, Elizabeth David—and my mother was a really brilliant cook. Both my parents were very much part of that gastronomic tradition of the '70s and '80s, and I think I aspired to where they were coming from, that French influence.

But my parents absolutely would not entertain the idea of me being a chef. I tried to be a good daughter and did what they said. I went off to university. Then I became a chef after I'd graduated, much to everyone's disapproval.

**Joseph**

I didn't study cooking, but I grew up having long summer holidays in Italy. My grandmother started cooking before we got up. I slept in a room where the only window was to the kitchen—there was no outdoor window, just a hatch to the cooker. Nonna was impatient for us grandkids to wake up. So she would open the hatch and put out cups of sweet coffee and do everything she could to entice us. That's how it got into me, but I had no idea that I could make it a career.

Then I got a job washing up in the kitchen for a guy called Chris, who's now a dear friend. One day he burned himself so badly he had to go to hospital, and I was left to make Sunday lunch. And I just loved it. That's when I thought, "Okay, I could really enjoy this."

**Sian**

I think I looked after you on your first day, Joseph. We both worked our way up through The River Cafe kitchen together, so we became friends. I remember once being on the cold section together and saying, "Joseph, how much oil do you think Ruthie will like on this dish?" We had a camaraderie. And we were on our same journey. All the way up to the top, to the point now that I get to work with my best friend.

**Joseph**

I was fortunate. I had an Italian grandmother who taught me a lot of things, but when I came to The River Cafe, Rose taught me—retaught me—how to make tomato sauce. I've no idea what kind of chef I'd be without Rose at home, let alone in a restaurant. I feel very lucky to have literally held on to her apron strings, probably being quite annoying as I tried to take it all in. I suppose a part of it as well, particularly in the early days, was trying to impress her. Three nice words from Rose could get you through half a year.

People always say, "You give up so much being a chef, especially in your twenties." But being here, cooking with Rose and Ruthie? "Oh, what—you can't come to the concert on Saturday night?" I didn't want to be anywhere else. I mean, are you kidding me?

**Sian**

From the minute I get up in the morning, I am in a constant dialogue about food. I cycle to the pool, and for half an hour when I'm swimming my lengths, I think about the menu. I think about who's working, what the weather's like—is it a scorcher, is it cold?—and no one can interrupt me because I'm swimming up and down. I remember once writing a menu in the early days at The River Cafe, and Ruthie said to me, "Every person who comes in is coming for a different reason. For one person it's a working lunch. For another it's a wedding, anniversary, or birthday." To write a menu that considers all those things—the fussy eater, the celebratory eater—is a real skill.

**Joseph**

I don't swim every day anymore, but I think about the menu cycling in, and when I'm writing it, I think about balance. Chili and lemon, say, and the colors in a dish.

**Sian**

Then I open the door to come down into the kitchen, and I've got my chef's outfit on, and I'm straight into my professional persona. "Morning," I say to everyone. I buoy myself up with my good-morning-ness. It really does create a feeling of goodwill and collaboration that I take really seriously.

I take a lot of pride in not being an aggressive chef, never raising my voice. Some people want to see you behave like that in the kitchen because they think that's what the head chef would do. I refuse to do that.

**Joseph**

Sian is a brilliant boss to the younger chefs. She's so focused on everyone being in the right zone all the time, which is so important.

**Sian**

We always say that being in a professional kitchen is like being in the West End. You've got two shows—two nonnegotiable deadlines a day where you have to be ready. It's curtain up and be ready to go.

**Joseph**

And the building. We haven't talked about the building. It's got this lovely feeling of calm. Even after twenty-two years of going into it, every morning I open the door and think, "This is impeccable." For us it's home.

*Sian and Joseph, what are your comfort foods?*

**Sian**

I reckon I could answer for Joseph. He'd say bread or pasta.

**Joseph**

A slice of bread, most definitely. If it's fresh and warm, nothing on it. And I could tell you what Sian's is. I've got a few choices, but I'll say spaghetti bottarga.

**Sian**

It's in my top five. Bottarga, it sounds not that appetizing. It's the cured, salted roe of a gray mullet, a Sardinian specialty. You grate it into spaghetti. Generally, I think chefs use about a third of a stick per person. I could eat a whole stick. I love it. You put it into the spaghetti with lots of olive oil, one tiny drop of lemon juice, and plenty of black pepper. Oh my God, I'm making myself hungry. And all the podcast

# Acknowledgments

Aimée Bell
Matthew Donaldson
David Kamp
Anthony Michael
Caroline Michel
Stephanie Nash
Adam Rapoport
Zad Rogers
Remo Ruffini

Kitty Alford
Vashti Armit
Ben Atkins
Phoebe Beber-Frankel
James Bedford
Josh Berger
Jennifer Bergstrom
Conal Byrne
Matilda Culme-Seymour
Mary Dean
Sierra Fang-Horvath
Olivia Gopnik-Parker
Charlotte Grocutt
Roger Guyett

Johnny Heah
Susanna Hislop
Michael Jackson
Jennifer Long
Sally Marvin
Jude Marwa
Leonie McQuillan
Caroline Pallotta
Will Pearson
Jean Pigozzi
Bob Pittman
Charles Pullan
Jaime Putorti
Bianca Roberts
Jennifer Robinson
Bella Salini
Jamie Selzer
Tilly Seymour
Ella Shindler
Chris Wilson

And all the podcast guests who have been on *Ruthie's Table 4*

# PHOTOGRAPHY CREDITS

Page vi: Ruthie Rogers interviews David Beckham (photograph by Matthew Donaldson)
Page 8: Ruthie Rogers (photograph courtesy of Jean Pigozzi)
Page 10: Ruthie Rogers and Paul McCartney (photograph courtesy of The River Cafe)
Page 16: Mary McCartney and Ruthie Rogers at The River Cafe (photograph courtesy of Atomized Studios)
Page 22: Stella McCartney (photograph courtesy of The River Cafe)
Page 28: Victoria Beckham (photograph courtesy of Victoria Beckham)
Page 32: Ruthie Rogers and David Beckham (photograph by Matthew Donaldson)
Page 38: Ruthie Rogers and Salman Rushdie (photograph courtesy of Atomized Studios)
Page 42: Rachel Eliza Griffiths (photograph courtesy of Atomized Studios)
Page 48: Matthew Rhys and Keri Russell with Ruthie Rogers (photograph courtesy of Atomized Studios)
Page 54: Ruthie Rogers with Elton John and David Furnish (photograph courtesy of Atomized Studios)
Page 62: Michael Elias at age four and more recently (photographs courtesy of Michael Elias)
Page 66: Ruthie Rogers with her son, Roo, in Venice (photograph by Bernadine Huang)
Page 72: Ruthie Rogers with Emily Mortimer and Vashti Armit (photograph courtesy of Atomized Studios)
Page 78: Ruthie Rogers and Tom Hollander look through his mother's recipe book (photograph courtesy of Atomized Studios)
Page 80: Clockwise from top: Greta Gerwig; Noah Baumbach with Ruthie Rogers; Noah and Greta (photograph courtesy of Alice Fisher)
Page 88: Linda Evangelista in Ontario, Canada, August 1977 (photograph courtesy of Linda Evangelista)
Page 94: Edward Enninful (photograph courtesy of The River Cafe)
Page 100: Ruthie Rogers and Mel Brooks (photograph by Zad Rogers)
Page 106: Wyclef Jean (photograph courtesy of The River Cafe)
Page 114: Tina Fey and Ruthie Rogers (photograph by Matthew Donaldson)
Page 122: Alfonso Cuarón (photograph courtesy of The River Cafe)
Page 126: Bob Pittman (photograph courtesy of Atomized Studios)
Page 132: J.J. Abrams and Ruthie Rogers at The River Cafe (photograph courtesy of Ruthie Rogers)
Page 138: Trudie Styler and Ruthie Rogers (photograph courtesy of Atomized Studios)

Page 144: Tom Hollander and Ruthie Rogers (photograph courtesy of Atomized Studios)
Page 150: Francis Ford Coppola and Ruthie Rogers (photograph courtesy of The River Cafe)
Page 156: Sarah Jessica Parker and Sian Wyn Owen (photograph by Matthew Donaldson)
Page 158: Ruthie Rogers and Michael Caine (photograph courtesy of Ruthie Rogers)
Page 164: Jake Gyllenhaal (photograph courtesy of Ruthie Rogers)
Page 168: Sarah Jessica Parker (photograph by Matthew Donaldson)
Page 176: Wes Anderson and Ruthie Rogers in Paris (photograph by Roo Rogers)
Page 180: Carey Mulligan (photograph courtesy of Atomized Studios)
Page 186: Jeff Goldblum in Florence (photograph courtesy of Jeff Goldblum)
Page 190: Ruthie Rogers and Fisher Stevens (photograph courtesy of Atomized Studios)
Page 196: Olivia Colman (photograph courtesy of Atomized Studios)
Page 202: Ruthie Rogers and Bob Iger (photograph courtesy of The River Cafe)
Page 206: Ruthie Rogers and Stephen Fry (photograph by Matthew Donaldson)
Page 214: Ruthie Rogers and Austin Butler play Tic! (photograph by Stefan Ratibor)
Page 220: Menu from The River Cafe (courtesy of The River Cafe)
Page 222: Norman Foster and Richard Rogers (photograph courtesy of Ruthie Rogers)
Page 226: Ruthie Rogers and Tracey Emin at the Lorcan O'Neill Gallery in Rome (photograph courtesy of Ruthie Rogers)
Page 232: Ruthie Rogers and Frank Gehry (photograph courtesy of Ruthie Rogers)
Page 238: Jony Ive and Ruthie Rogers (photographs courtesy of Ruthie Rogers)
Page 244: Frida Escobedo (photograph by Matthew Donaldson)
Page 250: Ed Ruscha and Dexter recording Ruthie Rogers's podcast (photograph courtesy of Atomized Studios)
Page 252: Ed Ruscha, 1969 (courtesy of Gagosian Gallery)
Page 254: Mala Gaonkar (photograph courtesy of Atomized Studios)
Page 256: Nancy Pelosi in London (photograph courtesy of Nancy Pelosi)
Page 262: Ruthie Rogers and Al Gore (photograph by Matthew Donaldson)
Page 268: Ruthie Rogers and Mala Gaonkar (photograph courtesy of Atomized Studios)
Page 274: Simon Sebag Montefiore and Ruthie Rogers (photograph courtesy of Atomized Studios)

Page 284: Darren Walker at age six (photograph courtesy of Darren Walker); Ruthie Rogers and Darren (photograph courtesy of The River Cafe)
Page 290: Mark Carney in Italy (photograph courtesy of Ruthie Rogers)
Page 296: Adam Schiff (photograph courtesy of Adam Schiff)
Page 302: Ruthie Rogers and Michael Bloomberg (photograph courtesy of Atomized Studios)
Page 306: The River Cafe (photograph courtesy of The River Cafe)
Page 308: Ruthie Rogers and Martha Stewart (photograph courtesy of Atomized Studios)
Page 314: Ruthie Rogers and Danny Meyer (photograph courtesy of Atomized Studios)
Page 320: Nigella Lawson (photograph by Richard Fox)
Page 326: Yotam Ottolenghi as a child and more recently (photographs courtesy of Yotam Ottolenghi and Atomized Studios)
Page 332: Ruthie Rogers and Wolfgang Puck in Los Angeles (photograph courtesy of Ruthie Rogers)
Page 340: Eric Ripert (photograph courtesy of Atomized Studios)
Page 348: Alice Waters in London (photograph by Sally Clark)
Page 354: Jamie Oliver in 1997 and 2023 at The River Cafe (photographs courtesy of Jamie Oliver and Atomized Studios)
Page 362: Sian Wyn Owen and Joseph Trivelli (photograph by Matthew Donaldson)
Page 369: Enjoying pasta (photograph courtesy of Noah Baumbach)
Page 370: Ruthie Rogers (photograph by Matthew Donaldson)

Table photography by Matthew Donaldson

Design by Michael Nash Associates

Gallery Books
An Imprint of Simon & Schuster, LLC
1230 Avenue of the Americas
New York, NY 10020

The essays in this book are adapted from the podcast *Ruthie's Table 4*, produced by Atomized Studios.

For more than 100 years, Simon & Schuster has championed authors and the stories they create. By respecting the copyright of an author's intellectual property, you enable Simon & Schuster and the author to continue publishing exceptional books for years to come. We thank you for supporting the author's copyright by purchasing an authorized edition of this book.

No amount of this book may be reproduced or stored in any format, nor may it be uploaded to any website, database, language-learning model, or other repository, retrieval, or artificial intelligence system without express permission. All rights reserved. Inquiries may be directed to Simon & Schuster, 1230 Avenue of the Americas, New York, NY 10020 or permissions@simonandschuster.com.

Copyright © 2025 by Atomized Studios Limited and The River Cafe, Ltd.

All rights reserved, including the right to reproduce this book or portions thereof in any form whatsoever. For information, address Gallery Books Subsidiary Rights Department, 1230 Avenue of the Americas, New York, NY 10020.

First Gallery Books hardcover edition October 2025

GALLERY BOOKS and colophon are registered trademarks of Simon & Schuster, LLC

Simon & Schuster strongly believes in freedom of expression and stands against censorship in all its forms. For more information, visit BooksBelong.com.

For information about special discounts for bulk purchases, please contact Simon & Schuster Special Sales at 1-866-506-1949 or business@simonandschuster.com.

The Simon & Schuster Speakers Bureau can bring authors to your live event. For more information or to book an event, contact the Simon & Schuster Speakers Bureau at 1-866-248-3049 or visit our website at www.simonspeakers.com.

Manufactured in Italy

10 9 8 7 6 5 4 3 2 1

Library of Congress Control Number: 2025934884

ISBN 978-1-6680-5589-2
ISBN 978-1-6680-5591-5 (ebook)

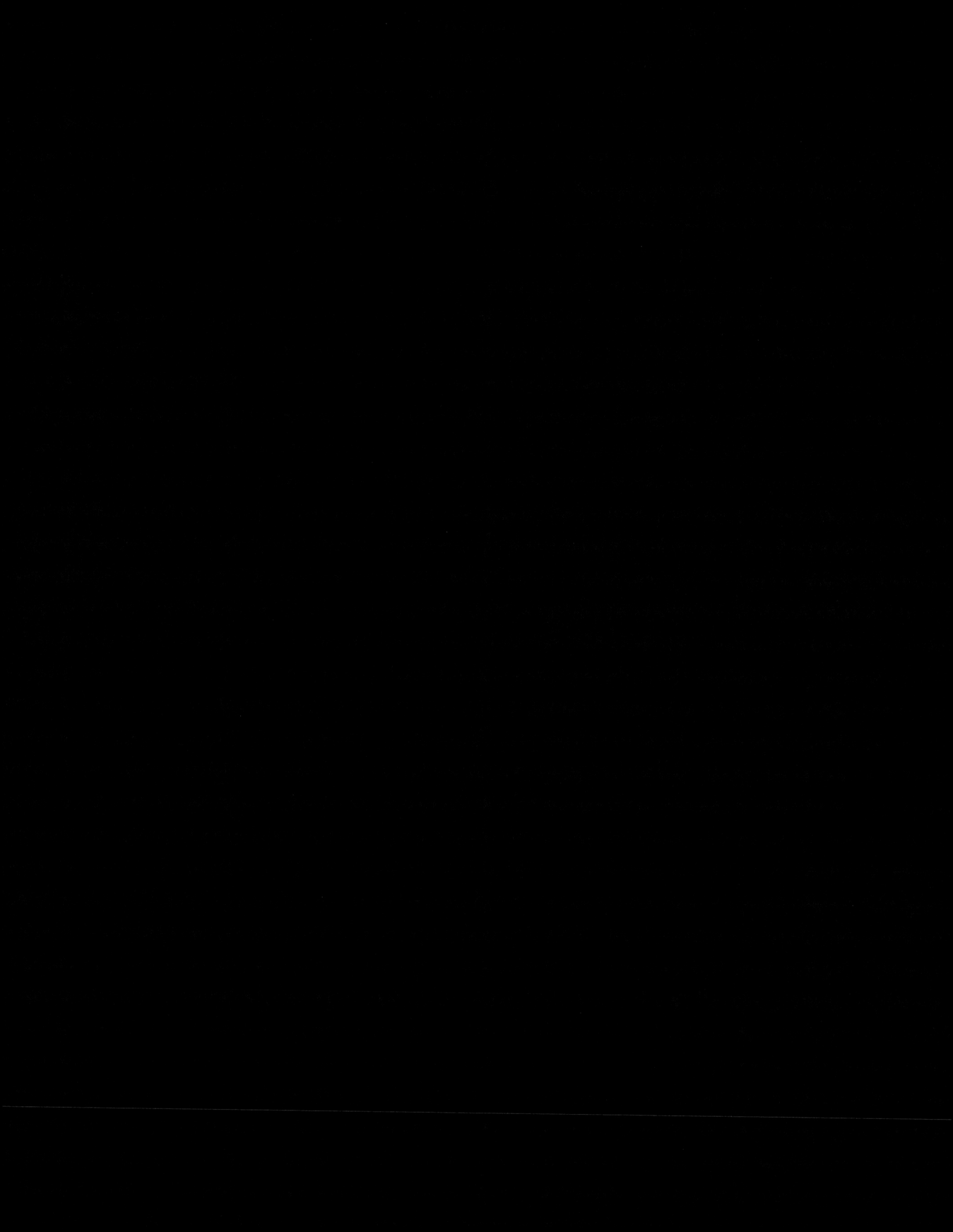